The New Philosophy for K–12 Education

Also available from ASQ Quality Press

Orchestrating Learning with Quality
David P. Langford and Barbara A. Cleary, Ph.D.

Academic Initiatives in Total Quality for Higher Education
Harry V. Roberts, editor

Kidgets: and other insightful stories about quality in education
Maury Cotter and Daniel Seymour

Using Quality to Redesign School Systems: The Cutting Edge of Common Sense
Peggy Siegel and Sandra Byrne

Total Quality for Schools: A Suggestion for American Education
Joseph C. Fields

Total Quality for Schools: A Guide for Implementation
Joseph C. Fields

Public Schools Should Learn to Ski: A Systems Approach to Education
Stephen E. Rubin

To request a complimentary catalog of publications, call 800-248-1946.

The New Philosophy for K–12 Education

A Deming Framework for Transforming America's Schools

James F. Leonard

ASQ Quality Press
Milwaukee, Wisconsin

The New Philosophy for K–12 Education: A Deming Framework for Transforming America's Schools
James F. Leonard

Library of Congress Cataloging-in-Publication Data

Leonard, James F., 1952–
    The new philosophy for K–12 education: a Deming framework for
transforming America's schools / James F. Leonard.
        p.   cm.
    Includes bibliographical references and index.
    ISBN 0-87389-363-8 (alk. paper)
        1. School management and organization—United States—Philosophy.
    2. Total quality management—United States.   3. Deming, W. Edwards
    (William Edwards), 1900–1993.   I. Title.
    LB2805.L386   1996
    371.2'00973—dc20   96-4055
                                                        CIP

Permission Acknowledgments
For excerpts cited as Deming 1986: Reprinted from *Out of the Crisis* by W. Edwards Deming by permission of MIT and The W. Edwards Deming Institute. Published by MIT, Center for Advanced Educational Services, Cambridge, MA 02139. Copyright 1986 by The W. Edwards Deming Institute.

For excerpts cited as Deming 1993: Reprinted from *The New Economics for Industry, Government, Education* by W. Edwards Deming by permission of MIT and The W. Edwards Deming Institute. Published by MIT, Center for Advanced Educational Services, Cambridge, MA 02139. Copyright 1993 by The W. Edwards Deming Institute.

10 9 8 7 6 5 4 3

ISBN 0-87389-363-8

Acquisitions Editor: Kelley Cardinal
Project Editor: Jeanne W. Bohn

ASQ Mission: To facilitate continuous improvement and increase customer satisfaction by identifying, communicating, and promoting the use of quality principles, concepts, and technologies; and thereby be recognized throughout the world as the leading authority on, and champion for, quality.

Attention: Schools and Corporations
ASQ Quality Press books, audio, video, and software are available at quantity discounts with bulk purchases for business, educational, or instructional use. For information, please contact ASQ Quality Press at 800-248-1946, or write to ASQ Quality Press, P.O. Box 3005, Milwaukee, WI 53201-3005.

For a free copy of the ASQ Quality Press Publications Catalog, including ASQ membership information, call 800-248-1946.

Printed in the United States of America

 Printed on acid-free paper

American Society for Quality

611 East Wisconsin Avenue
P.O. Box 3005
Milwaukee, Wisconsin 53201-3005
414-272-8575
Fax 414-272-1734
800-248-1946
Web site http://www.asq.org

This work is dedicated with love to my mother, who taught me; to my father, who coached me; and to my wife and children, from whom and with whom my learning continues.

By wisdom is a house built,
    by understanding is it made firm;
And by knowledge are its rooms filled
    with every precious and pleasing
        possession.
A wise man is more powerful than a strong
    man,
and a man of knowledge than a man of
    might.

Proverbs 24:3–5

Contents

Preface

The premise of this text is that U.S. schools do not need reform; the American education system is in need of *transformation,* and transformation implies a change in state. This book's purpose is to provide a framework and a philosophical foundation to help leaders in education begin or continue the transformation process in their schools, districts, and communities.

As a teacher and consultant, the late W. Edwards Deming developed a new management philosophy that continues to sweep this country. He devoted his life to helping leaders in business, education, and government service understand and implement a process for transformation. This book is intended to serve as a translation of Deming's philosophy, principles, and his system of profound knowledge for application in America's schools and school districts.

This text was written for anyone involved in school leadership and improvement efforts, including not only administrators, but also board members, teachers, parents, specialists, teacher union leaders, site-based decision-making team members, and department of education personnel. Because they play a critical role in the quality of education at local and state levels, business leaders, legislators, and community leaders and activists—in short, anyone interested in children and the quality of their education—should also benefit from reading this book.

This is also a textbook for faculty members and students in our schools of education, and for those who coordinate and attend administrator certification programs. Schools of education should not be working to perpetuate past and current practices of teaching, administration, and research. Rather, they should teach about transformation, teach profound knowledge, and prepare their graduates for the future.

Beyond the introductory first chapter, the text is organized to address three key elements of the transformation process.

1. Chapters 2 through 4 address the adoption of a systems perspective, the first key element of the transformation process. Among the topics covered are a model for viewing education as a system for skill and knowledge development; the importance of a clear, common purpose for the school, district, or any organization; and the need for leadership to ensure that all parts of the system are working well together to fulfill that purpose.

2. Chapters 5 through 7 address the essential statistical methods, the second key element of the transformation process. Emphasis is placed not on formulae and calculations, but on the core theory of variation and the role of statistical methods in helping leaders to understand and improve systems. In chapter 8, a basic procedure for improving a system is presented to guide efforts to improve teaching, learning, and administrative processes.

3. Chapters 9 through 11 take on the third and toughest element of the transformation process; that is, leadership to create, provide, and maintain a healthy environment for work, learning, and continuous improvement. Deming's system of profound knowledge is presented as the foundation of a new philosophy for education, and Deming's 14 points are restated as obligations of the school board and administration. The obligations serve as a model of the healthy environment that will exist after a transformation process guided by profound knowledge.

Chapter 12 presents a sequence of events and guidelines for getting started on the transformation. It is by no means comprehensive, nor is it intended to serve as a standard recipe for use in all settings. Instead, this chapter provides a framework for introducing the system of profound knowledge at a school or district level.

Finally, three appendices are provided for readers interested in further details and self-study. The first two provide summaries and examples of the basic statistical methods (appendix A) and of the intermediate statistical methods (appendix B). Appendix C is a short paper by Deming entitled "A System of Profound Knowledge." It describes the four components of profound knowledge as the foundation for leadership action to optimize work and learning systems, achieve continuous improvement of processes, and to more effectively understand and manage people.

Deming taught me that transformation must begin with the individual; all else follows. I hope this text helps you to begin or continue that journey.

Chapter One

Key Elements of the Transformation Process

Over the years, I've often opened my seminars with educators, their business partners, and community leaders by posing the following question: Is there a crisis in American education? Although a few seminar attendees have insisted that there may be a perceived crisis (but not a real one), the vast majority of them have agreed that the American education system is in crisis. When I ask what symptoms they observe that may lead them to conclude there's a crisis, a number of seminar participants have given the following responses.

- Businesspeople claim entry-level workers don't have the skills they need.
- There is an unacceptable and disturbing number of high school dropouts.
- The United States has the highest rate of teen pregnancy in the developed world.
- The United States has the highest rate of workplace illiteracy in the industrialized world.
- There is violence in schools.
- School districts are experiencing crises in funding because of state- and federally mandated programs that aren't funded and local property owners' resistance to higher school budgets.

- The United States has the highest prison incarceration rate in the world, with more than a million people in prison, and the number is growing.
- Students' average SAT scores are falling.
- Americans have a dramatically different family structure than we did in the past, with working parents unable to participate fully in their children's learning.
- Schools are burdened with programs to deal with society's problems (teen pregnancy, AIDS, counseling, and so on) in addition to academics.
- American students lag far behind their peers in other countries in tests of international comparison.

After discussing these and other symptoms, I always ask my seminar audiences a second question: Is the American education system broken?

The consensus answer to this question is a resounding no! The American education system is not broken; it's operating precisely as it was designed to operate; it's producing precisely what it was designed to produce.

On the one hand, we have this widely perceived crisis in American education. On the other hand, there is broad consensus that the system is not broken. When pondering this conundrum, I can come to only one conclusion: We do not need school reform! The system's not broken; why reform it? The system is operating as it was designed to operate; why reform it?

Our schools do not need reform or restructuring. The American education system is in need of transformation, and transformation implies a change in state. For example, if our vocational education system is water, and today's technological workplace needs ice, we cannot become ice and remain in liquid state. If our elementary schools are caterpillars, and today's child—faced with an increasingly complex society, provided a fractured family structure—requires a butterfly, we cannot become a butterfly and remain a caterpillar.

Yet, many of our alleged reform or restructuring efforts seem geared to flogging the caterpillar to get it to crawl faster! Many examples will be provided in the chapters to follow. One will suffice here. A school district in northeastern Connecticut went through a very long, very involved strategic planning process. Focus groups of parents, teachers, administrators, business partners, and community representatives worked for months to develop five long-range goals. All five goals called for higher scores on the Connecticut Mastery Test (the state's standardized test for elementary school students).

One may ask, "You mean this district has not been working to raise test scores in the past?" (Have they been working to *lower* test scores?)

This is not an example of transformation. This is an example of using new ways (a strategic planning instrument and focus groups) to work on the same thing (higher test scores). The means may be different, but the end is not.

Transformation, on the other hand, requires a complete change in state. Organizations truly working on transformation no longer have the same priorities, the same concerns, the same problems. As a teacher and consultant, the late W. Edwards Deming is credited with helping leaders in business and education understand and implement a process for accomplishing transformation.

We could study organizations that subscribe to Deming's teachings and are making unquestioned progress in the process of transformation. We could study Toyota, Matushita, and Fuji. We could study many other Japanese business organizations that have risen from the ashes of World War II to reach out and capture entire markets. Some people, however, are sick and tired of hearing about the Japanese. Forget the Japanese.

We could study Motorola, Intel, Ford, Greenwood Mills, and many U.S. business organizations that are making unquestioned progress in a process of transformation. After all, Ford lost more than a billion dollars in fiscal year 1980; it was on the brink of financial collapse. Study Ford and what its executives and union officials learned from Deming, and we'll see clear evidence of a change in state. Of course, educators are getting tired of hearing about how business has tried to learn and apply Deming's principles. Forget business.

Instead, we could study Mount Edgecumbe High School in Sitka, Alaska; or Ware Shoals School District 51 in Ware Shoals, South Carolina; or Enterprise School District in Redding, California; or any number of other schools and districts making unquestioned progress in the process of transformation. Encourage your school district to study all of these organizations making unquestioned progress. It doesn't matter if they're American or Japanese. It doesn't matter if they're schools or businesses. The district will find organizations that no longer have the concerns they once had; that no longer have the problems they once had; that no longer have the priorities they once had.

Your school district will also find it easy to lose heart. You'll quickly discover that there's no one right way to accomplish the transformation. There's no standard recipe, no cookbook.

A local school can't visit Toyota, copy step-by-step instructions of what it has done over the past four decades, plug it into the school community, and expect it to work. Your own district can't visit Sitka, Ware Shoals, or Redding; copy what those school systems have done over the past four to 10 years; plug it into your unique schools, with unique students, teachers, and histories; and expect it to work. There's no one right way to do it; no one right way to accomplish the transformation.

If, however, one were to study all the previously mentioned organizations making unquestioned progress, one would find three common threads. How those threads are woven into their unique fabrics may differ, may vary in terms of specific events or sequence; but we will find the following three common threads, the *key elements of the transformation process.*

1. Adopting a systems perspective

2. Applying the essential statistical methods

3. Providing leadership to create, provide, and maintain a healthy environment for work, learning, and continuous improvement

The balance of this book is devoted to exploring and expanding on the key elements of the transformation process. For now, a few introductory comments follow.

Adopting a Systems Perspective

When introducing their staff to the transformation model, I urge local educational leaders to avoid talking about Toyota or Ford or even other schools as examples. Instead, they should discuss situations from personal life as a first step to grasping the key elements of the transformation process.

For example, when a consumer buys a car, he or she does not want its engine to consist of perfect, individual components. The consumer wants an engine with components that work well together. By the same token, as a school board member, I would not want a district consisting of perfect, individual schools or programs. As a building administrator, I would not want a school made up of perfect, individual departments or classrooms. Rather, I would want a district whose schools and programs work well together and schools whose departments and classrooms work well together to facilitate child development. (This goal is addressed from the systems perspective in chapter 3.)

When educational leaders start teaching people about transformation, they should talk about systems so much that listeners get tired of the topic! When people start to complain about how much the superintendent talks about systems, the superintendent should consider that to be positive feedback. That's because there are so many fires to fight, so many problems to solve on a day-in, day-out basis, that people seldom have the opportunity to push their chairs back and start sharing ideas about how to get the many components of their "engines" to work better together!

Applying the Essential Statistical Methods

I do not intend to turn this book into a statistics text. Though examples will be provided, and the various statistical methods will be summarized, emphasis will be placed on the *role* of statistical methods in helping us to understand and improve systems.

Deming often said, "The statistical methods are essential, but they're relatively unimportant!" Indeed, the statistical methods are essential; we can't accomplish transformation without them. But compared to the importance of leadership, guided by Deming's system of profound knowledge, the statistical methods are secondary.

Deming long insisted that there will always be variation. He added, "The question is, What is the variation trying to tell us?" When faced with variation in test scores, student achievement levels, teachers' performance, or comparisons between or among districts, statistical methods are essential to understanding that variation, as well as what the variation is trying to tell us.

The question is not, "Are students different?" The question is, "Are they *significantly* different?" The question is not, "Are teachers different?" The question is, "Are they *significantly* different?" The question is not, "Are these schools different?" The question is, "Are they *significantly* different?" We shall see how statistical methods are essential to finding the correct answers to these questions. The correct answers are essential to taking the appropriate action for improvement in any teaching, learning, or administrative process setting.

Leadership to Create the Healthy Environment

This third key element of the transformation process is the hard part, the part that takes too long. One does not create and provide a healthy environment for work and learning overnight; it can't be done in an academic year or two. It may not even be in place by the year 2000, for which both the Bush and the Clinton administrations set some demanding goals. One, for example, calls for American students to be number one in the world in math and science by the year 2000. Another calls for the high school graduation rate to increase to at least 90 percent by the year 2000.

These goals have existed for years. The Clinton administration was so impressed with President Bush's America 2000 education goals, it copied most of them word-for-word in its own Education 2000 policies! How are we doing on these policies? Poorly.

Why? One can make a clear case that we're doing poorly because of a lack of leadership.

Deming long taught managers in business and industry, "In the absence of vision and leadership, set a numerical goal." How does this point translate to education? *In the absence of vision and leadership, give a test!*

Any farmer will tell you that you don't fatten a hog by weighing it. But what have we been doing as a result of the angst created by America 2000, Education 2000, and other so-called reform movements? We've been coming up with new and exciting ways to weigh hogs! A number of states have added proficiency tests at the high school level. New York, known years back for its demanding Regent Exams in high schools, has since added standardized Performance Evaluation Program (PEP) tests in elementary schools throughout the state.

A number of studies have found that such an emphasis on standardized testing hurts students! One three-year study by Boston College's Center for the Study of Testing, Evaluation and Educational Policy found that the most commonly used standardized tests emphasize low-level rote memorization, thereby assessing low-level skills and falling "far short of the current standards recommended by math and science curriculum experts . . . . [The tests] were found to have an extensive and pervasive influence on math and science instruction nationwide."[1]

Far too often, I've observed one common negative effect of this obsession with testing in the absence of leadership. Many school districts' strategic and annual plans include goals and time set aside to work with students on test-taking skills! There's no time to discuss that Hemingway novel; there's no time for a staff development seminar; there's no time to think through another set of algebra problems. These districts are too busy preparing students to stand on the scale!

In the interest of teacher or administrator accountability, state reform movements have used standardized test scores to rank districts. High-ranking districts get awards; low-ranking districts face probation and public ridicule. Some superintendents' tenure and raises are dependent on the district's test scores. The pressure flows downhill, and the central office uses district test scores to rank schools; schools use classroom test scores to rank teachers; and, of course, teachers have always used test scores to rank students.

Has anything changed as a result of school reform or restructuring? Clearly, the answer is no! School reform has taken student testing and ranking practices of the current system and expanded them to include teachers, administrators, and districts. The effects have been devastating, as reported in *Newsweek* magazine: "[The tests] skew the teaching process itself. Studies have found ample evidence that the anticipation of achievement tests narrows the curriculum and constrains both teachers' and students' creativity."[2]

When teachers feel forced to teach to the test, students end up learning less! Once again, we don't need any more school reform; the system never needed reform in the first place. What's needed is transformation, and transformation requires leadership. In Deming's words, "The required transformation of Western style of management requires that managers be leaders. Focus on outcome (management by numbers, MBO, work standards, meet specifications, zero defects, appraisal of performance) must be abolished, leadership put in place."[3]

One cannot help but notice that many so-called reform or restructuring proposals have not taken heed of Deming's warning. They call for focus on outcomes (test scores), pay for performance, merit pay for teachers, doing away with tenure, competition (choice) between schools based on test scores (results), and so on. For far too long our management system has accepted the myth that these practices work. For far too long, we've been locked in an age of mythology, and now we're trying to "reform" our schools by applying the same myths.

We don't need such reform. We need transformation.

The Age of Mythology

During a lecture in Chicago in September 1989, Deming made the following comment: "Two hundred years from now, management historians will look back at us and refer to ours as the 'age of mythology'." They'll wonder what pagan gods we were worshipping. They'll wonder why we had the management rituals we have.

Deming's simple observation triggered a great deal of thought on my part. What did he mean by the age of mythology? What were the myths he was criticizing? And how might this observation apply to the American education system?

During a subsequent conversation with him, Deming suggested that I ponder the systems perspective (see chapters 2 through 4). For decades, he insisted that managers must understand that most of the differences observed between workers have nothing to do with the workers. Most of the performance differences observed between workers are generated by the complex and dynamic system, of which those workers are only a part. In this regard, Deming wrote, "Would you sign your work? No: Not when you give me defective canvas to work with, paint not suited to the job, brushes worn out."[4]

The supposition that people have complete control over their performance is a myth. Exhortations for people to try harder, merit pay, sales commissions, incentives, grades, gold stars, and the like ignore the effect that many other factors in the system have on people's performance. A salesperson may control whether he or she visits customer A or customer B this morning, but the salesperson does not control the product design, production quality, delivery performance, billing practices, and many other factors that may please or displease the customer.

The sales commission system, however, ignores the fact that many variables influence whether or not the sale is made, whether or not there is a repeat sale. Locked in the age of mythology, our management rituals confound the salesperson with all the other variables. According to William Scherkenbach, we know that outcomes are the result of blending many factors. "Certainly we see differences in performance, but are those differences due to the system or the individual?"[5]

A commission or merit-pay system views end-of-month sales variance numbers and assigns them to the salesperson alone. Then the salesperson is rewarded or punished based on the numbers, as if he or she had complete control over those results!

As we shall see in subsequent chapters, outputs at work are the result of more than workers' individual skills or individual efforts. A third and powerful factor is the effect of the system on those outputs. This is perhaps the most radical challenge put forth by Deming and the systems perspective.

Systems thinking assigns most differences in student performance to the system, *not* the students. Transformation requires a change in state. Therefore, transformation requires that we be willing to question everything we ever learned and believed in the current system about testing, grading, ranking, tracking, grouping, and sorting students. Systems thinking requires that we be willing to question if the concept of a high school honor roll is a rational concept, because most of the differences we observe between students and use as the basis for placement on the honor roll have nothing to do with the students!

One way to consider the theory behind this radical new perspective is to try to solve the following math problem.

If $A + B + C + D + E + F = 73,$

then   What is the numerical value of F?

If thinking logically, one would conclude that this problem cannot be solved without knowing the numerical values (or sum) of variables A through E. If one is trapped in the age of mythology, however, one could apply the traditional grading system in our schools and find we *can* assign a numerical value to F as follows:

$$A + B + C + D + E \quad + \quad F \quad = \quad 73$$

Curriculum design, content, scope and sequence; text; supplementary materials; teacher; lesson plan; teaching methods; learning methods; the test itself; physical facilities and equipment; and many other variables	+ Student =	Test score

Traditional grading practices and other rituals take all of the many variables in the teaching and learning process, add the student, then assign their sum (test score) only to the student! (Molly got a 73 on her math exam, so she received a grade of C–.) When we take a serious look at learning as a process (chapter 4), it becomes clear that sources of variation in test scores include more than simply Molly and her fellow students.

Reference to Education

We cannot apply such process thinking and the three key elements of the transformation process to a school system in the same manner as we would apply them in business. In fact, many educators tell me that they're troubled by the effects on their staff when business partners try to help the district.

Well-meaning executives and business consultants will sometimes say something like, "Here's what we're doing in our factory. Just do it in the schools, and everything will improve." Many teachers cringe when the businesspeople go on to refer to our children as raw materials or products. The professional educator sits in the audience and thinks, "These people have no earthly idea."

In his text, *Out of the Crisis,* Deming made reference to how his principles apply to government service. Below I've paraphrased one of his paragraphs to make reference to education:

> In most [schools], there is no market to capture. In place of capture of the market, a [school] should deliver economically the service prescribed by law or regulation. The aim should be distinction in service. Continual improvement would earn the appreciation of the American public and would hold jobs in the [schools], and help industry to create more jobs.[6]

Let's break down Deming's insights by analyzing a few of the key points raised in this short paragraph.

1. *In most [schools] there is no market to capture.* Certainly, in higher education and parochial schools, there may be markets to capture. If William Bennett and other radical choice advocates have their way and get schools at each others' throats in destructive competition (choice) for limited resources at the expense of children, there will be markets to capture. But today, in the American public school system at large, there is no market to capture. Therefore, applying the key elements of the transformation process to education will differ from a business context.

2. *The aim should be distinction in service.* If not capture of market in an educational context, what is the aim? The aim is for distinction in service, and I defy any outcomes-based education advocate to figure out a way to measure it or set a mastery standard for it. And yet distinction in service is the aim!

Though it cannot be measured with any precision, it is easy to describe what distinction in service looks like or sounds like. I often ask my seminar participants if any of them owns a Toyota. When hands are raised, I ask them what they'd like to tell us about their Toyotas. A sample of common responses follows:

"It's a great car."

"I've got more than 100,000 miles on it, and it's never needed service."

"I'd buy another."

"I love it."

That's distinction in service! In your local community, this aim will be achieved when parents are out there bragging about the quality of their child's learning experience in your school's classrooms just like people brag about their Toyotas. The school board will know it's making progress when parents sit with visiting relatives during the holidays and rave about the quality of their child's learning experience in your school just like my seminar participants rave about their Toyotas.

Distinction in service cannot be measured, but it's the aim.

3. *Continual improvement would earn the appreciation of the American public and hold jobs.* When confronted with the transformation challenge, teachers and other staff members will sometimes ask, "What's in it for me? Why incur this pain?"

The response to their questions is often criticism from the board or community. "You're being self-centered, not student-centered. All you want is a paycheck."

Hold on a minute. If a district or school leadership decides to follow Deming's road map, it will be asking teachers and staff to consider deep, structural, fundamental change; transformation; change in state. It will be asking staff members to question everything they ever learned and believed about the current system (which cannot be reformed!).

It seems to me that if that's what we're going to ask of schoolpeople, it's a fair question on their part to ask what's in it for them. When they ask that question, they do not deserve criticism from school board members, they deserve an answer. So let's answer their fair question.

Achieving the aim (distinction in service), coupled with continual, never-ending improvements, will earn the appreciation of the local community, the state public, and, ultimately, the American public at large. Doing so will help protect jobs in education and contribute to the creation of jobs in the local community.

So, if I work on your local school's staff, what's in it for me? Why incur this pain? Because doing so will protect my job and those of my colleagues, not to mention that a more healthy work environment will help me to focus on my students and their learning, which is why I became a teacher in the first place.

Unfortunately, many so-called reform movements have not been geared to helping teachers, educating teachers, or answering their fair questions. Rather, in the interest of accountability, teachers are being held responsible for their students' test scores. Many so-called restructuring efforts have not restructured anything. They've merely invaded the current school structure and tried to hold people responsible for outcomes beyond their control!

Our children don't need such education reform. They need transformation.

Summary

Deming long taught that the first step to improving a system is finding out what's wrong with the current system. He provided a philosophy, principles, theories, and methods that can be applied to uncover myths and other flaws in the current system. He left us with a sound road map to accomplish the transformation. It all starts with the first key element of the transformation process, and the subject of our next chapter: adopting a systems perspective.

Notes

1. H. Stout, "Math, Science Tests Are Too Simplistic, New Study Finds," *The Wall Street Journal,* 16 October 1992, p. A5.

2. C. Leslie and P. Wingert, "Not as Easy as A, B or C," *Newsweek,* 8 January 1990, p. 57.

3. W. E. Deming, *Out of the Crisis* (Cambridge, Mass.: MIT Center for Advanced Educational Services, 1986), 54.

4. W. E. Deming, *Quality, Productivity, and Competitive Position* (Cambridge, Mass.: MIT Center for Advanced Engineering Study, 1982), 36.

5. W. Scherkenbach, *The Deming Route to Quality and Productivity: Road Maps and Roadblocks* (Rockville, Md.: Mercury Press, 1988), 55.

6. Deming, *Out of the Crisis*, 6.

Chapter Two

Adopting a Systems Perspective

In his texts, letters, papers, and lectures, Deming defined a system as follows:

> It is a series of functions or activities (sub-processes, stages—hereafter components), linear or parallel, within an organization that work together for the aim of the organization. The mechanical or electrical parts that work together to make an automobile or a vacuum cleaner form a system . . . .
>
> The aim of the system must be stated by the management thereof. Without an aim, there is no system. The components of a system are necessary but not sufficient of themselves to accomplish the aim. They must be managed.[1]

My friend Joel "Jim" McAbee, superintendent of School District 51 in Ware Shoals, South Carolina, attended one of my seminars, then continued his own learning via reading, reflection, and attending one of Deming's seminars. Months later, I met with him to discuss what he'd learned about his local system.

Jim mentioned, "Both you and Dr. Deming taught me that the first step to improving a system is to find out what's wrong with the current system. But Dr. Deming insists that without an aim, there is no system. Something finally dawned on me: I have no system! I have but three buildings united only by a common parking lot!"

In the context of the systems perspective, what does one find in Jim McAbee's district or those of Rodger Wutzl in Chaplin, Connecticut, and Ron Fitzgerald in Lexington, Massachusetts? One finds a great deal of work devoted to clearly defining and reaching consensus on the aim, or purpose, of the school or district.

What is the aim of a school district? Is it to achieve high (standardized) test scores? Or is it to effectively facilitate child development? It cannot be both.

If the stated goal, aim, or purpose of the district is to achieve high test scores, that district cannot effectively facilitate child development. Standardized tests assess development only along cognitive lines. (Many would argue that standardized tests don't really assess students' cognitive development. Rather, they argue that such tests measure facts and rote memorization. To give the devil his due, however, let's accept for now any claims that standardized tests assess cognitive development.)

Robert Audette, former commissioner of special education in Massachusetts and now elementary education coordinator at the University of North Carolina-Charlotte, taught me that child development occurs over time along four dimensions: physical, cognitive, emotional, and social. (Parochial schools would add spiritual.) There is no widely employed standardized test designed to measure child development along the dimensions of physical, social, or emotional development. Therefore, any district with the stated purpose of achieving high (standardized) test scores cannot effectively facilitate child development. Attention to development along dimensions other than cognitive will take a backseat to classroom time spent on test-taking skills and facts.

Such emphasis has negative effects in ways other than lack of attention to all aspects of child development. The following front-page story appeared in the June 9, 1994 issue of the *Austin American-Statesman*, Austin, Texas.

Cheating on TAAS Reported

Georgetown sophomores say some students took advantage of lax testing environment

by Linda Latham Welch

GEORGETOWN - Sophomores at Georgetown High School say they saw blatant cheating during the spring Texas Assessment of Academic Skills testing, including classmates who copied answers, left the room for long periods of time and whispered answers to others . . . . The TAAS is a basic skills test required by the state that covers math, reading and writing. High school students must pass it to graduate . . . .[2]

The state of Texas sends a very clear message to its high school students: Whether or not you walk across the stage at graduation depends on how you do on this test. Now, we're not going to tell you what's on the test. We're not even going to tell you if the required writing sample will be descriptive, expository, or some other form. But whether you walk across the stage or not depends on this test.

Then, it's front-page news that good kids do bad things in Austin! What would one expect? As noted in the previous chapter, numerous studies have found that emphasis on standardized tests retards student learning, restricts curricula, and constrains both teachers' and students' creativity. Students also learn what's important: not learning, but high test scores.

On October 22, 1994, C-SPAN broadcast a conference that featured a spokesperson for the Carnegie Foundation. He reported that their studies had found that the most common question asked by kindergarten children in this country is, why? By third grade, they no longer commonly ask, why? The most common question among third graders is, "Will it be on the test?"

What is the purpose of your school district? Is it to achieve high test scores? Or is it to effectively facilitate child development?

Defining a System

As noted in the previous chapter, communities don't need school districts made up of perfect, individual schools or programs. They want a local education engine (system) with schools and programs that work well together to drive in the direction they want to drive: a sound, high-quality education for their children. At the risk of oversimplifying it, one could illustrate a system as follows:

Regardless of the system or process under study, any time we can define some input or inputs, any time we can define what is done to those inputs to add value or transform the input into some output or outputs, we have defined a system. It doesn't matter whether we're analyzing a staff development planning process or budgeting or selecting a textbook or teaching math or strategic planning. Once we define and agree on the process inputs, value-adding activities, and outputs, we have defined that system. And, to jump ahead a little bit, any time we can define at least one key measure of the inputs, value-adding activities, and outputs, we can apply the essential statistical methods to better understand and improve that system.

When trying to apply the systems perspective, however, we encounter one major problem with the traditional American management system. (This does not apply to schools alone; it is found in management of education, government, *and* industry.) Traditionally, the American management system has locked the production worker, the process engineer, the field salesperson, the plant manager, the classroom teacher, the department head, the specialist, the building administrator, and others inside the value-adding functional box, as follows:

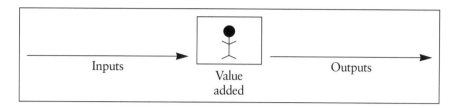

Traditional American management practices have then flogged those people to seek to optimize or perfect their local, value-adding, functional activities—with little or no attention paid to the effects of those local optimization efforts on other groups within the same system! Some common examples follow.

1. In many businesses, the sales incentive system rewards field salespeople with a commission based on sales—not margin or profit. Then, people in the plant want to throw stones at the field salesperson for selling stuff the plant can't make at a profit! It's not the field salesperson's fault. The system rewards salespeople for sales on which the company loses money!

2. Some years ago, I was conducting a seminar through the Board of Cooperative Education Services (BOCES) in Horseheads, New York. In attendance were school executives and site-based management teams from nearby towns and districts. On one site team was a third-grade teacher.

In her district, the state's standardized PEP test for math was administered in the third grade. During a break in the seminar, she talked to me about what it's like around PEP test time.

> I live in fear between when the PEP test is administered, and when the superintendent stands up at a districtwide meeting and shows how I and my third graders came out in comparison to the other third grades in the district. I live in fear. So what I do is, I teach to the test. In doing so, I may take instructional time away from science. But the science PEP test isn't 'til fourth grade, so that's not my problem.

In this age of mythology, obsessed with testing and ranking, how often does this happen in our schools? How often will we find one grade level of teachers trying their best to do a good job, but in doing so making life miserable for other grade-level teachers in the same building?

3. I'm amazed at the number of districts I've encountered in which the elementary schools' language arts program is based on whole language. Later, students move on to the middle schools in which the language arts program is still based on basal! Here we have a situation in which schools in the same district are not only using completely different methods and materials in their language arts program, they're using approaches based on completely different theories regarding how humans learn language!

And who suffers? Our children. Here we have the elementary schools trying their best. Here we have the middle schools trying their best; but those two components of the K–12 language development engine aren't working well together!

Therefore, educational leaders must stress that individual workers and groups are in fact a part of an extended process, as shown in Figure 2.1.

Every value-adding process in any organization includes suppliers, either internal or external. Every process also includes either internal or external customers (the person or group that uses the outputs). In the model for the healthy work and learning environment (chapters 9 and 10), the fifth of Deming's 14 points urges leaders to "Improve constantly and forever every process . . . ."

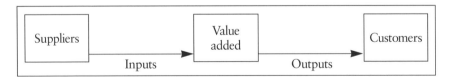

Figure 2.1. Extended process model.

Working to improve the process means the entire, *extended process*—not trying to come up with perfect, individual components. With this insight, that third-grade teacher in New York would understand that her math instruction process includes grades K–2 *and* grades 4–12. Her students need teaching and learning engines with components that work well together—not perfect, individual components.

When adopting the systems perspective, one challenge facing leadership is to get people working on improving extended processes; to help people understand the concept of optimization. On that topic, Deming wrote,

> Management's job is to optimize the total system. Without management of the system as a whole, sub-optimization is sure to take place. Sub-optimization causes loss . . . . An example of a system, well-optimized, is a good orchestra. The players are not there to play solos as prima donnas, to catch the ear of the listener. They are there to support each other. They need not be the best players in the country.[3]

Bowling team		Orchestra	School district
Low	Degree of interdependence (Need for optimization)		High

Elementary Questions for Improvement

In the context of the systems perspective and optimization, whenever any person or group sets out to improve something, leadership wants them to seek and take action on the answers to four fundamental questions.

1. Who are my customers? (Who uses what I produce?)

2. What are their needs?

3. How am I doing?

4. What can I do better?

There is a need to translate and communicate customer needs by using key measures. Then, everyone will understand what we mean by *good, bad, complete, incomplete, on time, late, mastery* . . . . The key measures are also used to translate customer feedback into evaluative data, derived from the key measures of the downstream customers' needs. As shown in Figure 2.2, feedback in the form of evaluative data forms the basis for plans and action to improve the value-adding process.

The answers to the elementary questions put people in a position to derive improvement efforts based on the needs and priorities of downstream customers. This contributes to optimization as local, functional, value-added process improvements are driven by the needs of the next group or process. However, when a superintendent asks district staff members the question, "Who are our customers?" responses often include the following:

• Students

• Parents

• Taxpayers

• Local business

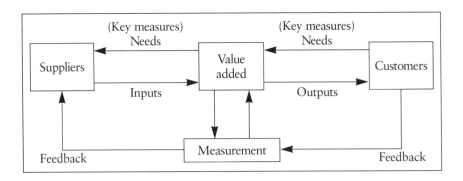

Figure 2.2. Basic systems model.

- Higher education
- Community
- Next grade-level teacher
- Society at large
- Others

After some discussion, one staff member will usually exclaim, "*Everybody's* a customer! How does this help us?"

In response to this question and understandable frustration, educational leaders have two options. First, they can introduce the concept of a process. Second, they can introduce their staffs to the major challenge facing educators today: educating the local community about the problems of education! For the balance of this chapter, we'll scratch the surface of these two options.

Focus on a Process

My older sister, Pat, is a lawyer. She had to be a lawyer; God made her to be a lawyer. Pat looks at her work and the world in general in a way that fascinates me. Ever since we were toddlers, it seems my sister has answered every question I've ever asked her by starting with the phrase, "That depends . . . ." (If I ask, "How are you feeling, Pat?" she'll reply, "That depends!")

The local school district is a complex, dynamic system of interdependent pre-K–12 teaching, learning, and administrative processes. In such a complex system, how should we respond when someone asks us, "Who is the customer?" I suggest that my sister Pat's response is appropriate: "That depends!"

It depends on the process under study. Therefore, the first duty of a district's or school's leadership is to focus on a process of concern. Then we can seek answers to the key questions: Who are the customers? What are their needs? How are we doing? What can we do better?

Who is the customer? Whoever uses the output of the process under study! For example, staff development is a critical process;

one that any enlightened leadership would like to continually improve. Who are the customers of the staff development process? One could make a case for teachers, support staff, administrators, specialists, and parents who serve on various teams and committees. But one could not make a strong case that students, higher education, a local factory, taxpayers, or society at large are direct customers of the staff development process!

By first focusing people on a process of concern, local educational leaders can realize at least three benefits.

1. It becomes easier for people and teams to define their customers (whoever uses the outputs of the process). In turn, the definition of customer needs, key measures, and strategies for improvement flow more easily, too.

2. Focus on the process also helps people grasp the concept of the extended process. For example, trying to improve a staff development process will be difficult without engaging the staff (the customers or users of the process outputs).

3. Focus on a specific process helps people understand that the transformation to continuous process improvement is feasible—it *can* be done! Too often, cries to reform or restructure education are accompanied by a litany of all the symptoms of crisis in American education. Commonly cited symptoms are that the United States has the highest teen pregnancy rate in the developed world and the highest prison incarceration rate in the entire world.

Put yourself in the place of your child's second-grade teacher. In the face of all the problems reported in the media, that teacher is put in a hopeless position: "How does what I do every day in my classroom directly affect teen pregnancy? What can I do tomorrow that will directly impact our society's high rate of prison incarceration?"

On the other hand, if we focus teachers and staff on some specific process, we can eliminate their feelings of hopelessness. Engaging them in process improvement efforts will restore not only hope, but also the pride and joy they once felt as new teachers.

Finally, by introducing the concept of a process, educational leaders can not only address but also reduce the fear and frustration inherent in the reaction, "Everybody's a customer! How does this help us?"

Educating the Local Community

Some years ago, I had the honor of assisting Deming in one of his four-day seminars. I had the opportunity to meet with him in the evening and pick his brain about how his principles can and should apply to American education. During our discussions, he kept repeating one particular phrase. If he said it once, he said it 20 times: "The major problem you face is educating the local community about the problems of education!"

Educating the community about the true problems in education would be daunting enough. But the community education challenge is now more difficult because of many widely publicized, simplistic reform proposals for solving those problems. People have been led to believe that the solution to the crisis is as simple as holding teachers accountable, issuing school vouchers, or merely setting goals for higher levels of achievement. One critic, Thomas Sowell of the Hoover Institution, simplified the source of the crisis with this observation.

> There is really nothing very mysterious about why our public schools are failures. When you select the poorest-quality college students to be public school teachers, give them iron-clad tenure, a captive audience, and pay them according to seniority rather than performance, why should the results be surprising?[4]

Columbia University's Linda Darling-Hammond exposed the inherent oversimplification of such proposals by noting:

> These proposals reflect one of the rationales for establishing national goals: that schools can be made to improve if standards are set and incentives

established that force schoolpeople to pay attention to them. Essentially, this line of thinking assumes that problems exist either because educators don't have precise enough targets to aim for, because they aren't trying hard enough, or both. Supplying concrete goals and using both carrots and sticks to move educators to pursue them are the presumed answers to underperformance . . . .[5]

The simplistic goal setting so common in education reform not only defies the true complexity of child development, teaching, learning, and education in general; it also denies reality. Like it or not, children bring many factors with them into the classroom that are beyond the control of their teacher: poor nutrition; dysfunctional home environment; lack of study space; parental absence or unemployment; abuse; peer pressure; and so on. Calls to hold teachers accountable do nothing to address many other factors that affect student learning.

This is not to suggest that there aren't turned off, burned out, or ineffective teachers in our classrooms. However, calls to hold teachers accountable, use merit pay, eliminate tenure, and get rid of deadwood and no-good teachers are overly simplistic reactions to complex problems. Of Sowell and others who think these are good ways to improve our schools, I'd like to ask a few questions.

- What control do teachers have over the long-range plans and policies of the school?

- What say do teachers have about state-mandated curricula and programs?

- What control do local teachers have over the selection of the textbooks used in the mandated curricula?

- What control do teachers have over the selection, skills, knowledge, interest, and previous education of the students assigned to their classrooms?

- What say do teachers have over the design, selection, and use (or misuse) of standardized tests (which may or may not be accurate measures of the school's effectiveness)?

The obvious answer to these questions is, or should be, "Not much!" Therefore, it's not right to blame teachers for the poor performance of our schools. We must turn our attention to the root cause of the crisis: the total school system for which the board of education, senior administrators, and the community are responsible.

Viewing Education as a System

In August 1950, Deming introduced Japanese executives to a model of production viewed as a system. "The Japanese had knowledge, great knowledge, but it was in bits and pieces, uncoordinated. This [model] directed their knowledge and efforts into a system of production . . . . The whole world knows about the results."[6]

Derived from the simplified, basic systems model provided earlier in this chapter, Figure 2.3 shows an illustration of education as a system for the development of skills and knowledge. As the Japanese grew to understand production as a system, they discovered numerous opportunities for improving quality, productivity, and competitive position. Just as in the case of Japanese executives in 1950, there is a need today for educators and others to view education from a similar systems perspective.

What are the inputs? Students

Where do they come from (suppliers)? Families and the local community

What is the value-adding process? The complex system of interdependent K–12 teaching, learning, and administrative processes

What comes out? Value-added students, skills, and knowledge

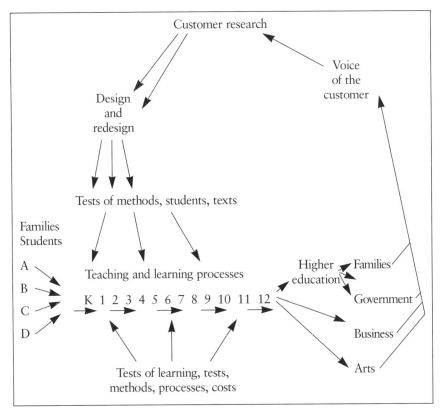

Source: J. F. Leonard, "An Introduction: Applying Deming's Principles to Our Schools," *South Carolina Business* 11 (1990): 84. Used with permission.

Figure 2.3. Education as a system for skill and knowledge development.

Where do they go (customers)? Some go directly on to an institution of higher education. Others go directly out to work in local businesses, government service, the armed forces, families of their own. All move on to the community at large.

Summary

According to Deming, in order to address the crisis in American education, there is a need to educate the local community about the problems of education. A solid first step in that local education effort is to help the community view and understand education as a system. In the next chapter, we will derive several key insights from the model of education as a system for skill and knowledge development, then move on to begin to address the issue of variation.

Notes

1. W. E. Deming, "A System of Profound Knowledge" (March 3, 1990), 2.

2. L. Welch, "Cheating on TAAS Reported," *Austin* (Texas) *American Statesman*, 9 June 1994, 1.

3. Deming, "Profound Knowledge," 3.

4. T. Sowell, "Excuses, Excuses," *Forbes*, 14 October 1991, 43.

5. L. Darling-Hammond, "Achieving Our Goals: Superficial or Structural Reforms?" *Phi Delta Kappan* (December 1990): 287.

6. W. E. Deming, *The New Economics* (Cambridge, Mass.: MIT Center for Advanced Educational Services, 1993), 58–60.

Chapter Three

Lessons of the
Systems Perspective

Deming's model of production as a system, introduced to the Japanese in 1950, and the model for viewing education as a system, introduced in chapter 2, are useful for helping people begin to apply the systems perspective. Both models are incomplete, however. Neither shows a layer of complexity that is a part of the day-in, day-out life of the local school district and its staff—what I refer to as the return loops of influence on families and learning. Figure 3.1 provides a revised view of education as a system for skill and knowledge development with those return loops added to the original model.

Let's say I live in your community, and two of my children attend the elementary school. I work for a local business that does not value learning. Managers don't encourage learning; they don't stroke it; they don't provide opportunities for learning on the job; they have no tuition refund plan or other programs to help me if I choose to take some college courses at night for my own self-improvement. My employer does not value learning. That will influence my behavior as a parent in the role of supplier of my children in your school.

On the other hand, let's say I work for Greenwood Mills, a company that does value learning. Managers encourage it; they stroke it; they provide ample opportunities for it on the job; they

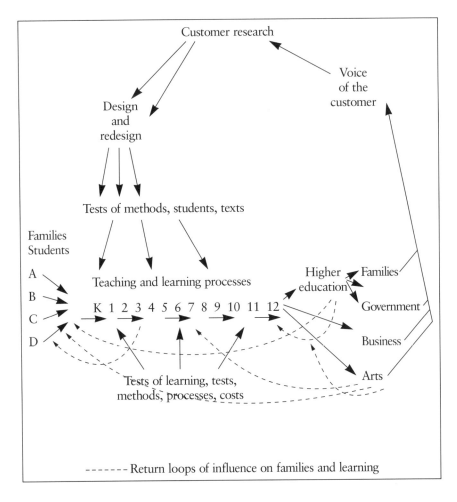

Figure 3.1. Refined view of education as a system for skill and knowledge development.

offer some college and GED-equivalency courses during work hours; they have tuition refund and other programs that help me if I choose to take other college courses at night. As an employer, Greenwood Mills values learning. That too will influence my behavior as a supplier to your school. I will be more prone to work with my children on their studies and learning. I will be more inclined to make sure my children are prepared for their school experience.

Mat Self, president of Greenwood Mills, made the following comments in a speech before the Southern Association of Chamber of Commerce Executives on May 4, 1992.

> For a quality process to have any chance for success, authority and responsibility must be pushed down throughout the organization. This is empowerment, but you must also realize that this requires a tremendous amount of training, education, and cultural awareness . . . .

Local employers with leaders like Self can and do exert a positive influence on their employees and their families. Unenlightened employers exert a negative influence. But all employers, in one way or another, influence their employees, families, and learning.

Nowhere will one find a clearer illustration of the fallacy of school reform than in the phenomenon of these return loops of influence. Most state reform mandates are focused exclusively on school governance and funding. For example:

1. The state of Texas developed a matrix for evaluating schools and districts. Among the indicators are standardized test scores, graduation rates, graduates receiving advanced seals on their transcripts, retention rates, pass rates, dropout rates, and college admissions test scores.

2. In Buffalo, New York, a business newspaper annually publishes a ranking of districts in the western New York region. Among the rating criteria are dropout rates, percent of high school graduates receiving a Regents diploma, pupil-teacher ratios, per-pupil spending, and standardized test scores at both high school and elementary school levels.

Where is the matrix for evaluating Texas business organizations? Where is the ranking of companies in western New York? Who is auditing those businesses to determine whether or not they're behaving as responsible customers of the local district? Who is evaluating their practices to see if they're acting as a responsible component of the local education system?

Among the criteria I'd like to see are whether or not local businesses are clearly defining and communicating to the district their needs and key measures of those needs; whether or not the company is providing periodic, systematic feedback (as opposed to after-the-fact complaints); and whether or not local businesses are supplementing that feedback with suggestions for improvement, as well as help and resources to accomplish the desired improvement.

To begin to educate the local community about the problems of education, there is a need to display Figure 3.1 during meetings and argue about it! Understanding the influence of employers and other components on families and learning is one of many insights that can be drawn from the adoption of a systems perspective. A few other insights follow.

Lessons of the Systems Perspective

Lesson 1

There is and can be no such thing as an optimum curriculum. In the model illustrated in Figure 3.1, ongoing research to learn about child development and other customers' needs will drive continuous design and redesign activities to improve value-adding processes. Therefore, there is and can be no such thing as an optimum curriculum.

As noted, there is a need to get the systems model in front of groups to educate the local community about the complexity and problems of education. However, I always urge administrators to start with their own staff. Some of them may find it heartbreaking to learn that, despite all the effort poured into the current curriculum design, it's written in sand! That's because ongoing curricular improvements will result from the energy generated by continually seeking and taking action on answers to the question, "What can we do better?" In any district guided by the systems perspective, it would be impossible to find a high school teacher using the same lesson plan used five years ago! The continuous improvement energy provided by the systems perspective will yield ongoing enhancements such that today's lesson plan will be quite different from the one used just a few years ago.

Lesson 2

We will find numerous opportunities to improve the education system outside the four walls of our schools. Once again, here's where most alleged reform mandates break down. They're geared to school governance, school funding, and educator accountability. Few address, to any depth, the role of local businesses, local government, or even, for that matter, higher education. Lawrence Sherr, of the University of Kansas, offers the following indictment of the higher education component of the broader system.

> What does this have to do with higher education? I believe that very few of our institutions have any idea of who our customers are . . . . Somehow we have lost our way. We don't know who our customers are. How did this happen? We like to find excuses. We like to blame people and we in higher education, I claim, are just as guilty of doing that as any business leader I have met.[1]

One conference at the Massachusetts Institute of Technology determined that teaching at research universities leaves a lot to be desired. As reported in the *Boston Globe,* "The prevailing view at the conference seemed to be that not enough attention was being paid to how well professors communicate knowledge. Teaching assistants are not trained to teach—students in the audience said some assistants had difficulty speaking English."[2] So, it's not that serious problems aren't recognized; it's just that, to date, higher education has remained exempt from the zeal and attention of school reformers.

Even though groups outside our school buildings have not been effectively engaged in transformation, many practices of those groups are being proposed as ways to improve our schools. Deming reported on President Reagan's proposals to start paying teachers on merit rather than seniority. "The problem lies in the difficulty to define a meaningful measure of performance. The only verifiable measure is a short-term count of some kind . . . . Where were the President's economic advisors? He was only doing his best."[3]

More recently, California's Governor Pete Wilson proposed that merit pay be applied to teachers. A number of other states have introduced the concept under the umbrella of reform. Several years ago, schools in one southeastern state could not get funding unless they agreed to teacher incentive pay. (After all, 85 percent of American businesses have merit pay. Why not use it to reform schools?)

The theory behind these proposals is that merit pay is a motivator; that the chance to make more money will drive dramatic improvements; that getting teachers at each others' throats for limited merit budgets will solve the crisis in American education.

Lesson 3

The term healthy competition *is an oxymoron.* In my seminars, I use a simple demonstration of the fallacy of merit pay as a means for improvement. I suggest to participants that three others and I serve on their staff. One activity we're working on is pen-clicking and I figure out a way to click my pen faster and better than the others. Under the traditional evaluation or merit pay system, will I share my technique with the others? The answer from seminar participants is always a resounding no!

Why won't I share my technique with my colleagues? Because the traditional ranking and merit pay system rewards me for keeping my pen-clicking technique to myself, allowing my peers to remain mediocre. In doing so, I get high ratings, high rank, big raises, recognition, the teacher-of-the-year award, the employee-of-the-month parking space.

The prevailing system of ranking and merit pay punishes me if I share my pen-clicking technique. If I share it, I won't stand out. I'm punished for sharing, even though sharing my technique is clearly what's best for me, my colleagues, our students, the administration, the board of education, parents, and the community at large!

Some years ago, I used my pen-clicking demonstration with a state superintendent of education and 32 of her executive directors in the department of education. Based on that insight, the superintendent started working hard with legislators to eliminate the mandated, yet destructive, teacher incentive pay system. As a result of her work and leadership, that state eventually did away with the teacher incentive pay system. It was replaced with a campus incentive system, under which the top 25 percent of schools in the state were rewarded with a thousand-dollar bonus for the principal and all staff members. In other words, they found a way to take their disease orally instead of anally. It went down a little easier, but they had the same disease—destructive competition!

In the interest of so-called reform, some states have raised the competition to a building level. Now, I'm a school principal with an effective new pen-clicking technique. The campus incentive system, the Excelsior Awards in New York, the Exemplary Schools Awards in Texas, and so on, reward me for keeping my pen-clicking technique to myself. They reward me for allowing other principals in the same district to remain mediocre!

From a systems perspective, such insight clearly illustrates that the two-word phrase, *healthy competition,* is an oxymoron. It's the same as *safe sex* or *cruel kindness.* Any competitive practice, broken down to its foundation, is fundamentally based on the attitude, "I win, you lose." In our schools, I win, you lose in the short term leads to "we lose" in the long term! In the campus incentive system, if I win the award this year, the only way one of my three colleagues can win it next year is at my expense.

If there are administrators in a district who cannot tell the difference between games and child development, remove them from the central office and return them to the coach's office. If we have teachers and staff who cannot differentiate between sports and child development, the school board should revise its staff selection and placement policy because it's flawed!

In the context of transformation, optimization, and the systems perspective, there is and can be no such thing as healthy competition. What's needed is not competition, but cooperation; not win-lose, but win-win; not efforts to become perfect, individual schools, but schools and other components that work well together.

Last year I experienced an example of such cooperation in Dallas, Texas. I flew into the airport there, rented a car, and stepped out to the curb to wait for my rental car company's courtesy van. Minutes later, a bus pulled up with the following words stenciled on its side: "National, Hertz, Budget, Avis."

I thought to myself, How smart these Texans are! Before me was a sterling example of cooperation. At many airports, those four major rental-car companies practically share the same lot. Despite such close proximity, most of them run separate fleets of courtesy vans. But in Dallas, they're cooperating rather than competing, and *everybody wins.* The companies win, with savings on capital investments, route and terminal coverage, and lower maintenance costs. Their equipment and maintenance services suppliers win because they're able to carry smaller inventories of spare parts, not to mention that they need to service just one type of bus. Every customer wins, with lower rental charges and no longer having to experience the frustration of watching three other vans drive by before ours shows up! And none of this keeps anyone from going into the rental car business. None of this is an unlawful restraint of trade. Rather, it is a prime example of Deming's call for leaders to strive for optimization, for cooperation, for win-win relationships. It is the new economics in action, as described in Deming's text of that title.

MIT's Peter Senge adds that vision often gets confused with competition.

> Competition can be a useful way of calibrating a vision, of setting scale. To beat the number-ten player at the tennis club is different from beating number one. But to be number one of a mediocre lot may not fulfill my sense of purpose. Moreover, what is my vision after I reach number one?[4]

The belief that competition is good and healthy is yet another belief from the age of mythology. (Again, I draw a distinction here between games and child development, between sports and American business, in which people's jobs and livelihoods are at stake.) Based on the myth that competition is good, many reform leaders are calling for school choice, for voucher systems.

In his text, *The New Economics,* Deming implied that school choice would be destructive from a systems perspective by noting:

> A system of schools (public schools, private schools, parochial schools, trade schools, universities, for example) is not merely pupils, teachers, school boards, boards of regents, and parents working separately to achieve their own aims. It should be, instead, a system in which these groups work together to achieve the aims that the community has for the school—growth and development of children . . . . Such a system of schools would be destroyed if some group of schools decided to band together to lobby for their own interests. They together with all other schools would in time be losers.[5]

The school choice advocates' theory is that competition will drive school improvements. Because they'll be fighting to attract students (and their tuition vouchers), schools will improve quality, reduce costs, become more efficient, and improve the effectiveness of their teaching and learning processes. The cream will rise to the top.

Unfortunately, the effects of school choice disprove the theory. In Massachusetts, which adopted a modified choice system a few years ago, there is growing evidence that competition is having a negative effect. The following article appeared in an issue of the *Maynard Beacon,* Maynard, Massachusetts.

Educator: Schools' Relationships Hurt

by Peter Dunn

Maynard - Over the course of the past year, educators at the Green Meadow Elementary School have been working to revise the school's reading/language arts curriculum. When such projects are undertaken, according to school Principal Frank Hill, it is common to ask neighboring schools for their curriculums. "We've done it for years," he said. "It's a cross-check. Have we left something out? . . ." This year, Hill sent out 12 requests to other school systems for copies of their reading curriculums. In the past, he would have received between 8 and 10 responses. "Now that choice has got us competing with each other, I did not get one single response," said Hill.[6]

How can such choice possibly improve quality? Reduce costs? Improve efficiency? In this article is clear evidence of the lesson that the phrase *healthy competition* is indeed an oxymoron. School choice stifles cooperation across school and district lines.

The alternative to adversarial competition is cooperation. For example, two adjacent small towns have separate high schools. Local budgets are currently funding facilities and programs for the arts and vocational education in both high schools. Adopting the systems perspective on a regional basis may lead to a decision to have one of the towns' high schools concentrate on an arts program and the other to channel its limited resources into the vocational program.

Such cooperation would result in a win-win situation, as opposed to counterproductive competition, for all involved. Taxpayers would win, because they'd no longer have to fund the two programs in each individual high school. Students and parents would win because they'd have better choices for focused, high-quality educational programs. And the schools would win because their limited budgets, time, and other resources would no longer be diluted by trying to be a one-size-fits-all high school.

Lesson 4

Parents (families) are an integral part of the school system. When Deming taught them to view production as a system, Japanese executives recognized that their customers were the most important people on the production line. The adoption of a broad systems perspective also led to a breakthrough in Japanese management thinking relative to how they viewed their suppliers.

Those suppliers came to be viewed as an integral part of the production process. They were no longer viewed as outsiders, as sources for cost savings alone. Over time, a transformation occurred in company purchasing operations. Partnerships were formed with suppliers based on cooperation, sharing, and a win-win relationship.

Viewing education as a system of skills and knowledge development provides a wonderful opportunity to clarify or validate the definition of parents' roles. For example, the model of education as a system clearly illustrates that parents (families) are an integral part of the system. In recent years, there has been great progress in engaging parents in school programs. Representation on site-based management teams, as well as their inclusion in focus groups and strategic planning, are cementing better relationships between educators and parents. At the same time, these efforts are tapping parents' talents for school improvement efforts.

Looking at the broad systems model, parents (families) can be viewed as customers of the K–12 system, together with local business, higher education, the community at large, and other groups. But the same model clearly illustrates that parents (families) also play the role of suppliers to the K–12 component.

How many parents in your community sit in a passive state, as if they are just customers, asking your schools' teachers, "What have you done for us lately?" How many of them have had an opportunity to view themselves as suppliers, of whom our classroom teachers have the right to ask, "What have *you* done for *us* lately?" Adopting a systems perspective creates opportunities for parents to understand their dual role.

Lesson 5

Students' roles must be clarified, if not redefined. Just as challenging is defining the role of students from a systems perspective. Clearly, students are customers (consumers) within the teaching and learning process; but they may also play a role of value-adding resources in a cooperative learning environment, as well as a source of assessment and feedback.

During one of my seminars, a high school English department head explained that, due to staff reductions, all the high school English teachers had to take on an extra class period. With between 100 and 125 students moving through their classrooms every day, the department head said, "My English teachers don't have time to learn these concepts. Nor do they have time to experiment with them in their classrooms." When I asked why they didn't have time, she replied, "That's a lot of papers to grade every week."

I asked her, "What are high school English teachers doing grading papers every week?" Some of those English students may end up at a university next year—in a 350-student freshman lecture hall. Some of them may be working in the warehouse at a local manufacturing company next year. In those settings, do you think someone's going to grade their papers every week?

If that high school's students don't graduate well-schooled and comfortable developing and applying some rubric to their own work to determine how they're doing, they're dead at the university next year. If they graduate unable to develop personal plans for improvement, and with their peers plans for group improvement, they're dead at the local manufacturing company next year.

No wonder those high school English teachers had no time to learn; no wonder they had no time to experiment in their classrooms. They were too busy retarding adolescent development by grading their students' papers every week!

A second-grade teacher was interested in seeing how her students could fill the role of source of assessment and feedback. So, she engaged them in the development of a three-by-four rubric (see Figure 3.2). Students apply this rubric to their own writing samples. Then they pass their work across the aisle, and their neighbor applies the rubric. The teacher occasionally audits the rubric applications to make sure they're accurate and also uses the rubric scores as one answer to the question, "How am I doing?" At the same time, she is freed up to concentrate on her teaching and learning process, as well as individual students' needs and learning styles. If these second-grade students can develop and apply a rubric to determine how they're doing, high school English students can too!

William Glasser shed another light on the role of the student with the following observation.

> If we accept the idea that the purpose of any organization, public or private, is to build a high-quality

3	2	1
You underlined your adopted word.		You did not underline your adopted word.
You drew and colored your picture neatly.	You drew and colored your picture sloppily.	You did not color your picture.
You wrote a complete sentence, beginning with a capital letter and using . , ? or !	You left out a beginning capital letter, or you left out . , ? or !	You did not use capital letters or . , ? or !
You printed your sentence neatly.		You did not print your sentence neatly.

Figure 3.2. Second graders' rubric.

product or perform a high-quality service, then we
must also accept the idea that the workers in that
organization must do high-quality work . . . . In our
schools, students are the workers, and today almost
none are doing high-quality work . . . .[7]

I do not suggest that we try to hang any one label on any one
player in a system of education's complexity. As noted by Glasser,
students are indeed workers. But they're also suppliers (of effort
and energy), value-adding resources, a source of assessment and
feedback, as well as customers (consumers). My friend Robert
Audette helped me to clarify in my own mind the role of students
by reviewing the core theory of child development.

According to Audette and others, child development occurs
along four dimensions: physical, cognitive, emotional, and social.
(As noted previously, parochial schools would add spiritual.)
Children begin development in a dependent state. Then, as development occurs, at varying rates and stages, children achieve an
independent state. They are able to take on more and more responsibility for their own physical hygiene, homework assignments,
participation in social events, and so on. Finally, development has
occurred when children achieve an interdependent state—able to
do things not only on their own, but also with and through others.

Based on Audette's insights, I arrived at the following three-
stage definition of the role of the student in the education system.

1. We can view the dependent child as customer *of* the system.
   (What are his or her needs? Development along physical,
   emotional, cognitive, and social dimensions.)

2. As children develop at varying rates and stages, we can view
   the independent child as worker *in* the system.

3. What do we want to see emerge *from* the K–12 component
   of the education system? The interdependent self-manager—
   capable of, excited by, and looking forward to pursuing a
   process of lifelong learning.

Once the roles of students are clarified, understood, and agreed upon, the challenge facing educational leaders is to manage the interface among the various components of the system to facilitate child development. Cooperation and partnerships must be forged with parents, local businesses, local government, service agencies, and other community groups so those components work well together to help children achieve the status of interdependent self-managers.

Lesson 6

Teachers' roles must be clarified, if not redefined. If we accept Glasser's view that one role (perhaps even a primary role) of students is that of worker, we must recognize the implications that definition will have for how we define the role of their teachers.

In a manufacturing setting, if one wants high quality work from production workers, they must be provided with high-quality machines, raw materials, methods, other resources, and supervision. Similarly, viewing students as workers in the school system—from whom we want high-quality work and learning—makes clear the need for providing them with good texts, curricula, instruction, materials, other resources, and supervision.

If the role of the student is that of worker, the role of the teacher may be viewed by some as that of supervisor. Many educators may resist that definition, however, especially if they interpret supervisor to mean boss or, worse yet, the foreman of the factory model. Therefore, some people may prefer to define the role of the teacher as that of facilitator, mentor, or coach.

Still others may insist that the role of the teacher is that of coworker. Resist such an interpretation! After all, if I have to undergo open heart surgery, the last thing I want to hear from the surgeon as I sink into anesthesia is the comment, "Let's brainstorm on how to best make this cut!" I do not want my surgeon to be a coworker, along with others on the operating room support staff. I want a surgeon who knows what to do and how to utilize the talents of others on the support staff.

Optimally, we can define the teacher's role as *leader*. Why are we so hesitant to confer that status on our classroom teachers? They are leaders of the local classroom teaching and learning processes and the students who work therein.

Here, the teachings of Deming transfer cleanly from the so-called business model to education. For years, Deming taught certain general behavioral attributes of a leader, in the context of the seventh point of his 14-point model of a healthy work environment, "Institute leadership." The following is a restatement of those general attributes.

Attributes of the Effective Leader/Teacher

1. Understands how the work of his or her class fits into the overall aims and curricula of the school. The assumption here is that the school board and senior administrators have done their job. They have clearly defined and communicated the district's purpose, aims, and curricula, so classroom leaders/teachers can figure out how they and their students fit in.

2. Focuses on the customer, both internal and external.

3. Is coach, counsel, and teacher—not a judge. What systems and practices does your local district have that help classroom teachers learn and fulfill the role of coach and counsel? What systems and practices exist that require classroom teachers to pass judgment?

4. Removes obstacles to joy in learning.

5. Understands variation. Uses systems thinking, statistical thinking, and statistical methods to determine who (if anyone) is outside the system, in need of special help. Effective leaders/teachers understand that the question is not, "Are my students different?" Rather, they understand that the appropriate question is, "Are they significantly different?" Statistical methods and an understanding of variation help leaders/teachers strike that distinction and then take appropriate action to improve their teaching and learning processes to help their students' development.

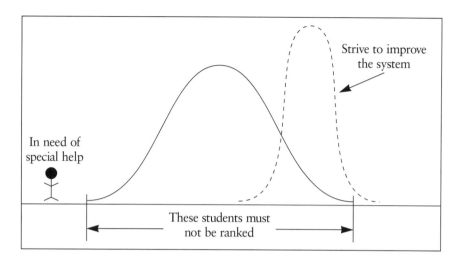

6. Works to improve the teaching and learning process in which he or she and the students work. Effective leaders/teachers strive continually to improve the teaching and learning process. They do not sort kids, track kids, grade kids, or rank kids—they improve the process!

7. Creates trust.

8. Forgives a mistake.

9. Listens and learns.

Unfortunately, today many teachers encounter systemic barriers to learning and exhibiting these attributes.

It will take a long time to transform the system and remove barriers to teachers' creativity and students' joy in learning. In the meantime, learning and adopting a systems perspective can help to clarify roles. I urge any school district interested in transformation to view the attributes list as an outline for their teaching staff development planning over the next three years. Ask yourself, What is our plan for teaching these attributes to our classroom teachers? What is our strategy for helping them to exhibit those attributes behaviorally?

Lesson 7

Variation is the enemy! Let's climb inside the system model (Figure 3.1) and consider just three teaching, learning, and administrative processes: math instruction in the elementary school; building maintenance and repairs; and budgeting in the central office. Outputs from these processes include

Math instruction: Math skills, knowledge, methods

Maintenance: Repairs, preventive maintenance, building safety inspections

Budgeting: Spending forecasts, budget variance reports, reports to state agencies

Key measures of these process outputs may include test scores, maintenance response time, and the plus or minus variance of actual expenses compared to the budget. Are all of these measures always exactly the same? Do all students achieve exactly the same raw score on standardized tests? Are all maintenance repairs completed in exactly the same amount of time? Are all budget variance numbers always zero?

The obvious answer to these questions is, "Of course not." At the output of these and other processes we will always find variation. Some students get high scores; others low; most score around some local average. Some maintenance repairs take a long time; others are completed quickly; most cluster around some average completion time. Deming taught that there will always be variation. We'll find it at the output of any and every value-adding process in the district.

A final lesson to be learned from adopting a systems perspective is that variation is the enemy! Even though variation will always exist, it is nonetheless the enemy. Consider the following examples.

1. In accounting, costs are already within or over budget by the time the business manager cuts the check. The enemy is the variation and sources of variation in and around the cost and budgeting system.

2. In transportation, students are already on time or late by the time they climb off the bus in the front of the school. The enemy is the variation and sources of delays in and around the bus scheduling and transportation system.

3. In manufacturing, products are already good or bad by the time an inspector looks at them. The enemy is the variation and sources of variation in and around the design and production process.

4. Students already know or do not know the material by the time they are tested. The enemy is the variation and sources of variation in learning and achievement in and around the teaching and learning process.

Summary

A transformation in Japanese management thinking and behavior occurred when they adopted a broad systems perspective as it relates to production. Once executives began to view external suppliers and customers as integral parts of their manufacturing system, they discovered numerous opportunities for improving quality, productivity, and competitive position.

Similarly, a transformation in people's thinking will follow the adoption of a broad systems perspective in American education. Roles will be clarified and better understood. Barriers to optimization in the current system will be recognized. New sources for improvement will be identified and pursued.

Educating staff members and communities about the problems and complexity of education will help eliminate short-sighted, ineffective, and dysfunctional reform proposals. In their place will emerge rational improvement strategies, guided by the systems perspective—the first key element of the transformation process.

To complete an examination of the systems perspective, it is now time to explore the concept of a process. In the next chapter we'll do so, beginning with some more detail on the seventh lesson of the systems perspective: variation is the enemy.

Notes

1. L. Sherr, "Is There a Better Way to Manage Higher Education?" (paper presented at the 29th Annual Forum of the Association for Institutional Research, Baltimore, Md., May 1989), 40.

2. A. Flint, "Teaching at Research Universities Gets a D," *The Boston Globe,* 10 October 1991.

3. Deming, *Out of the Crisis,* 103–104.

4. P. Senge, *The Fifth Discipline: The Art and Practice of the Learning Organization* (New York: Doubleday/Currency, 1990), 149.

5. Deming, *The New Economics,* 64.

6. P. Dunn, "Educator: Schools' Relationships Hurt," *The Maynard* (Massachusetts) *Beacon.*

7. W. Glasser, "The Quality School," *Phi Delta Kappan* (February 1990): 426.

Chapter Four

Concept of a Process

As noted in the previous chapter, the seventh lesson of the systems perspective is that variation is the enemy. Outputs are either good or bad by the time we look at them; the enemy is the variation and sources of variation in and around the process that produced the output.

Deming referred to the Taguchi loss function (developed by Genichi Taguchi in Japan in 1960 and illustrated in Figure 4.1) as an excellent model for understanding not only the concept of optimization, but also the loss that is generated by variation. He wrote, "A loss function describes the losses that a system suffers from different values of some adjustable parameter . . . . The most important use of a loss function is to help us [move toward] continual reduction of variation . . . through improvement of processes."[1]

As an example of the Taguchi loss function, let's say Kate is most comfortable and works most efficiently when the temperature of her office is 68 degrees Farenheit. If the temperature drops to 67 degrees or rises to 69 degrees, any loss of comfort is imperceptible. On the other hand, if the temperature plunges to 48 degrees or jumps to 88 degrees, Kate feels it! And she experiences loss in both comfort and work efficiency. That's the whole theory behind the Taguchi loss function. As variation increases, loss goes up. As variation is reduced around some target or optimum value, loss is minimized.

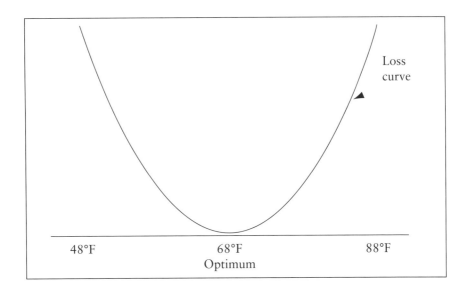

Figure 4.1. Illustration of the Taguchi loss curve.

Figure 4.2 illustrates variation in sixth graders' math learning, achievement, and aptitude. It is the distribution of assessed math skills of students who entered the sixth grade from the K–5 components of the district's math teaching and learning system. In the face of this wide variation, the sixth-grade teacher has to stretch to meet the individual needs of his students. While he's working with students at the low end, students on the high end experience loss; while he's working with students at the high end, the students on the low end experience loss.

What if a tighter distribution of assessed learning, achievement, and aptitude (illustrated in Figure 4.3) arrived in the sixth grade from the K–5 components of the system? The sixth-grade teacher would still have to stretch—but not as far! The teacher and all of the students would experience less loss.

Once again, the whole idea behind Taguchi's model is that variation brings with it some waste, cost, and loss. Therefore, variation is the enemy.

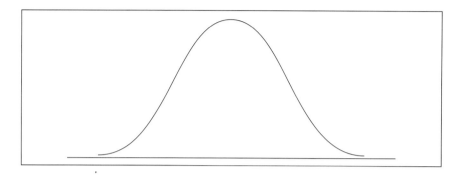

Figure 4.2. Distribution of sixth graders' assessed math learning, achievement, aptitude.

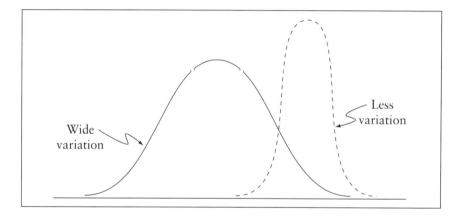

Figure 4.3. Revised distribution of sixth graders' math assessments.

New Definitions

Based on the lessons of the systems perspective and Taguchi's model, we must help people to ponder the theory that variation is the enemy. Then, if we agree that variation is the enemy, we can derive some new definitions for *quality* and *quality improvement,* as follows:

Quality = minimal variation around some target or optimum value

Quality improvement = reduced variation around the target or optimum value

The beauty of these new definitions is that I need not have a manufactured widget in my hand to apply them. Nor do I need a blueprint, specification, or standard. All I need is for an enlightened local leadership to focus me on a process of concern, then help me derive appropriate key measures of the process outputs. The wider the variation found in the evaluative data, the lower the quality, the greater the loss. The tighter the evaluative data cluster around some target or optimum value, the lower the loss, the higher the quality.

Some people may have a hard time accepting these new definitions. Among the objections we can anticipate are

• *Quality = minimal variation.* Resistance is manifested through comments such as, "That definition doesn't apply here! We have no control over the variation in readiness to learn that showed up on our kindergarten doorstep last August. Besides, manufacturing companies can drop bad suppliers; they can bring the best on board. But as a public school district, we can't go out to dysfunctional families in our community and tell them not to send their kids here."

• *Quality improvement = reduced variation.* Resistance is manifested through comments such as, "That doesn't apply here! We don't want some cookie-cutter approach to education that makes students walk alike, talk alike, think alike, and act alike. That will stifle students' individuality; that will stifle creativity."

How can school leaders and others reply to these objections? Let's take them one at a time.

Minimal Variation

People are right to observe that we had no control over whatever variation that arrived on the kindergarten doorstep last August— but only in the short term! Longer term, schools can and must manage their supplier base to reduce future incoming variation in readiness to learn. For example, districts can reach out to work with local Head Start programs, preschools, and day care facilities in their communities to improve preschool preparation over time.

Some districts are working on parent education, especially among teenage mothers. One goal of these efforts is to encourage parents to more actively and formally prepare their children for the school experience.

Finally, bear in mind that today's third-grade children are tomorrow's parents. Their future behavior as parents (suppliers) will in large part be influenced by their experience as students.

It may be true that we had no choice but to work with whatever variation in readiness to learn that showed up in our kindergarten last August. However, work over time with parents and other preschool components of the system can and will reduce future incoming variation.

Reduced Variation

When applying this definition of quality improvement, we are not talking about adopting a cookie-cutter approach to education. We are not talking about trying to get students to walk alike, talk alike, think alike, and act alike. (The obsession with standardized testing in some quarters of this country is doing too good a job at that now!) Nor are we talking about extinguishing the beauty of the child's individuality, race, gender, or ethnic origins. We are talking about reduced variation in learning and achievement.

This does not mean that we're interested in dumbing down curricula or speeding up the slow students at the expense of the fast. To picture what we mean by improvement, let's consider how an avid golfer would define improvement.

Figure 4.4 illustrates the distribution of the golfer's scores from last summer. As you can see, she had some low scores and some high scores, but most of her scores clustered around an average score, used to calculate her handicap.

Improving her golfing process would not result in the distribution illustrated in Figure 4.5. Granted, she reduced variation in her scores, and she was shooting more consistently. But in doing so she lost her best scores.

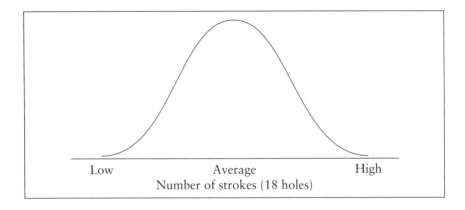

Figure 4.4. Distribution of golf scores from last summer.

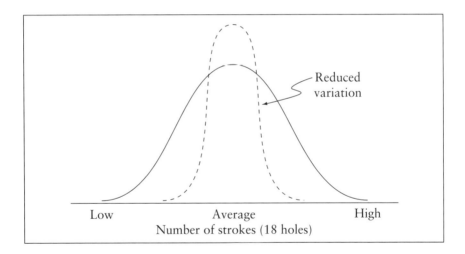

Figure 4.5. Reduced variation in golf scores.

Figure 4.6 does illustrate improvement in the golfer's process. She is not only shooting more consistently, but she's doing so around a lower average score. If she were interested in continuous improvement, she'd continue to work on improving her stance, grip, backswing, clubs, and other elements of her golfing process to

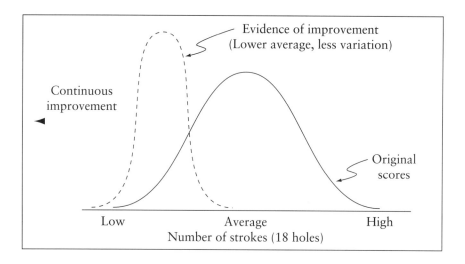

Figure 4.6. Results of improved golfing process.

continually reduce her average score and to achieve less variation and greater consistency around that lower average score.

To apply our new definition of quality improvement to education, one need only picture the inverse of the improved golfing process! (See Figure 4.7.) Improvement of teaching and learning processes yields continuing higher levels of average student learning and achievement, with less variation and greater consistency around those higher average scores. In the case of student learning and achievement, optimum will always mean *higher;* it will not be defined by some minimum standard imposed by the state department of education!

Sorting Versus Education

Adopting the systems perspective will require a significant change, a transformation, in the traditional approach to managing variation in student learning and achievement. According to Frank Newman, president of the Education Commission of the States, the traditional approach has had a negative effect: "The prime job of the education system is sorting more than education."[2]

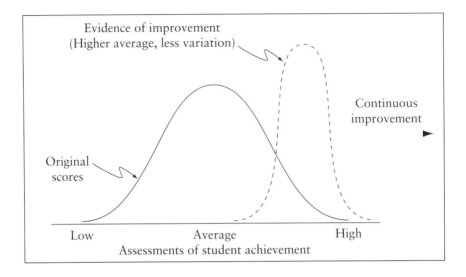

Figure 4.7. Results of improved teaching and learning processes.

This sorting begins at a very early age. A number of states begin to use standardized tests in second grade, with seven-year-olds. Those test results, together with other inputs, determine the distribution of student achievement and/or aptitude. Figure 4.8 illustrates a typical distribution. This information is often used to identify the bottom 5 percent of students for special programs. These students, beginning at the age of seven, get to stand up five days a week during normal school hours and figuratively hang a sign around their necks that reads, "I'm stupid!" Then, they head off to their special programs for the "stupid kids."

I met one of those children several years ago at a Board of Cooperative Education Services (BOCES) facility in upstate New York. I was in the Staff Development Center one July morning, setting up for one of my seminars. A child entered the lobby. He looked to be about 12 years old, and he was attending a summer school class. I introduced myself, and told him what I was doing there. When I asked who he was, he replied, "I'm a BOCES student."

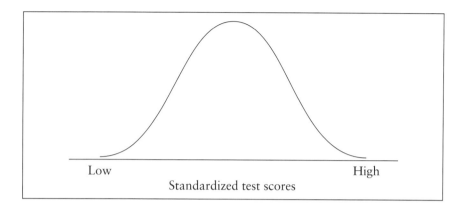

Figure 4.8. Distribution of second graders' assessed achievement.

That child had no name! I did not ask, "What are you?" I asked, "Who are you?" He did not reply with his name; he replied, "I'm a BOCES student."

Then I asked him, "What's a BOCES student?"

He answered, "We ride the short bus with the seat belts."

Look what the system has done to that child. Beginning at an early age, it sorted him out for the special programs, and it took away his name.

Later, I pondered the conversation I had with that youngster. I imagined that I was doing a graduate research project on higher order thinking skills. As a part of that project, I was conducting interviews and looking for evidence of employed higher-order thinking skills among my interviewees. If I asked that boy, "What's a BOCES student?" and he replied, "We ride the short bus with the seat belts," would I record that response as evidence of employed higher-order thinking skills? Yes, I would. That child is gifted, and I'd have the evidence to prove it. But he doesn't know he's gifted. By the age of 12, he no longer had a name.

Back to Figure 4.8, the same information is used to identify the top 5 percent of students for gifted programs. These kids, beginning at the age of seven, get to stand up five days a week during normal school hours and figuratively hang a sign around their necks that reads, "I'm gifted!" Then, they head off to their special, more interesting, challenging, and enriching programs for the talented and gifted students.

What happens to the other 90 percent of the kids? The current system retards them by using the state standardized test scores to determine the standard, and the standard often falls at the average. Half the kids are capable of going beyond the standard (average), but we say, "Stop! Our reading program teaches only the standard requirements."

Note that none of these sorting and grouping practices address the source of the enemy: the core teaching and learning processes that produced the variation in student learning and achievement to begin with!

Results of Sorting: Increased Variation

Adopting a systems perspective requires that we question all of these practices. Somehow, we have developed a vocabulary that sends a message to 95 percent of our children, beginning at the age of seven, that they are not gifted! We cling obsessively to the vocabulary and sorting practices to continually reinforce that message throughout the balance of their grade school career. What gives us the right to extinguish the self-esteem of 95 percent of our children? In our age of mythology, we act as if 100 percent of our children—including those learning disabled children, outside the system in need of special help—are not gifted!

What is the effect of these sorting practices? What happens to the distribution we started with in second grade by the time the same population of students emerges from the eighth grade and moves on to high school? Unfortunately, the slow get slower and the median drops. The fast may get faster, but only in the short term! Longer term, the fast have been retarded by the current system, too. See Figure 4.9 for the effects of sorting.

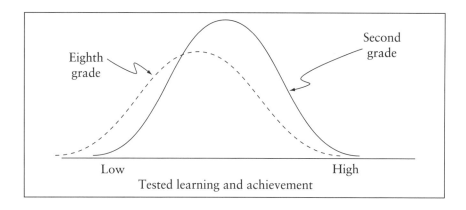

Figure 4.9. Destructive effects of sorting and grouping.

Then, we wring our hands over a 29 percent high school dropout rate nationwide. Frank Newman once asked, "What happens to the 29 percent of people who do not graduate from high school in this country? The answer, we know, is that this country is developing an underclass. We've developed the highest rate of teenage pregnancy in the developed world. Even more alarming is the highest rate of [prison] incarceration."[3]

Why do we have a 29 percent high school dropout rate? Because in the absence of a systems perspective, the elementary and middle school components of the system failed to do their job! (Please note that I refer to the elementary and middle school *components*, not schools alone; to all of the components, including parents, not teachers alone.) Their job was to take the distribution of learning and achievement in second grade and, through continual improvement of K–8 teaching and learning processes, pass a distribution with a *higher* average and *less* variation on to the high school. (Refer to Figure 4.7.)

A Word from the Defense

In attendance at one of my seminars in Austin, Texas, was a group of gifted and talented program specialists. One of them stood up and said, "Mr. Leonard, you'd better know what you're talking about before you criticize pull-out gifted and talented programs. I've got something you'd better read."

She gave me a prepublication copy of a report, signed by Richard W. Riley, Secretary of Education, entitled, *National Excellence: A Case for Developing America's Talent.* That evening, I read the report; then I re-read it; then I re–re-read it. I am critical of pull-out gifted and talented programs, referring to them as, among other things, a disease. Never in my personal experience and research, however, had I found more clear evidence of the destructive effects of these practices than I saw in the gifted and talented lobby's own data!

The forward of the report notes, "More than twenty years have elapsed since the last national report on the status of educating gifted and talented students . . . . Americans can celebrate improvements over the past two decades in how we educate gifted and talented students . . . . The number of programs for gifted and talented youngsters has grown substantially."[4]

The same report then goes on to cite evidence of the crisis facing our so-called gifted and talented students. On most of the instruments cited and by practically every measure reported, the data clearly indicate that our top students are doing more poorly today than they were more than 20 years ago—before the adoption of pull-out gifted and talented programs! The gifted and talented lobby's own report, their own data, prove beyond a shadow of a doubt that the program they champion has been an abject failure; the fast have indeed gotten slower.

Among the indicators described in the report are the following.

1. "Since 1972, the number of students with high scores (over 600 out of a possible 800) declined by more than 40 percent on the verbal portion [of the SAT]."[5]

Most reports of the drop in SAT scores must be taken with a grain of salt. A lot more students take that test today than 20 years ago, and the reports usually deal with the average scores. However, the gifted and talented lobby's report deals only with the top students, and, despite the fact that a lot more students are taking the SAT today, a lot *fewer* students are scoring over 600! (See how the fast have gotten slower or, if not slower, certainly fewer.)

2. "We can turn to a study comparing U.S. seniors taking Advanced Placement (AP) courses in science with top students in 13 other countries . . . . The study found that American students were

- 13th out of 13 in biology;
- 11th out of 13 in chemistry; and
- 9th out of 13 in physics." [6]

Once again, I take tests of international comparison with a grain of salt. After all, what other education system in the world is asked to take on all of society's problems? How many hours a week do you think Korean or Japanese schools spend on AIDS awareness, diversity, Drug Awareness and Resistance Education (DARE), multilingual education, and the many other mandates placed on American schools?

But these data are dealing with our top students, the ones who are taking advanced placement courses, many of whom have undoubtedly been labeled gifted and talented.

3. "In mathematics, the top 1 percent of students in the United States scored very poorly . . .

- 13th out of 13 in algebra and
- 12th out of 13 in geometry and calculus." [7]

At the risk of being repetitive, please bear in mind that these U.S. Department of Education data are dealing only with our top students. They clearly indicate that these top students are doing more poorly than they were years ago—before the pull-out, talented and gifted interventions were introduced!

I am not suggesting that we stop trying to develop enriched material and learning opportunities; nor am I suggesting that we get rid of all the gifted and talented specialists. We need those people.

We need them for one of the potentially most exciting interventions in local education: *integrating enrichment into the standard curricula.*

We cannot depend on Washington, D.C. From there we're getting numerical goals, not leadership. We cannot wait for our state legislators. At a local district level we must take action. We must stop sorting and start working to improve our teaching and learning processes, so that all students experience enrichment.

Outcomes Quality Versus Process Quality

According to Wheeler, Chambers, and others, reduced variation (improvement) in outcomes can only be achieved via careful study of the sources of variation in a process, followed by action to reduce or eliminate sources of extraneous or excessive variation.[8] In other words, if we're not happy with the results (outcomes) of a process, we must change the process. If we do not change the process that's producing an unacceptable output, we'll continue to produce that unacceptable output!

To illustrate this concept, let's say we operate an oil distribution company. Our output is oil and, if all goes well, we produce good oil, accept it, put it in a barrel, and pass it on. Our process is our piping system through which the oil passes. (See Figure 4.10.)

Now, let's say that in our company we're most concerned about the quality of our output, the quality of our oil. We want to make sure it's good and acceptable versus customer requirements, internal standards, and so on. We're focused on the quality of our outcomes.

A few weeks later, the pipe cracks. Through the crack, all kinds of dust and dirt and other contaminants enter the oil. At the end of the pipeline and driven by our concern about our output quality, we immediately determine that the oil is bad. We cannot pass it on. From this outcomes quality focus, what corrective action will we take?

We could patch the crack, but we're not looking at the pipe. We're focused on the output, oil. From this outcomes quality focus,

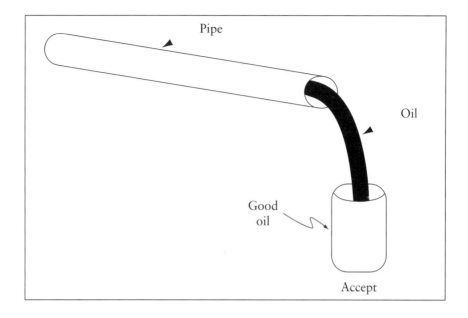

Figure 4.10. Piping system and its output (oil).

we'll add a filter to the end of the pipeline to correct the situation. The filter will detect and screen out the contaminants. Now the oil is good again. It's acceptable; we can put it in a barrel; we can pass it on. (See Figure 4.11.)

Please note that the filter, in and of itself, does nothing about the source of the contaminants (the crack in the pipeline). It detects them, it screens them out, but the filter adds no value! All it does is get the oil back up to where it should have been all along when it first came out of the pipe.

What filters have we installed in the local school district? One, addressed earlier, is testing. Children already know or do not know material by the time we test them. The test adds no value. (This is not to say that we will eliminate all testing. We wouldn't have answers to the question, "How are we doing?" without measurement and assessment. Within the context of the systems perspective, however, let's recognize that testing adds no value.)

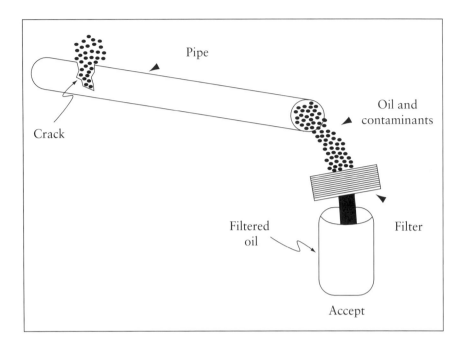

Figure 4.11. Piping system and its output (oil) with filter added.

Another non–value-adding filter in a school or district is sorting students for remedial programs. Such programs add no value. All they do is get the students to where they should have been all along when they first emerged from the teaching and learning pipeline.

In manufacturing, such filtering practices are called inspection and rework. In our schools, they're called testing and remediation. As my five-year-old, Emma, might say, "Same difference."

For years, this focus on outcomes quality in American management worked, until we eventually started to discover that the filter gets dirty. So, American management created quality control (QC) people. Their job was to stand at the end of the pipeline and look at the oil as it came out. If it was clean, they were to put it in the accept barrel and pass it on. If it was dirty, they were to put it in a reject barrel, then call maintenance and have them change the filter.

Later, the American management system added redundant inspection: auditors. The auditor looks at the oil that was deemed clean to determine if it is indeed clean. They also look at the oil that was deemed dirty to determine if it is indeed dirty. And, they check to make sure the filter was changed as scheduled.

One beauty of such redundant inspection and auditing practices is that no one's responsible! The managers of the pipeline aren't responsible for the quality of outputs; it's the job of the inspector to catch it. The inspector's not responsible; it's the job of the auditor to check it. The auditor's not responsible, either; it's the job of those working in the pipeline to do it right in the first place.

The result: finger-pointing, blame-placing, discontent, and excuses. In our age of management mythology, it's so much easier to engage in finger-pointing than it is to work on improvement.

At the risk of oversimplifying it, all Deming was getting at was for leaders to ponder the oil and pipe analogy for a nanosecond. Upon doing so, they would recognize all of the investment of value-adding resources that, from an outcomes-quality focus, add no value. (Remediation adds no value; rework adds no value; inspection adds no value; testing adds no value; auditing adds no value.)

Instead, Deming urged us to shift the emphasis from output (or outcomes or product) quality to *process quality.* Leaders must provide the strategy, plan, training, tools, and help for people to shift the emphasis to the quality of the process. As soon as they do that, they'll see the crack. As soon as they see the crack, they'll patch it. As soon as they patch the crack—compared to what it was—they'll have improved not only the process, but also its future outputs. And if we can keep people focused and working continually to maintain and improve the quality of the process (pipeline), 100 percent of the output (oil) will be good!

Shewhart's Concept of a Process

Figure 4.12 shows a model developed and proposed by a physicist, Walter Shewhart, who worked at Bell Telephone Laboratories in the

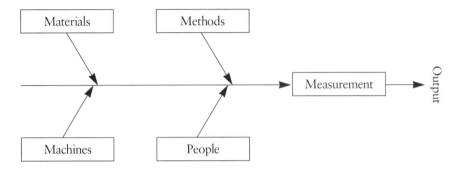

Figure 4.12. Shewhart's concept of a process.

1920s. Shewhart's concept was that most of the variation, waste, loss, cost, contamination, and defects found at the output of any process were produced by what Deming later labeled common causes of variation, waste, loss, cost, contamination, and defects from within the process.

Shewhart's model was developed from a manufacturing context; however, the same concept can help school leaders to get a picture of a process (of the pipeline) into people's minds whenever we talk about quality. Since outcomes will be improved only if processes are changed and improved, it is critical that we help people to think this way.

Of course, in administrative processes, we don't talk about raw materials. We talk about information; that's our raw material, and it may be good or bad, accurate or inaccurate, available or not. In administrative processes, we don't talk about methods as much as we do policies or procedures. Once again, they may be good or bad, complete or incomplete, clear or unclear, up-to-date or out-of-date, user-friendly or not. Finally, in administrative processes, we don't talk about machines. We talk about our information-processing technology, and that would include hardware, software, form or format of the information. And, in our school and central offices, there are people and there is measurement and reporting. (See Figure 4.13.)

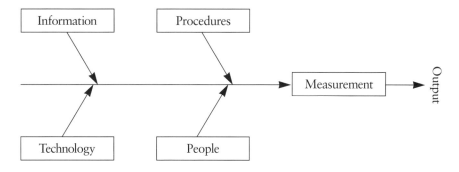

Figure 4.13. Shewhart's model revised for administrative processes.

Many people have found Shewhart's concept of a process to be clear, understandable, and rational. In a manufacturing setting, people understand that we can have the best-trained, hardest-working staff in the universe, but if we get garbage raw materials from suppliers, what comes out of our process? (Garbage!) Despite this clarity, local leaders may have months of work ahead of them to help people think this way—to start thinking about process quality rather than just outcomes quality. That's because in our society we have learned and experienced a completely different model! We have experienced what I like to call the process model from the age of mythology (see Figure 4.14).

It's interesting how so many calls for education reform seem to be based on the model in Figure 4.14. A real catchword among reformers is *accountability*. They all seem to be looking for someone they can hold accountable for the flaws and problems of our complex system. As noted earlier, many recommend merit pay for teachers, based on the belief that teachers will do a better job and students will learn more if the teacher has a merit carrot to pursue. (Welcome to the age of mythology!)

The most common example I encounter of this process model from the age of mythology existent in our management culture is the widespread practice of performance appraisal and staff evaluation. How would your organization answer the following simple questions?

Figure 4.14. Process model from the age of mythology.

Do you conduct a formal, sit-down, periodic, measured, recorded, reported, analyzed, and acted-upon appraisal of every raw material and service that enters the organization? Of every policy? Every procedure? Of every measurement and reporting system? Do you conduct a formal, sit-down, periodic, measured, recorded, reported, analyzed, and acted-upon appraisal (capability study) of every machine, including the copiers, so they don't break down or run out of toner any more?

Though answers to all of these questions are seldom in the affirmative, most organizations sure do conduct formal, sit-down, periodic, measured, recorded, reported, analyzed, and acted-upon appraisals of all the *people* through the widespread practice of performance appraisal and staff evaluation! Why? Because we're busy trying to hold people accountable. There's no time left to study processes to identify and deal with other sources of waste, mistakes, and defects.

Why are performance appraisals, staff evaluations, merit pay, incentive pay, and other such practices so common? Probably because we all attended American schools and were conditioned to accept test scores as a measure of the student alone. As noted previously, most of the measured, test score differences we find between students have nothing to do with the students. They are generated by the complex and dynamic teaching and learning process, of which the students are only a part.

It is impossible to measure student achievement. I don't know why we keep trying to do so, except perhaps for the influence of the age of mythology. It is impossible to measure student achievement separate from other components of the system, including the test itself. Students alone do not produce their test scores. The teaching and learning process produces the test scores. (See Figure 4.15.)

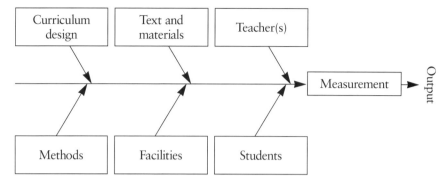

Source: J. F. Leonard, "An Introduction: Applying Deming's Principles to Our Schools," *South Carolina Business* 11 (1990): 85. Used with permission.

Figure 4.15. View of the classroom as a process.

What produces low test scores? They are generated by the curriculum design and content; the texts and supplementary materials; the teachers; the teaching and learning methods, including homework assignments and the effects of the home environment; the physical facilities and equipment; the students, and all the baggage they bring with them into the classroom beyond the direct control of the teacher; the test itself; and the interaction between and among all of those factors. That's what produces low test scores!

From a systems perspective and based on Shewhart's rational concept of a process, if we're not happy with low test scores, we must study and improve the process. If we do not change the process that produced the low test scores, we'll continue to get the low test scores. The only alternative is to remain locked in the age of mythology, sorting and remediating students, adding no value.

Summary

At the output of any process, one will find variation. As Deming wrote, "Life is variation. Variation there will always be, between people, in output, in service, in product. What is the variation trying to tell us about a process, and about the people that work in it?"[9]

The Taguchi loss function is an excellent model for understanding the concept of systems optimization, as well as the loss generated by variation. Any variation brings with it some waste, cost, and loss. That loss may be great, or practically imperceptible, but variation always produces some loss. Therefore, variation is viewed as the enemy in the context of the systems perspective.

Based on the theory that variation is the enemy, we can define *quality* as minimal variation around some target or optimum value. We can define *quality improvement* as reduced variation around some target or optimum value. The challenge then becomes one of determining how best to improve quality, how best to reduce variation.

Shewhart's concept of a process clearly illustrates that the most common sources of waste, cost, and loss are found inside a process. Therefore, if we want to achieve a significant reduction in the variation and waste found at the output of a process, we must change the process. If we don't change the process that's producing the waste, it will continue to produce the waste.

The tools we apply to learn about our processes, the tools we apply to improve processes, are the essential statistical methods. We'll begin to address this second key element of the transformation process in chapter 5.

Notes

1. Deming, *The New Economics*, 219.

2. F. Newman, "Commencement Address" (remarks to graduates of the Worcester Polytechnic Institute, Worcester, Mass., 18 May 1991).

3. *Ibid.*

4. P. O'Connell Ross, *National Excellence: A Case for Developing America's Talent*, U.S. Department of Education (Washington, D.C.: GPO, 1993), iii.

5. *Ibid.*, 7.

6. *Ibid.,* 9.

7. *Ibid.*

8. D. Wheeler and D. Chambers, *Understanding Statistical Process Control* (Knoxville, Tenn.: Statistical Process Controls, Inc., 1986), 4.

9. Deming, *The New Economics,* 101.

Chapter Five

The Role of Basic
Statistical Methods

The second key element of the transformation process is a body of essential statistical methods. Joseph M. Juran observed, "The temptation to start with remedies instead of diagnosis is so common that it merits separate discussion. The peril exists because many people are engaged in 'hard sell' of remedies, but few are engaged in hard sell of diagnosis."[1] How true Juran's observation seems to be in light of the many reforms being proposed for our schools. People are arguing for and against whole language, national standards, outcomes-based education, vouchers, and other remedies.

Few people seem to have a clear definition of the core problems that these proposals are supposed to remedy, however. In the context of the systems perspective, statistical methods are the tools we apply to clearly define problems with the current system, then to diagnose and improve the processes that are producing those problems.

In chapter 2, we considered four elementary questions for driving the continuous improvement effort: Who are my customers? What are their needs? How are we doing? What can we do better? With an understanding of the systems perspective comes the realization that variation will be found at the output of any process. The Taguchi loss function illustrates that any variation brings with it some waste, cost, and loss. Thus, improvement efforts are guided by a definition of quality as minimal variation, and quality improvement as reduced variation over time, around some target or optimum value.

Based on these insights, we can expand on the elementary questions to end up with a seven-step formula for driving the continuous improvement of quality.

1. Who are our customers? (Who uses the process outputs?)
2. What are their needs?
3. How can we best meet those needs?
4. With minimal variation (or maximum consistency)?
5. And showing continuous improvement (as measured by reduced variation or improved consistency over time)?
6. How are we doing?
7. What can we do better?

The challenge facing leadership is to eventually get to a point where every person and group in the organization is actively seeking and taking action on answers to these questions. Statistical formulae won't get you to that point; nor will a calculator move people into a position of seeking and taking action on the answers to these critical questions. Only leadership will get you there!

Shewhart's concept of a process teaches us that the answer to the question, "What can we do better?" will not be found in some report of output (or outcomes) quality. Rather, the answer to that question will be found inside the process that produced the output. The essential statistical methods provide the means for not only diagnosing how we're doing, but also taking action on answers to the question, "What can we do better?"

Who Needs Statistical Methods?

Over the years, I've had the opportunity to work with administrators, school boards, site-based teams, planning committees, and other groups, helping them to develop local action plans for applying Deming's principles to their districts. One topic that must be addressed in any such plan is training. I'll often pose to those groups the question, "Do all of your staff members have to learn statistical methods?" Among the responses people offer are, "Yes," "No," and occasionally, "I hope not!"

Remember that our intention is to get to the point where all of our staff members are actively seeking and taking action on the answers to the questions listed earlier. The answer to the seventh question, "What can we do better?", will be found inside the process. The tools we apply to learn about and improve processes are the essential statistical methods. How can we ask people to find and take action on answers to the question, "What can we do better?", but not provide them with the tools they'll need to find and take action on the answers to that question?

Indeed, if we're serious about accomplishing the transformation, if we're serious about successfully and continuously improving our processes for the good of our children, leaders must provide training in the statistical methods for all of their staff members. When I refer to the essential statistical methods, however, I like to break them down into three sets.

1. *Basic statistical methods (or the basic tools).* Some statisticians refer to this set of statistical methods as the simple tools, because to use them one does not need a calculator. They include

    a. Flowcharts used to paint a picture of the process under study

    b. Brainstorming to generate creative ideas

    c. Cause-and-effect (or fishbone) diagrams to organize brainstorming ideas, and, at the same time, reinforce process thinking

    d. Data collection

    e. Organizing those data in the form of a Pareto diagram, scatter diagram, run chart, frequency distribution (or histogram), or some other basic graphing technique to help people view and, at a basic level, begin to analyze the data

None of these techniques requires a calculator. When developing plans for training, districts and their leaders should plan on 100 percent of their staff—including the school board—eventually learning and using these basic tools.

2. *Intermediate statistics.* These are the techniques most people think about when they hear the word *statistics.* Local business partners would view statistical process control charts to be part of this set of tools and concepts. Wheeler and Chambers noted, "Management must learn to study the process. [Outputs] should be constantly improved by searching out the sources of variation and eliminating them. [Statistical process control] charts should be used as a guide to pinpointing these sources."[2]

In chapter 7, we will explore how the intermediate statistics are employed to study and understand variation, but not all staff members need to learn these methods. As it relates to training in these principles, I recommend that a district plan on about 30 percent of its staff eventually learning and using these intermediate tools. The aim is for the district to develop internal resources and become self-sufficient. When a team of people uses the basic tools and finds that getting better gets harder, they need to be able to call in help.

3. *Advanced statistical methods.* In this set of the statistical methods, most people will think about statistical design of experiments (DOE), regression analysis, and other advanced tools and concepts. Regarding designed experiments, J. Stuart Hunter noted, "Statisticians by themselves do not design experiments, but they have developed a number of structured schedules called 'experimental designs,' which they recommend for the taking of measurements. These designs have certain rational relationships to the purposes, needs, and physical limitations of experiments."[3] Despite their usefulness in certain settings, however, not everyone on the staff needs to be trained in these tools.

Once again, the district's aim should be to become self-sufficient. Therefore, when planning for training, the district should plan on ensuring that a few staff members learn advanced statistical methods.

They will then be available to provide help should some individual or team need it at some point in the future.

Advanced statistical methods and concepts are beyond the scope of this text. People interested in learning more about them are encouraged to contact technical and engineering groups in local business organizations or professors at nearby colleges or universities for guidance.

A Word of Caution

When planning for training in the statistical methods, it is strongly recommended that the following formula be kept in mind.

$$\text{Training effectiveness} = f[(\text{Quality of the subject matter}) \times (\text{Probability of use})]$$

In English, this equation states that the effectiveness of any training will be a function of the quality of the subject matter (taught in the training program) times the probability of use. So if the probability of use is zero, the training effectiveness will be zero—no matter how many bells and whistles we build into the training program!

Therefore, district leaders are cautioned to avoid conducting mass, districtwide training in the statistical methods. Rather, they should start on a small scale and ensure that trainees are provided a high probability of using the tools soon after their training.

One excellent means for providing this high probability of use is assignment to formal, cross-functional, process improvement project teams. The projects are selected by district or school leadership and guided by the systems perspective. Thus, leaders recognize that systems problems, by their very nature, cut across and involve different groups within the district.

For example, a concern about student reading skills in the sixth grade affects parents, reading specialists, administrators, and classroom teachers in the pre-K–6 components of the system. One way to attack this issue would be to form a team of these people and give them an assignment such as, "Study the major causes of low student reading achievement levels in the sixth grade. Return to district leadership with recommendations, supported by data, for changes we can make to our pre-K–6 reading programs to improve sixth-grade students' reading skills."

Once teams return to district leaders with recommendations for process improvements, those leaders accept responsibility for seeing that the changes are implemented. The essential statistical methods—with great emphasis on the basic techniques—are the tools such teams employ to guide their diagnosis of the systems problems, as well as to generate ideas for improvement.

The balance of this chapter will be devoted to an exploration of some basic statistical tools and concepts. Emphasis will be placed on general concepts and the role of the statistical methods, not on procedures. (For greater detail and summaries of basic and intermediate statistical methods, see appendices A and B.)

The Basic Statistical Methods: First Steps

When project teams are first formed, they should apply the statistical methods in a logical sequence to guide their process diagnosis and improvement effort. Therefore, the first tool they employ will not be a statistical process control chart (intermediate tool) or a full factorial designed experiment (advanced tool)! Rather, as a first step, cross-functional teams should define the process under study. Recall that the first question they must address is, "Who are our customers?" The answer to that question will depend on the process under study; in other words, whoever uses the output of the process. Therefore, before worrying about any data collection or analysis, teams must define their process.

Where appropriate, the basic tool teams employ to define the process is the flowchart, or flow diagram. It illustrates, in sequence, the value-adding steps of the process. Another use of the flowchart is in the area of process design. The flowchart in Figure 5.1 was developed by Randy Flack, superintendent of schools in Knoxville, Iowa, and his district leadership team. It illustrates the process for selecting, defining, and managing cross-functional process improvement project teams in their district.

Once the process has been defined, teams next want to develop clear operational definitions. Deming defined an operational definition as "a procedure agreed upon for translation of a concept into measurement of some kind."[4] Another way to view an operational definition is as a clear response to the question, "What do you mean by . . . ?"

For example, a project team may be working on the identification of barriers to effective parental involvement and suggestions for removing those barriers. District leadership would want to ask that team, "What do you mean by effective parental involvement?" The answer to that question must be clear, along with plans to collect data in order to understand the current situation and track future progress. To lend that clarity is the role of the operational definition.

Having defined their process and developed clear operational definitions, a team's next step would be to generate creative ideas about the major causes of current problems or major barriers to future improvement. Here teams employ the basic tool of brainstorming. (Note that we have briefly summarized three basic statistical methods and concepts, and have yet to need a calculator!)

After the brainstorming technique generates a large number of creative ideas, teams must organize those ideas. The basic tool used at this diagnostic step is the cause-and-effect, or fishbone, diagram. Figure 5.2 shows the fishbone diagram developed after brainstorming by a team of teachers, administrators, and parents. (They were trying to get a handle on the causes of any lack of student motivation to learn.)

As a diagnostic tool, the fishbone diagram yields three distinct benefits. In fact, no other statistical method—basic, intermediate, or advanced—provides the following advantages of a fishbone diagram when used immediately after brainstorming.

1. Transferring brainstorming ideas to this format facilitates discussion of the ideas and, at the same time, reinforces process

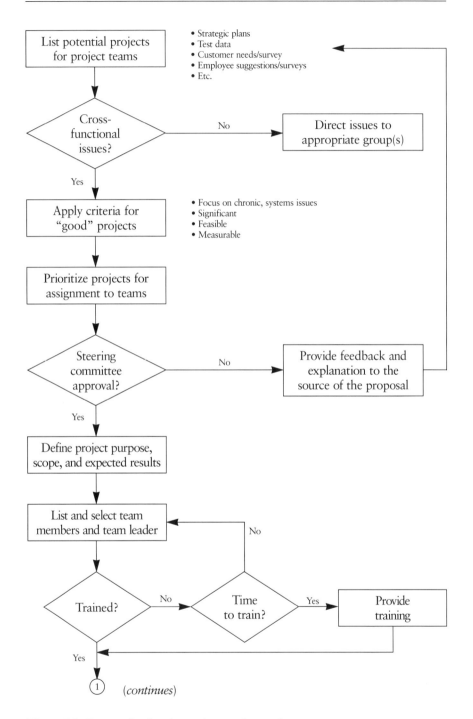

Figure 5.1. Process for forming and managing project teams.

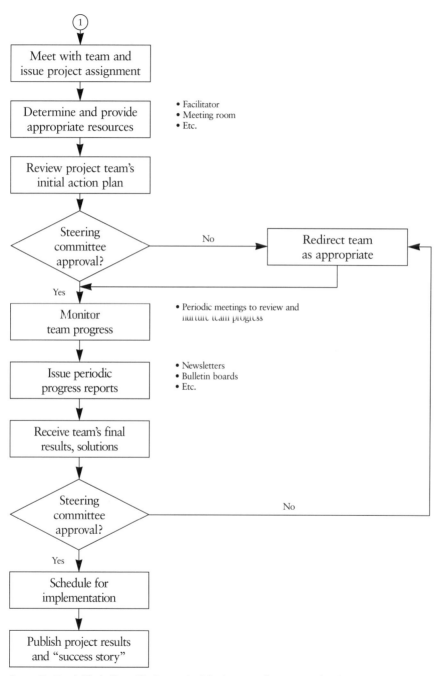

Source: Dr. Randy Flack, Knoxville Community Schools, Knoxville, Iowa. Used with permission.

Figure 5.1. (*continued*).

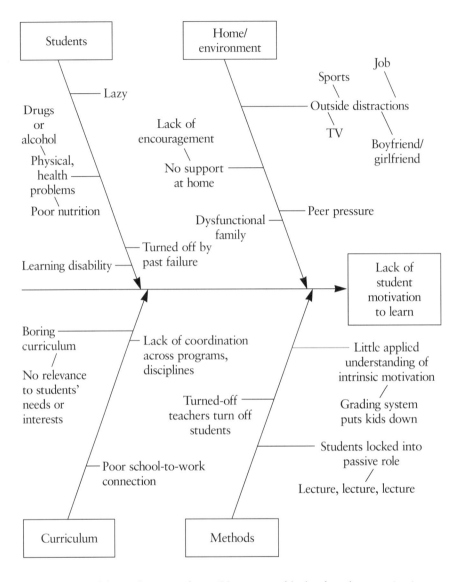

Figure 5.2. Fishbone diagram of possible causes of lack of student motivation to learn.

thinking. During brainstorming, no interruptions or discussion are allowed. As ideas are placed on the fishbone diagram, team members can seek clarity by asking, for example, "What do you mean by lack of awareness? Do you think that's a people problem or a communication (methods) problem?"

Beyond such clarification, the fishbone diagram also helps to facilitate process thinking. In other words, it illustrates that cause-and-effect relationships are not all cut and dried; that students alone do not control the curriculum, texts, selection of their teachers, and other sources of barriers to motivation. (This basic tool helps people to step beyond the *person = output* model from the age of mythology.)

2. Once completed, the fishbone diagram provides a very organized summary of the brainstorming ideas. It can be stapled to the meeting minutes; it can be posted on a bulletin board; it can be placed in the project folder. During one of his lectures, Juran added that the fishbone diagram has a lot more eye appeal than a long list of brainstorming ideas that were posted on a flip chart as they came up.

3. Finally, cause-and-effect analysis invites "operator self-inspection." On a team, we have limited time, people, and resources. Teams can examine their fishbone diagrams to ensure that they're not out of balance, with a large number of theories crowded on one branch, while other branches remain empty or almost so.

Another way to view this advantage is to think about building a house. We can use the most expensive building materials in the world, but if the foundation is flawed, the house will fall down! Fishbone diagrams can be viewed as the team's theoretical foundation for its process improvement effort. If that foundation is flawed, any future improvement plans will fall down too.

Once a team drafts the fishbone diagram, it has a model of theories of what is causing a particular problem or situation. The next step is to clarify or test those theories. Here the basic technique of data collection helps the team begin to test its theories and form a foundation for building an effective plan for improvement.

Data Collection

Of all the executives, academicians, and consultants who continued Deming's work in Japan, perhaps none was more influential than Kaoru Ishikawa. On the critical topic of data collection, Ishikawa wrote, "The word 'statistical' implies data, and data reflect facts. For a situation to be correctly analyzed and control to be realized, data must be collected carefully and accurately."[5]

In other words, in order to move from the opinions generated during brainstorming to a strong foundation of facts, teams want to ensure that they are dealing with key measures of the situation. The data they collect and analyze must be in the form of counts that count.

One way to derive appropriate key measures is to first select a process, then list what comes out of it (outputs) and who uses those outputs (customers). Teams can then seek answers to the question, "What are (the customers') needs?" Key measures translate those customer needs into useful data that, in Ishikawa's words, "reflect facts."

As an illustration, superintendent Ginny Tresvant and a site-based decision-making team from the school district in Snohomish, Washington, worked to define appropriate key measures. To do so, they took the following steps.

1. *Select a process.* The team selected the elementary schools' reading instruction process. To reinforce the idea of the pipeline, team members pictured a large pipe that started where the wall meets the ceiling and came down at an angle to desktop height. On the side of that pipe was stenciled, "Elementary schools' reading instruction process."

2. *List the outputs.* Next, the team listed what comes directly out of the pipe. Among the outputs listed were reading skills, knowledge, methods, and materials.

3. *List the users (or customers of the process).* At this step, the team listed students as the primary users of the reading process outputs. It also recognized that middle schools and parents should be viewed as customers of the reading instruction process, too—especially as it relates to parents' concerns about the texts and materials used in the process.

On the team's list of customers, however, one would *not* find higher education, local businesses, society at large, government service, the arts, and other groups that are customers of the macro education system. Note how, by starting with the process, this group avoided the trap and frustration inherent in the statement, "Everybody's a customer! How does this help us?"

4. *List the customers' needs.* The team started with students as customers and used the brainstorming technique to answer the question, "Students need reading skills, knowledge, methods, and materials that are *what*?" The resulting list of responses included such needs as applicable, effective, transferrable, and interesting.

5. *List key measures.* Here, the team sought answers to the question, "How can we put a number on these (customer) needs?" Their list included the following:

Students need reading skills, knowledge, methods, and materials that are	Key measures
Applicable	Number of portfolio entries, book reports, and so on that exhibit the students' application of the reading program content to their personal life or situation.
Effective	Standardized test scores, quiz scores, rubric scores on assigned homework and classwork projects, and so on.

Transferrable	Number of portfolio entries, book reports, and so on that document how students transferred the reading program content to other academic subjects.
Interesting	Number of extra books or stories that students read on their own. Percent favorable responses on student surveys that provide feedback from students on how interesting they are finding the texts, assignments, material, and so forth.

Data in the form of these key measures are used to answer the question, "How are we doing?" They also serve as the basis for driving people back into the reading instruction process pipeline to take action on answers to the question, "What can we do better?" In other words, these key measures in Snohomish are used primarily to drive process improvement efforts—not to sort kids, rank kids, grade kids, remediate kids, or label kids.

Note that the district's standardized test scores were included as a key measure of the effectiveness of the reading program. They were, however, but one answer to the question, "How are we doing?" Other data can help to answer the same question, and most of those data are more robust, available, and generated more frequently than the once-a-year snapshot provided by a standardized test.

This is not to say that Snohomish will or must do away with standardized tests. It's just that the district's leaders understand that they must resist dependence on standardized tests. These tests not only fail to provide a frequent response to the question, "How are we doing?", they tell us nothing about how the process is performing relative to customer needs for interesting and applicable reading skills, knowledge, methods, and materials.

Data Collection Guidelines

Once key measures are identified, a team's next step is to collect data on those key measures to diagnose the current level of process performance and to test any theories about causes or remedies. To guide data collection efforts, Ishikawa offered the following reminders.[6]

1. *Clarify the purpose for collecting the data.* Why are we collecting the data? Who will use it? What action should result once the data are collected and reported?

2. *Collect data efficiently.* Ishikawa long insisted, and Juran and others in this country long agreed with him, that in many cases all the data we need to learn about a process are already available to us in the form of prior in-house data. It's sitting in somebody's file drawer; it's recorded on a printout somewhere. In the case of the reading process key measures derived in Snohomish, team members recognized that they already had some data on every one of the key measures they listed—except the student survey data.

3. *Take action according to the data.* Literally, Ishikawa seemed to be saying, "If the data you're collecting results in no action, stop collecting the data!" In the American public school system, how often do people find themselves in a position of having to collect and report data that result in no action? (The issuance of the report is an end in itself!) What could those people be doing to make things better if they weren't tied up collecting and reporting numbers that result in no action?

In the face of such concerns, districts are encouraged to study their current data collection and reporting systems. (What is being reported? By whom? To whom? What action is being taken?) As a result of such a study, many districts have uncovered staggering redundancy and obsolescence in current reporting systems. When action is taken to eliminate the redundancy and discontinue obsolescent reports, time is freed up for working on improvement.

Finally, teams should strive to report their data in an appropriate form. We want to effectively communicate the facts and, in doing so, encourage action for future improvement. As noted earlier, New York uses standardized PEP tests in elementary schools. The results are reported in the form of the percentage of a district's students who tested above the statewide reference point (SRP), the state's minimum standard.

One district in upstate New York found it difficult to use its PEP test data in this form. Year after year, 92 percent or more of its students scored above the SRP in reading, math, and other basic skills. Because of such good performance, the district's leadership kept encountering barriers to improving their teaching and learning processes. A common response to proposals for improvement was, "If it ain't broke, don't fix it!" (Note how such standards are and will forever be inhibitors to continuous improvement.)

To remove this barrier to improvement, district administrators changed the form of their reports. Instead of reporting the percentage of students scoring above SRP in each grade in the district, the data were converted into the form of a histogram. This basic tool provides a snapshot of variation around one key measure. In this case, the key measure selected was the raw score students achieved on the PEP test. The highest raw score a student could achieve was a 66; the SRP (minimum standard) fell at a raw score of 23. (Recall that only 8 percent or less of their students scored at or below the SRP.) Figure 5.3 shows the histogram of the district's raw scores.

Once the data were viewed in the form of a histogram, district leadership could start to emphasize the idea of improvement as the inverse of a golfer's scores. In other words, future process improvements would be reflected by a shift to the right: higher average scores, with less variation and greater consistency around those higher averages.

In order to follow through on Ishikawa's third reminder for collecting data (take action), the district had to report the data in an appropriate form. The old reporting system proved to be a barrier to improvement because people concluded, "We're already over

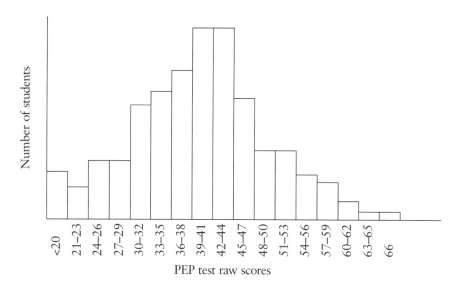

Figure 5.3. Histogram of district PEP test raw scores (grade 6).

90 percent. Why get better?" However, once the data were reported in the form of a histogram, improvement could not only be pictured, but also pursued. The old minimum standard no longer served as a barrier to improvement.

Histograms, scatter diagrams, Pareto diagrams, and run charts are basic statistical tools (graphing techniques) that help in organizing and clearly communicating data. Appendix A provides step-by-step procedures for setting up these charts, as well as a few examples. For now, we'll examine the role of just one of the remaining basic statistical methods: the Pareto diagram.

Pareto Diagrams

Pareto diagrams are particularly useful tools for guiding leaders' decisions throughout a continuous improvement process. They are based on the principle that most of the waste found at the output of any process is the result of a vital few causes of waste from within the process.

Peter Scholtes noted, "Since they draw everyone's attention to the 'vital few' important factors where payback is likely to be greatest, Pareto charts can be used to build consensus in a group. In general, teams should focus their attention first on the biggest problems . . . ."[7]

The Pareto principle is named after an Italian economist, Vilfredo Pareto. Late in the nineteenth century, Pareto observed that most of the wealth in Europe was held or controlled by relatively few people. Conversely, most of the population of Europe as an aggregate held or controlled relatively little of the total wealth. More specifically, Pareto's study found that about 80 percent of Europe's wealth was controlled by only about 20 percent of the population. (See Figure 5.4.)

Others in this century picked up Pareto's observation and suggested that it is a universal principle. In business, most of a company's sales will be generated by relatively few (large) customers. Most of its individual customers will generate relatively little of the company's annual sales revenue.

In budgeting processes, beyond staff salaries and benefits, most of a district's annual spending will be generated by relatively few

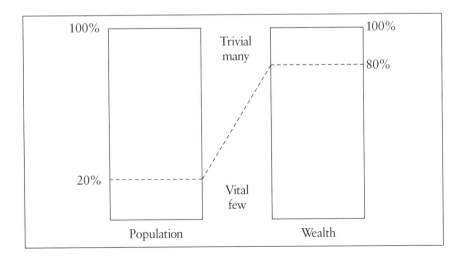

Figure 5.4. Illustration of the Pareto principle.

(often capital) purchases. Conversely, most of the district's individual purchases will account for relatively little of the total spending. Most staff absenteeism will be traceable to relatively few district employees. On the other hand, most employees, as an aggregate, miss very little time!

Once again, this universal principle is applied to identify those vital few causes of wasted time, low test scores, and other problems with outcomes. Action to reduce or eliminate those major causes of variation and waste will result in a significant reduction of that waste both in the short and long terms.

Another use of Pareto diagrams is for summarizing and reporting survey and test data. For example, a district can report the number of incorrect responses on standardized tests by specific skills tested by that instrument. Survey responses can be reported by number (or percent) of positive or negative responses by question.

Jim Anderson, who works for the Heartland Area Education Agency (AEA) in Des Moines, Iowa, was interested in collecting data on students' opinions, feelings, and feedback about their school experience. He surveyed hundreds of students from elementary and high schools in central Iowa for their responses to a number of questions. Among the questions asked were[8]

- Which word best describes at this time in your life your greatest concern? (What do you worry about more than anything else?)

- Which word best describes at this time in your life your greatest need? (What do you need right now more than anything else?)

The Pareto diagram is the best basic tool for reporting the type of data generated by such survey questions. Figure 5.5 summarizes the responses from 255 high school males in response to the question, "Which word best describes at this time in your life your greatest concern?"

The Pareto diagram presents a very clear, very understandable summary of Anderson's survey results, and one need not have a

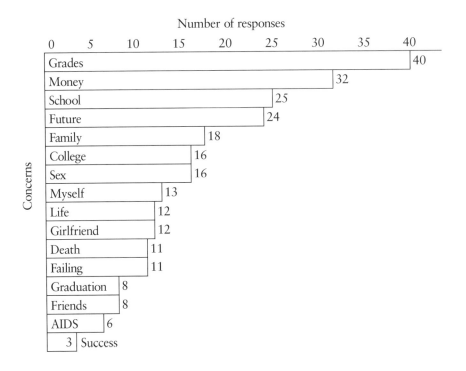

Figure 5.5. Pareto diagram of 255 high school males' greatest concerns.

single course in statistics to be able to view and understand the Pareto diagram shown in Figure 5.5. When I first saw Anderson's data, I was struck that, when asked to describe what they worry about more than anything else, the highest number of high school males wrote, "Grades." Just as interesting is how this concern was reported by two to four times more students than concerns like college, life, or even death!

Figure 5.6 is the Pareto summary of responses from 569 high school students (male and female) to the question, "Which word best describes at this time in your life your greatest need?"

What Anderson discovered in his survey is fascinating. When asked what they worry about more than anything else, the highest response from 255 high school males was "grades." When asked what they need more than anything else, the *lowest* response from

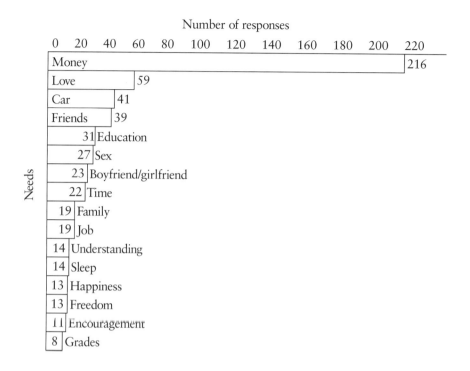

Figure 5.6. Pareto diagram of 569 high school students' greatest needs.

569 central Iowa high school students was grades. (Less than 2 percent of students surveyed gave that response.) Our obsession with grading and ranking in our age of mythology has put these kids' concerns 180 degrees out of phase with their perceived needs!

Equally fascinating is not only that the highest response (40 percent of students surveyed) was "money," but also that not one student surveyed replied that what they needed more than anything else is "God"! (When Anderson first talked to me about his plans for the survey, I formed a thesis that at least one student from America's heartland would give that response. The data disproved my thesis.)

We now come full circle to Juran's observation that opened this chapter: that many people are engaged in the hard sell of remedies, but few are engaged in hard sell of diagnosis. In the interest of school reform, many people are engaged in the hard sell of putting prayer back in our schools and other similar recommendations for reconnecting our education system with the Scripture-based history of our country. These suggestions may have merit, but will an insincere prayer or a moment of silence at the beginning of the school day significantly change these high school students' perceptions of their needs?

As either an alternative or supplement to putting prayer back in schools, perhaps these high schools should study their current American history and American government curricula. Are these students learning about our Declaration of Independence and Constitution? Are they doing research on the lives of the authors of those documents; what those people meant by inalienable rights; their beliefs regarding the divine source of those rights?

In the absence of transformation, such meaningful study and learning will not occur. Students will remain locked in the age of mythology, concerned about their grades, not learning; concerned about class rank, not knowledge. Short of transformation, there will be no time for learning. Students will continue to spend instructional time boning up on test-taking skills; attending preparation courses prior to taking their SATs.

The transformation needed in America's schools is much broader, much more involved, much too complex to be accomplished by mere remedies. As a first step to improving any system, we must determine what's wrong with the current system. The basic statistical methods and data collection can and will guide the initial diagnosis of systems problems, and, in turn, lead to the development of effective strategies for improvement.

Summary

The second key element of the transformation process is a set of essential statistical methods. They facilitate the diagnosis of systems and processes to yield accurate answers to the question, "How are we doing?" Beyond that, they are the tools teams apply to change and improve systems, guided by the question, "What can we do better?"

Once appropriate key measures are derived from downstream customers' needs, data are collected and reported in the form of Pareto diagrams, run charts, histograms, and other basic graphing techniques. Run charts and histograms provide pictures of variation found at the output of processes under study.

Since one lesson of the systems perspective is that variation is the enemy, the next step to be taken is to learn from that variation. In Deming's words, we need to determine "what the variation is trying to tell us about the process, and the people that work in it." The role of the intermediate statistical methods is to guide the study and understanding of variation. Before addressing those methods and concepts, in the next chapter we'll explore the core theory of variation.

Notes

1. J. M. Juran, *Managerial Breakthrough* (New York: McGraw-Hill, 1964), 88.

2. Wheeler and Chambers, *Understanding Statistical Process Control*, 11.

3. J. S. Hunter, "Design and Analysis of Experiments," in *Juran's Quality Control Handbook*, 4th ed., eds. J. Juran and F. Gryna (New York: McGraw-Hill, 1988), 26.6.

4. Deming, *The New Economics*, 108.

5. K. Ishikawa, *Guide to Quality Control* (Tokyo: Asian Productivity Organization, 1986), 30.

6. *Ibid.*, 4.

7. P. Scholtes et al., *The Team Handbook* (Madison, Wisc.: Joiner Associates, 1988), 2-25.

8. J. Anderson, "Missing the Mark: How the National Educational Goals Ignore the Real Needs of Students," working paper, Heartland Area Education Agency, Des Moines, Ia., 1993, 2.

Chapter Six

Theory of Variation

As noted in our review of the systems perspective, at the output of any process one will find variation: in test scores, in maintenance response time, in budget variances, in number of favorable survey responses, and in other key measures. In our set of basic statistical methods, the run chart and the histogram are used to illustrate patterns of variation. The run chart shows the pattern of variation over time, while the histogram provides a snapshot of variation around one key measure.

For example, Figure 5.3 in chapter 5 showed a histogram of variation in test scores. The variation in the data ranged from raw scores of below 20 to the maximum possible score of 66. Figure 6.1 shows a run chart of one district's standardized test scores over a five-year period. Specifically, it plots the percentage of grade 5 math Stanford Achievement Test (SAT) scores that fell at or above (norm-referenced) average in the district's elementary schools from 1989 to 1993.

If variation is the enemy, we must first seek to determine what type of variation we're dealing with. Absent an understanding of the type of variation present, any discussion of accountability is a burlesque! Why? Because different types of variation require different types of corrective action for which different people will be accountable!

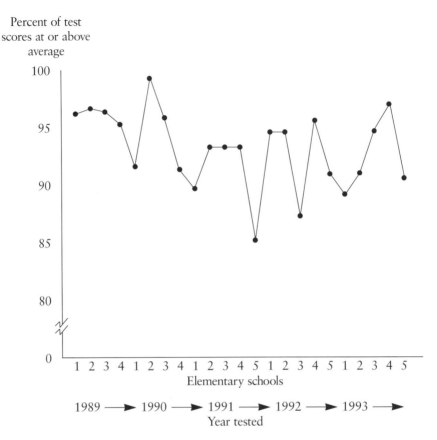

Figure 6.1. Run chart of grade 5 math SAT scores.

Recall that, in the area of student test scores, the question is not, "Are these students different?" The question is, "Are they significantly different?" Thus, there is a need to determine what's different and what's significantly different. The theory of variation helps leaders to make this distinction.

Viewing the run chart in Figure 6.1, one will see fluctuations in tested results from one year to the next. For example, in elementary school 1, 97 percent of students tested at or above average in 1989, but that percentage dropped to 92 percent the following year. In 1991, the percentage dropped to 90 percent, but then rose four points to 94 percent in 1992. Clearly, this school's year-to-year results are different; but are they significantly different?

Bonnie Small and her colleagues reported that such fluctuations can fall into either normal or abnormal patterns.

> Fluctuations in the data are caused by a large number of minute variations or differences: differences in materials, equipment, the surrounding atmospheric conditions, the physical and mental reactions of people. Most of these differences are extremely small. They cause the pattern to fluctuate in what is known as a "natural" or "normal" pattern.
>
> Occasionally, however, there will be a large or unusual difference, much more important than all the other differences put together . . . . These large differences make the pattern fluctuate in an "unnatural" or "abnormal" pattern.[1]

Fluctuations in Driving Time

Yesterday, it took Justin 20 minutes to get from home to work. Today it took 25 minutes. What could cause the additional travel time (five minutes, 25 percent longer)? Possible causes of a five-minute delay might include traffic congestion, weather conditions, traffic signals, school bus or slow-moving truck, and any number of other such sources of driving delays.

In other words, there are many, many variables Justin encounters during every drive to work. Any one or more of these variables could contribute to the extra driving time. Justin's drive could take 25 percent longer today, but he may not be able to put his finger on the precise, assignable cause of the five-minute delay.

On the other hand, what if it took Justin two hours to get from home to work tomorrow? What could cause that great an increase in his travel time? Possible causes may include a catastrophic car breakdown or perhaps he slammed into the back of another vehicle!

In other words, Justin would probably be able to identify some precise, assignable cause of taking two hours to complete a trip that's usually only about 20 minutes.

In this simple illustration we find that there are two very different types of variation occurring. One type is generated by normal causes of delays in a typical drive to work. But the second type is clearly something that's unusual, its cause undoubtedly something other than natural sources of delays encountered during Justin's typical trip from home to work.

While working at Bell Laboratories in the early 1920s, Walter Shewhart conducted studies of variation. As reported by Wheeler and Chambers, Shewhart reached the following conclusion: "While every process displays variation, some processes display *controlled* variation, while others display *uncontrolled* variation."[2]

Controlled Variation

Among other characteristics, Shewhart found that controlled variation was random and that it was mathematically predictable. He wrote that control could be conceived as "a mathematical state characterized by the quantitative aspects of the end results and describable in mathematical terms and an operation of drawing at random."[3]

Deming once commented on Shewhart's highly technical style of writing: "He said that his writing had to be fool-proof. I thereupon let go the comment that he had written his thoughts so damned fool-proof that no one could understand them!"[4] Some people find Shewhart's style of writing difficult to follow. But just as difficult to grasp was his theory that controlled variation was at the same time both random *and* predictable!

A simple illustration of this phenomenon can be found in the process of rolling dice. Though we cannot predict the precise results of one roll of the dice, we can predict that the result will fall at random within a predictable range of outcomes.

When Cailin rolls a pair of dice, she can mathematically predict that the result will come out somewhere between a two and a 12, inclusive. Over a series of dice rolls, Cailin would learn that there is only one combination on the dice that will give her snake eyes (1-1). However, there are six ways to roll a seven (1-6, 2-5, 3-4, 4-3, 5-2, 6-1). So, over a series of dice rolls, Cailin could mathematically predict that she will roll a seven more often than a two or a 12.

Shewhart described controlled variation as being due to random chance. Back to our drive to work example: Roll the dice, Justin, tomorrow it may be foggy. Roll the dice, Justin, tomorrow those traffic signals may be red. Roll the dice, Justin, tomorrow you may be behind that school bus.

Uncontrolled Variation

Shewhart determined that another type of variation is not random. Rather, it was neither (statistically) controlled nor mathematically predictable. If Cailin were to roll her dice, rolling a 13 would not be predictable. There's no way she could mathematically predict that some fly would come along and drop a miscellaneous dot on one of her sixes! Furthermore, Shewhart postulated that uncontrolled variation is due to some assignable cause. He wrote, "As these assignable causes are found and eliminated, the variation gradually approaches a state of statistical control."[5]

As noted, if it took Justin two hours to get to work tomorrow, he'd be able to put his finger on some precise, assignable cause of the two-hour delay.

Deming's Contribution to Shewhart's Concept

According to C. S. Kilian, Deming first heard about Shewhart when he worked at the Hawthorne plant of the Western Electric Company during the summers of 1925 and 1926. "The men [there] were talking about . . . Dr. Walter A. Shewhart, saying that they did not understand what he was doing, but that it was important."[6] Ten years later, Deming was in charge of courses in mathematics and statistics in the department of agriculture. One of his duties was to invite leading authorities in the field to give lectures.

Recalling his experience at Western Electric, Deming invited Shewhart to share his knowledge.

Deming was, to say the least, impressed with what he learned from Shewhart and his theory of variation. He wrote, "Even if only ten percent of the listeners absorb part of Dr. Shewhart's teachings, the number may in time bring about change in the style of Western management."[7] Shewhart conducted four lectures at the department of agriculture, and Deming later worked with him to reduce those four lectures into the manuscript published in 1939 as *Statistical Method from the Viewpoint of Quality Control.*

Deming refined Shewhart's theory of variation by adding the concept of a process. He started to refer to controlled variation as common cause variation, and to uncontrolled variation as special cause variation.

Deming agreed with Shewhart that controlled variation was random, mathematically predictable, and due to random chance. He added, however, that it was due to common causes of variation from within the process that produced the output.

Recall from the systems perspective our theory that variation is the enemy because it always brings with it some degree of loss. The role of intermediate statistics is to determine what the variation is trying to tell us: what type of variation we're dealing with. Another way to look at it would be that we're searching for the source of the enemy—common causes of variation from within the process or some special cause(s) of variation from outside the process.

Thanks to Shewhart and Deming's contributions, if the data indicate a random pattern, then we know that the source of the enemy (variation) is common causes of variation from within the process or system.

For example, Justin designed his drive-to-work process. He sets the alarm; he picked the car; and he selected the route. If he's not happy with a five-minute delay, and it's the result of controlled, or common cause, variation, he must change the process. (Set the alarm an hour earlier so the traffic's lighter; pick a different route; buy a helicopter!) In the face of random, common cause variation, the appropriate strategy for improvement is to change the process. If Justin does not change the process that's producing the five-minute delay, he will forever experience five-minute delays at random!

When test data plot in a random pattern, the source of the enemy is illustrated in Figure 6.2. In any situation where analysis of test data indicate the presence of controlled, common cause variation, the appropriate improvement strategy is to change the process. As in the case of Justin's drive to work, if we do not change the teaching and learning process that's producing the low test scores, we'll forever get low test scores. When faced with random, common cause variation, the only alternative to improving the process is continuing to sort and remediate, adding no value, forever!

Adding the concept of a process to Shewhart's concept of variation, Deming started to refer to uncontrolled variation as special cause variation. Thus, uncontrolled variation is not only nonrandom, not mathematically predictable, and the result of some assignable cause, it is also generated by some special cause of variation from outside the process or system.

Special causes produce outputs that are not only different, they're significantly different. When a pattern of variation indicates

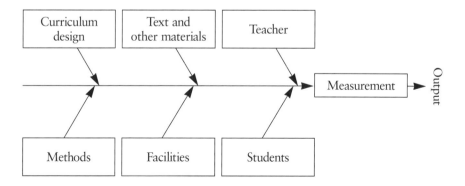

Figure 6.2. Source of controlled, common cause variation in test scores.

such significant differences, then we know the source of the enemy is some special cause from outside the process, and no amount of work on the process will address it!

Let's say the special cause of Justin's two-hour delay was that his brakes failed, resulting in his running off the road. In this case, he'd have to take action to address that special cause—get a new set of brakes. Justin did not design brake failure into his drive-to-work process. Any time there's evidence of a special cause, the appropriate corrective strategy would be to identify and deal with that special cause. Work on the process will not help to eliminate a special cause because, by its very nature, special cause variation comes from outside the process.

Justin would not increase the frequency of routine maintenance checks (on the methods branch of his process). Nor would he change the standard maintenance procedure to have new brakes installed during every 3000-mile lube-oil-filter servicing! Driving to work by a different route wouldn't get him what he needed, either. Again, no amount of work on his standard process will address a special cause; it requires special, focused action to find and deal with that special cause.

Costly Mistakes

Deming long insisted that the failure to understand variation is a source of staggering waste in American industry. One example has to do with rising costs of malpractice insurance, not to mention the costs of settling malpractice suits. Deming wrote,

> Every suit for malpractice in medicine, or in engineering or accounting, implicates the event to a special cause—somebody was at fault. Study with the aid of a bit of knowledge about variation leads to a different conclusion: the event could well have come from the process itself. It could have been built in, guaranteed.[8]

Deming reduced the costly mistakes generated by failure to understand the theory of variation to two categories.[9]

Mistake 1. To react to an outcome as if it came from a special cause when actually it came from common causes of variation.

Mistake 2. To treat an outcome as if it came from common causes of variation when actually it came from a special cause.

In American education, the costs of mistakes in reacting to variation are even more staggering than those found in business because in education the stakes are so much higher. In our schools, we risk not merely money or raw materials or machine downtime, we affect raw human potential. Following is some elaboration on the two common and costly mistakes generated by failure of leaders to understand variation.

Mistake 1

In many manufacturing settings, quality control personnel publish reports of every defect they discover during final inspection. Then engineers and supervisors are required to investigate every defect and take action to eliminate it. Later people can't understand why the level of defects doesn't go down over time; why it remains steady at 5 percent or 10 percent or higher. Deming insisted that, in this case, people were "confusing common causes with special causes. Every fault to them was a special cause, to track down, discover, and eliminate."[10] They ended up making things worse because they were so busy chasing random events there was no time or energy left to change or improve the process that was the source of the defects to begin with!

In chapter 3, we examined just one facet of the staggering cost of mistake 1 in American education. If we conclude that low-scoring students are in need of special help, we sort them out for tutoring and remediation. If we conclude that high-scoring students need more enrichment than others, we sort them out for the gifted and talented program. (See Figure 6.3.) If, however, the variation in test

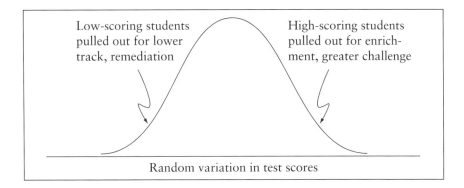

Figure 6.3. Mistake 1 reaction to random variation in teaching and learning outcomes.

scores is random, then there's nothing special about the low scores and high scores. Instead, they resulted from common causes of variation from within the teaching and learning process. Sorting in no way addresses the true source of the enemy (the process that generated the wide variation in test scores).

Sorting and tracking students for special programs have made things worse because over time the slow have gotten slower, the median has dropped, and the fast have been retarded, too! This phenomenon will be found in any objective review of SAT scores over time and is illustrated in Figure 6.4.

Mistake 2

In a manufacturing setting, let's say scrap levels jump dramatically due to a significant change in a supplier's process. Increased contamination in the incoming raw materials actually caused the quality problems. The manufacturer responds to this dilemma by purchasing and installing new machines. In other words, it changed its own manufacturing process by investing capital in new equipment.

In this case, the manufacturer will have made a very costly mistake. Because uncontrolled variation is by its very nature not predictable, the special cause from the supplier's process will come screaming in without warning and disrupt the new machines just as

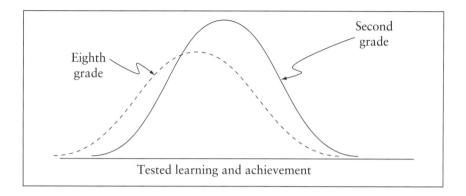

Figure 6.4. Disastrous effects on mistake 1 on student learning and achievement.

it did the old machines. The manufacturer will have flushed that capital investment right down the toilet!

Once again, the cost of such mistakes is even greater in a school setting because we're dealing with raw human potential—not merely capital. A few years ago, a superintendent attended one of my seminars on applying the statistical methods to teaching, learning, and administrative process data. The day he returned to his district, the report of his first graders' reading test results landed on his desk.

The report showed the actual number of words first graders read in a 100-word story. More specifically, it listed, by student and classroom, the number of words the first graders read correctly (out of 100 words in the story) in each of the district's 12 first-grade classrooms. The results ranged from 0 to 100 words read correctly. Students who read below a certain number of words correctly were identified for Chapter 1 help and were provided that help.

Use of intermediate statistics indicated that most of the first graders in the district fell into a group that constituted a system. In other words, their test results were different, but they were not significantly different. They rolled the reading program and test dice, and all of them rolled somewhere between a 2 and a 12.

A few students' scores in each of the schools feel statistically significantly low in comparison to all the test scores. These students rolled the reading program and test dice, but rolled a negative number! Figure 6.5 illustrates what the superintendent discovered about his first graders.

The first graders whose test scores fell significantly low were in need of special help like that provided by Chapter 1 or Reading Recovery initiatives. That special help would not be provided by the regular classroom reading program. But three out of every four first graders in the district who were in need of special help did not receive it! The arbitrary standard for Chapter 1 aid had been placed at a score lower than theirs.

Bear in mind that norm-referenced standards are derived from national or state scores. But this leader was not the superintendent for the United States of America or the state of California. He was superintendent of schools in his own town. The norm-referenced

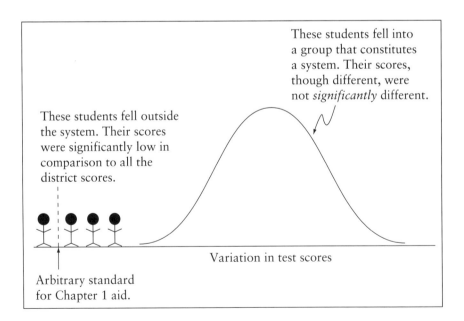

These students fell into a group that constitutes a system. Their scores, though different, were not *significantly* different.

These students fell outside the system. Their scores were significantly low in comparison to all the district scores.

Variation in test scores

Arbitrary standard for Chapter 1 aid.

Figure 6.5. First graders' reading test scores.

standard had dictated who among his children would receive help and who would be denied that help. Only when he applied the intermediate statistics to his own first graders' raw scores was he able to remove the barrier imposed by the standard. Only then was he able to understand the variation in his own district and understand the needs of his own unique first graders.

In the absence of this understanding, tragically three out of every four students in need of special help remained in their regular classrooms—in need of special help, but not getting it. When the superintendent called me to report his findings, he said he felt physical pain as a result of what he'd learned. He'd realized that these first graders were sitting in their regular classrooms, falling farther and farther behind in their language development, not understanding why they couldn't keep up, why they were failures. What struck the superintendent was that at the tender age of a first grader, within a few short years they'll be lost! He said, "It's devastating to realize that I have spent most of my career hurting children."

He hadn't meant to hurt children. He hadn't meant to fail to provide special help to children in need of special help. But because he didn't understand variation, he indeed ended up spending most of his career hurting kids.

Now this problem is not a people problem; it is not the fault of the superintendent. It's not his fault that he graduated from the University of California at Berkeley not understanding variation. It's not his fault that he received bachelor's, master's, and doctoral degrees without learning about variation. It is a fault of the system, and the costs are devastating. The costs are incalculable because they involve children and their future.

How many so-called reform mandates have called for widespread study and understanding of Shewhart's theory of variation? Clearly, we do not need reform, we need transformation. Without transformation, well-meaning and caring educators will continue trying their best to help children, but only end up hurting them.

Filters and Pipes

One way to picture mistake 1 (treating outcomes as if they came from a special cause, when in fact they were produced by common causes of variation) is to return to the oil and pipe analogy, described in chapter 4. There, defective outcomes were produced by a crack in the pipe. Adding a filter to the end of the pipe does nothing to address the source of the problem. Thus, remediation increases cost because it employs value-adding resources in a manner that adds no value. Additional costs are generated as the process (pipe) itself erodes over time due to lack of appropriate attention and process improvements.

On the other hand, Chapter 1, Reading Recovery, and other remedial initiatives are not filters when used to help students in need of special help. Significant differences in assessed student performance are not produced by the pipeline because special causes intervene from outside the process.

When, then, is remediation a filter? It depends on the type of variation present! In the face of random, common cause variation, the appropriate corrective strategy is to study and improve the process. After-the-fact remediation would be a filter.

On the other hand, nonrandom patterns of variation in outcomes indicate the presence of special causes. In that case, providing Chapter 1 aid for students whose cognitive scores fall outside the system would not be a filter. Rather, it would be the district's appropriate strategy for providing special help to those students in need of special help.

Understanding Variation: The Dilemma

Understanding the core theory of variation and differentiating between common cause and special cause variation are essential to avoiding the mistakes just described. Beyond that, such understanding is essential to the development of appropriate strategies for improvement. In trying to do so, however, leaders encounter a problem.

The human brain is incapable, by eye or feel, of determining just what type of variation is present. The statistician's brain is incapable of looking at a run chart or a histogram of Justin's drive-to-work times and determining, by eye or feel, just where we'll find the line of demarcation that indicates where the effects of common causes of delays from within the process leave off and where the effects of special causes of delays from outside the process begin to intervene.

We may agree that the line of demarcation may fall somewhere between 20 minutes and two hours, but we don't know where! We need help. The statistician needs help. We need some practical statistics.

Summary

At the output of any process, we will find variation. The challenge facing leaders is to determine what that variation is telling them about their processes and the people who work in those processes.

Shewhart developed a theory regarding two distinct types of variation: controlled variation and uncontrolled variation. Deming contributed to Shewhart's work by adding the concept of a process. Thus, when key measures of a process outcome fall into a random pattern, the variation is the result of common causes of variation from within the process. In such a case, if one is not happy with the outcomes, the only appropriate corrective action is to change the process.

On the other hand, if key measures of process outputs exhibit a nonrandom pattern, then the theory of variation teaches that those outcomes are the result of some special cause(s) of variation from outside the process. Corrective action must be taken to identify and remove the special cause of variation. No amount of work on the standard process will correct this type of variation, because it's coming from outside the process.

Deming defined two costly mistakes from failure to understand variation: treating special cause variation as if it were generated by common causes, and reacting to an outcome as if it resulted from a special cause when in fact it was generated by common causes of variation from within the process.

Shewhart's theory, together with Deming's refinements, yield knowledge of variation. This knowledge is the foundation for leaders being able to differentiate between the two types of variation: common causes of variation from within a process and special causes of variation from outside the process. Helping leaders apply knowledge of the theory of variation and to differentiate between these two different types of variation is the role of the intermediate statistical methods. Those methods and concepts are the subject of the next chapter.

Notes

1. B. Small et al., *Statistical Quality Control Handbook* (Charlotte, N.C.: Western Electric Company, 1956), 6.

2. Wheeler and Chambers, *Understanding Statistical Process Control,* 5.

3. W. A. Shewhart, *Statistical Method from the Viewpoint of Quality Control* (1939; reprinted, New York: Dover Publications, 1986), 8.

4. C. Kilian, *The World of W. Edwards Deming* (Rockville, Md.: Mercury Press, 1988), 57.

5. Shewhart, *Statistical Method,* 37.

6. Kilian, *The World of Deming,* 53–54.

7. *Ibid.,* 58.

8. Deming, *The New Economics,* 193.

9. *Ibid.,* 178.

10. *Ibid.,* 186.

Chapter Seven

Applying Intermediate Statistical Methods and Concepts

Knowledge of variation is crucial for guiding leaders' decisions and actions throughout the transformation process. Failure to understand and differentiate between the two types of variation leads to mistakes and staggering waste. The human brain, however, is incapable of determining by eye or feel whether patterns of variation indicate the presence of special cause or common cause variation. There is a need to go beyond the pictures of variation provided by some of the basic statistical methods; there is a need to put numbers on those pictures. We need some practical statistics.

Some Practical Statistics

Figure 7.1 shows a frequency distribution (histogram) of 35 observations, or measurements. They range from a low of 13 to a high of 21. Any time we set out to put numbers on such pictures of variation, we're interested in two types of numbers. One is a measure of central tendency, or average. The second is a measure of dispersion.

Central tendency refers to the point about which the data tend to cluster when plotted as a frequency distribution. Today, most districts use two common measures of central tendency: the arithmetic mean and the median. (For clarity's sake, whenever we refer to the average, we're talking about the mean.) As districts move

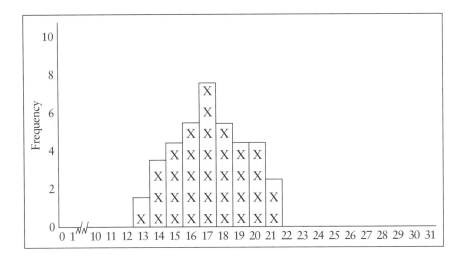

Figure 7.1. Histogram of 35 observations.

forward to apply the intermediate statistics, they'll continue to use the same measures.

$$\text{Mean} = \bar{X} = \frac{\text{Sum of all measurements}}{\text{Number of measurements}} = \frac{\Sigma X}{n}$$

For the histogram in Figure 7.1, the mean would $= \bar{X} = \dfrac{602}{35} = 17.2$

$$\text{Median} = \tilde{X} = \text{Middlemost value in a set of numbers} \\ \text{when arranged from lowest to highest}$$

The histogram in Figure 7.1 includes 35 measurements. To determine the median, one would start at the lowest value (13) and count up 18 observations. This would yield a median, or middle value, of 17.0.

A measure of average is an important statistic. For example, if I work in municipal water management, it's important to know that the average depth of the river is 10 inches. Is it possible for one to drown in a river with an average depth of 10 inches? Of course it is; and one need not be 9 inches tall in order to drown in a river that averages 10 inches deep! That average measure doesn't tell me that the depth of the river ranges from 2-inch ripples to 10-foot pools, and it's the 10-foot pools people drown in! (It's the 10-foot pools of variation in many reading programs that children drown in.)

Therefore, whenever we set out to apply the practical statistics—whenever we begin to put numbers on our pictures of variation—we must always accompany our measure of average with some measure of dispersion. One easy-to-calculate measure of dispersion is the range, designated by the symbol R. It is simply the difference between the largest measure in the distribution and the smallest measure in the distribution. For the data illustrated in Figure 7.1,

$$\text{Range} = R = X_{max} - X_{min} = 21 - 13 = 8.0$$

Thus, putting numbers on our picture of variation in Figure 7.1, we would report that we have a distribution that averages (mean) 17.2, with a range of 8.0.

Returning to the distribution in Figure 7.1, what if we were to take one more measurement, and it measured 30? Now, we would have a histogram, or frequency distribution, of 36 observations. Putting numbers on that picture would yield:

$$\text{Mean} = \bar{X} = \frac{\Sigma X}{n} = \frac{632}{36} = 17.6$$

$$\text{Range} = R = X_{max} - X_{min} = 30 - 13 = 17.0$$

Note that, with the addition of one measurement, our measure of average (mean) increased by only four-tenths. However, our measure of dispersion (range) more than doubled! This increase occurred despite the fact that the original 35 measurements remained right where they were in the distribution. Their location did not shuffle up and change by a factor of greater than two! For this reason, the measure of range is a very misleading measure of dispersion for other than small sample subgroups. Such subgroups may be made up of four rubric scores at a time, time taken to close out five maintenance repair requests at a time, budget variances in three monthly reports at a time, and so on.

For large samples or local student populations, however, the measure of range can be misleading because all it considers are the largest measure in the distribution and the smallest measure in the distribution. The range ignores all the other measures!

Another measure of dispersion is available that avoids the pitfalls of the range. Instead, it includes all the measures in a sample, then provides an estimate of the dispersion in a much larger group. This measure is the standard deviation, designated by the Greek letter *sigma* with a prime symbol (σ').

Literally, the standard deviation is a number that ranges from zero to big. The bigger this number, the greater the variation, spread, dispersion, or difference we observe in a frequency distribution, or histogram. It is calculated with the following formula.

$$\text{Standard deviation} = \sigma' = \sqrt{\frac{\Sigma(X - \bar{X})^2}{(n - 1)}}, \text{ where } n = \text{sample size}$$

For the original 35 measurements in Figure 7.1, the standard deviation would equal 2.11. Adding to that distribution a 36th measurement equal to 30 yields a standard deviation (σ') of 2.98.

Unlike the range, the standard deviation provides a measure of dispersion that includes all of the measures in a sample. It is then used to estimate the total dispersion, or variation, that exists in an entire population—the limits of a process. Before proceeding, let's define what is meant by the terms *sample* and *population*.

Population: All of the students in one grade level; all of the reports in process; all of the phone calls coming into the central office; or any other description of the whole

Sample: A part of the population, used as the basis for estimating the characteristics of the entire population or process output

It is important to note that, in the realm of practical statistics, we will never be able to measure an entire population. As it relates to third-grade reading assessments, in order to measure the entire population (outcomes from the reading instruction process), one would have to assess all of the third graders who have passed through that program, all of the third graders currently in the program, and all of the third graders yet to come!

Therefore, the practical statistics are calculated with measures of a representative sample of third graders. These are used to derive an estimate of the entire population; to determine for that reading instruction process the limits of random, controlled variation. Only then can one determine if the reading assessments are being generated by common causes of variation from within the process or if there is indeed something special about some of our students.

Applying Practical Statistics: The Normal Curve

When dealing with variables data, or measurements, the practical statistics of the mean ($\bar{X}$) and standard deviation (σ') are used to estimate the extent of random variation produced by a process. The foundation for this application is the normal distribution, or normal curve. Small and her colleagues at Bell Laboratories noted, "When statisticians speak of a 'normal' distribution, they mean one which is specifically defined by a certain mathematical equation. This distribution is symmetrical about its mean and has the familiar 'bell shape.'"[1]

Let's say a team collects a random sample of 30 to 50 measurements from a process and plots them on a histogram. The pattern of the distribution takes the familiar bell shape. The team can then calculate the average ($\bar{X}$) and the standard deviation (σ') from its sample data.

As illustrated in Figure 7.2, by moving up and down three standard deviation measures from the average, the team will have defined the extent of random variation for 99.7+ percent of the entire population, based on that small sample of 30 to 50 measurements.

Wheeler and Chambers added that the most straightforward way to use the normal distribution is for describing where certain parts of the population are located relative to the population average. This description is provided by a three-part empirical rule.[2]

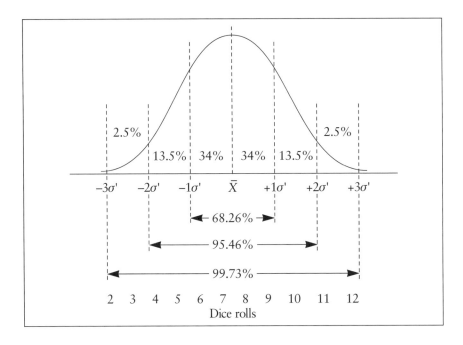

Figure 7.2. The normal distribution curve.

Part 1. Roughly 60 percent to 75 percent of the data will be located within a distance of one standard deviation on either side of the average.

Part 2. Usually 90 percent to 98 percent of the data will be located within a distance of two standard deviations on either side of the average.

Part 3. Approximately 99 percent to 100 percent of the data will be located within a distance of three standard deviations on either side of the average.

In other words, based on the normal curve theory, the average plus and minus three standard deviations defines the extent of random variation for virtually all of the outputs of a process. Thus, at a distance of three standard deviations above and below the average we will find that which the human brain cannot determine by eye or feel. We will find

1. The upper and lower limits of random, controlled, common cause variation

2. The lines of demarcation that indicate where the effects of common causes of variation from within a process leave off and the effects of special causes of variation from outside the process begin to intervene

3. The means to differentiate between that which is different and that which is significantly different

4. A model for transferring the theory of variation into appropriate decisions and action for improvement

As noted, all measures that fall within the limits defined by the average plus and minus three standard deviations are different, but not significantly different. Across the bottom of Figure 7.2 are shown possible results from dice rolls. On every roll of the dice, the result will fall at random between a 2 and a 12, inclusive.

In other words, in any dice roll, Cailin could roll a 2 or she could roll a 12. One result is six times higher than the other, but that difference is not significant! Why? Because both results fall within the realm of random, common cause variation; both results fall within the lines of demarcation that indicate where the effects of common cause variation from within the dice-rolling process leave off.

On the other hand, if Cailin were to roll the dice and roll a 13, she would conclude that something special happened. Even though a 13 is but one count higher than a 12, that difference is significant! Why? Because it falls beyond the three-sigma limit; beyond the line of demarcation and into the realm of statistically significant variation produced by some special cause(s) of variation from outside the dice-rolling process.

Converting Sample Data to Process Limits

Referring back to the 35 measurements plotted on the histogram in Figure 7.1, recall that the average ($\bar{X}$) was 17.2, and the standard deviation (σ') was 2.11. Figure 7.3 shows the limits of the process, as defined by moving up and down three standard deviations from the average value.

Our 35 measured outcomes were produced by a process. The limits of random, controlled variation for that process range from 10.87 to 23.53. In other words, nothing special would have to happen for the next output from our process to measure as large as 23—even though its highest outcome to date was 21. A measured outcome of 23 would be different from other outcomes, but not significantly different.

On the other hand, recall that we added a 36th measurement equal to 30. That value falls beyond 23.53—beyond three standard deviations ($3\sigma'$) above the average value; beyond the upper limit of

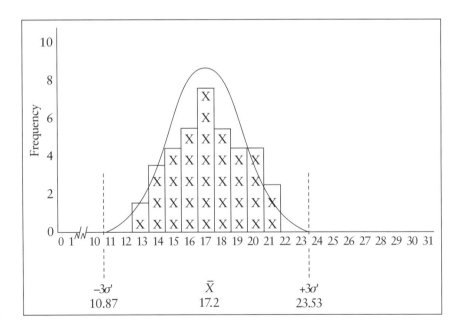

Figure 7.3. Process limits derived from a sample of 35 measurements.

controlled, common cause variation. Therefore, we would conclude that something special had occurred. Some special cause from outside the process must have produced that outcome. The measure of 30 in this case is not only different, it's significantly different from all the other outcomes!

Characteristics of Common Cause and Special Cause Variation

What if the measure of 30 was in our original sample? What if we had started our process study with a sample of 36 measurements? As noted previously, the 36 measurements averaged ($\overline{X}$) 17.6, with a standard deviation (σ') of 2.98. Moving up and down three standard deviations from the average (17.6 plus and minus 3×2.98) yields process limits ranging from 8.66 to 26.54.

Note that the measure of 30 falls beyond the upper limit of 26.54—even though we used that measure to calculate the statistics in the first place! That's what special cause variation is all about. It generates such significant differences in outcomes that it falls beyond the limits we use all the data to determine.

There are many, many common causes of variation at work in any process—no one of which will be significant. Common causes result in fluctuations in output measurements that fall in a normal pattern.[3]

On the other hand, there are a lot fewer special causes of variation at work on any process—any one of which *will* be significant. Their impact on process outputs is so significant, measures under their influence will fall outside the limits we use the same measures to calculate. Unfortunately, they defy identification by the naked eye or gut feel. Deming added that special causes "can be detected only with the aid of proper statistical techniques."[4]

Lessons of the Normal Curve

Let's say I select 10 employees at random and take them out into the parking lot to run a 40-yard dash. I use a precise stopwatch.

According to the normal curve theory, I would learn the following lessons.

1. One of my 10 runners—and only one—will end up in the top 10 percent of that timed 40-yard dash.

2. One of my 10 runners will and must come out in the bottom 10 percent of that timed 40-yard dash.

3. Five of my 10 runners' times will be equal to or above the average dash time.

4. Five of my 10 runners' times will be equal to or less than the average dash time.

5. And that's normal!

In other words, there's nothing special about the above-average runners in comparison to the below-average runners. Half of them will be above average because they have to be—that's normal. Half of them will be below average because they have to be—that's normal.

Grades in school, merit pay, honor rolls, ranking, sales commissions, gold stars in recreation league athletics, gifted and talented programs—all of these practices spread across America's societal landscape—are based on a different theory. The theory underlying such practices teaches different lessons from the normal curve theory.

1. All 10 runners can come out in the top 10 percent of the same timed 40-yard dash.

2. All 10 runners can come out in the bottom 10 percent of the same timed 40-yard dash.

3. If all 10 runners come out in the top 10 percent, they'll all be labeled gifted.

4. If all 10 runners come out in the bottom 10 percent, they'll all get no raise.

5. But since only one runner came out in the top 10 percent, that's special. That person is gifted.

6. And since only one runner came out in the bottom 10 percent, that's special. That person will get no raise.

This is the theory that lies at the foundation of grading, ranking, and merit pay. The reader must decide if it's rational. When applying intermediate statistical methods, we're guided by a completely different theory. We're guided by a theory that flies in the face of everything we've been conditioned to accept in the age of mythology.

After all, one of the worst things you can say to an American citizen is, "You are a below-average thinker." But half the readers of this book, in comparison to all the readers of this book, will be below-average thinkers—and that does not make them defective! That's normal. Half the readers of this book, in comparison to all the readers of this book, are above-average thinkers. That does not mean they're anything special. That's normal.

I recall attending an open school board meeting some years ago. At one point, the superintendent stood up and announced, with much pomp and circumstance, that the school had scored above the state average during the last round of state standardized testing. He thought it was something special; he expected applause.

He got it. The applause thundered from the ceiling of the gymnasium as board members, teachers, parents, and others cheered themselves for being above state average. Eventually, the applause subsided. I raised my hand from the back of the gym and observed, "Half the schools in the state are above state average. That's nothing special. Half the schools in the state are below state average. That's nothing special.

"I'm no more excited to learn that this school is above state average than I would be concerned if I learned that it was below state average. My question is, What are we doing to make things better for kids?"

Unfortunately, that superintendent and board of education did not understand variation. They thought that to be above average was somehow good (if it ain't broke, don't fix it). Content with being above average, they did not seek ways to continually improve teaching and learning processes for the good of their students. They lacked knowledge of variation, so they ended up retarding children.

Limitations of the Normal Curve

The model of the normal distribution has a few limitations. One is that it applies only to variables-type data, or measurements. Counts (for example, number of disciplinary referrals) and attributes data (number or percent of test scores above or below standard) are not normal. Rather, they follow the properties of the Poisson distribution (for counts) or the binomial distribution (for attributes data).

This limitation of the normal distribution is not insurmountable. When dealing with counts or attributes data, we merely use different formulae for deriving upper and lower limits of random, controlled variation. Once those limits are established (using the appropriate intermediate statistical methods), the same theory and principles of variation apply.

Beyond this surmountable issue, the normal distribution has only one major limitation. It is a static model, whereas in American education we exist in a dynamic process world. Many teachers end the semester with a different number of students than they had at the beginning of the semester. Child development is a dynamic process. The depth and difficulty of subject matter changes over time.

The histogram, a basic statistical method, is a static tool. Looking at the pattern of variation on a histogram will provide no clue about significant trends or shifts over time. The dilemma we face is how to apply the rational theory of variation, which is based for the most part on a static model, in our dynamic process world.

Recall that the basic tool of the run chart does illustrate process performance over time. Unfortunately, it does not have the built-in alarm system of the normal distribution. It cannot signal the presence of special causes of variation; it cannot answer the question, "What is the source of the enemy?" It illustrates differences in process outputs, but does not indicate whether those outputs are merely different, or significantly different.

Wouldn't it be nice if we could combine the strengths of the run chart and the normal distribution? If we could develop some way to apply the static model of the normal curve in our dynamic process world?

Introduction to Control Charts

Statistical process control charts are intermediate statistical tools that combine the dynamics of the run chart with the alarm signals of the normal distribution. Ishikawa viewed the control chart as a means to see what changes in data occur over time, as well as the impact of various factors in the process that may change over time. He added that failure to grasp these two factors may lead to "irrational evaluations." (Deming referred to them as mistakes.) "When irrational evaluations are made, necessary action may be missed or unsuitable action may be taken in haste, thus causing confusion."[5]

In essence, the control chart turns the normal distribution on its side; extends the upper and lower limits (plus and minus three sigma) of controlled, common cause variation; and adds the element of time. Illustrated in Figure 7.4, the control chart then enables us to plot key measures of dynamic process outputs over time and determine—real time—what is the source of the enemy!

There are several different types of control charts to select for analyzing processes and their outputs. Which control chart should we use? As my sister, the lawyer, would say, "It depends!" It depends on the type of data used to measure the process outputs.

For variables data, or measurements, the most common control chart is the X-bar and R chart, on which we plot sample subgroup averages and ranges. For processes that provide very slowly evolving

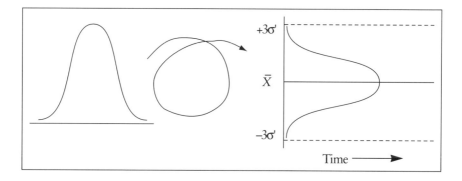

Figure 7.4. Foundation of the control chart.

data, we employ the moving average and moving range chart, or the individuals chart, accompanied by a moving range chart. Examples of variables data include average rubric scores, budget or schedule variance, report processing time, and instructional time.

For attributes data, we use the *np* chart (for number of defectives) or the *p* chart (for percent or proportion defective). Examples of attributes data include the number or percentage of test scores that fall above or below standard and vendor delivery performance (on time or late).

For counts data, we employ the *c* chart for number of defects or a *u* chart for rate of defects per standard unit. Examples of counts are number of disciplinary referrals, number of complaints or grievances, number of grammatical or factual errors in a term paper, and number of discrepancies found during school bus or building safety inspections.

Details and all of the formulae for these different types of control charts are provided in appendix B. No matter which control chart we're using, however, they all have three things in common.

1. A central line (CL), which falls at the process average

2. An upper control limit (UCL)

3. A lower control limit (LCL)

Recall that in his original studies of variation, Shewhart referred to "controlled variation" and "uncontrolled variation." On a control chart, the UCL and LCL define the upper and lower limits— the lines of demarcation—for controlled, random, common cause variation. A random pattern of measured process outputs that all fall within the upper and lower limits of controlled variation would indicate that those outputs are the result of common causes only from within the process or system.

A Key Vocabulary Term: Stable Process

Whenever points on a control chart plot in a random pattern, clustered around the CL, with no points falling outside the UCL or

LCL, we conclude that the process is stable. This is a key vocabulary term that I urge educational leaders to help everyone on their staff and school board to understand. Referring to a process as *stable* means

1. The process is in statistical control. Drawing from the work of Shewhart and his core theory of variation, statistical control means that the outcomes are random, mathematically predictable, and due to random chance.

2. All of the variation illustrated on the control chart is the result of common causes only from within the process or system. Therefore, if we're not happy with the outcomes, we must develop and pursue a strategy to change the process (not filter defective outcomes).

3. There is no special cause variation present from outside the process. Figure 7.5 provides a portrait of a stable process. Anyone can see that the first measured output is higher than the third, but it is not significantly higher. Adding filters to address apparent high's and low's in a stable process is falling prey to Deming's mistake 1: treating outcomes as if they came from a special cause when actually they were produced by common causes of variation.

On the other hand, when key measures plot in a nonrandom pattern, or if one point falls outside the UCL or LCL, the process

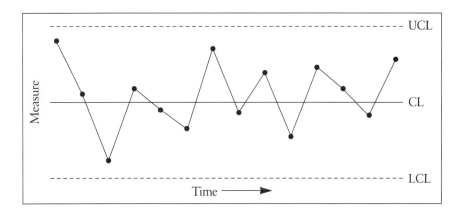

Figure 7.5. Portrait of a stable process.

is (or has gone) out of statistical control. Such a condition would indicate the presence of special causes. In that case, the appropriate corrective strategy would be to find, remove, and/or address the special cause.

In summary, statistical process control charts are intermediate statistical tools that combine the power of the theory of variation with the dynamics of a run chart. They are used to determine what type of variation is present at any given time.

Understanding the type of variation present guides the development of appropriate strategies for corrective action and improvement. In the case of a stable process, the appropriate corrective action is to change the process. In the case of special causes, the appropriate corrective strategy is to find, remove, or to otherwise address that special cause.

Process Capability

Just because a process is stable does not mean it's acceptable. A control chart passes no judgment whatsoever whether an outcome is good or bad. All control charts do is tell us the source of the enemy. Beyond that, people must try to understand the capabilities of their processes, how they compare to requirements, then set their priorities and work to accomplish improvement.

Literally defined, the capability of a process is the random, inherent, common cause variation we observe. Statistically, it will be defined by the average plus and minus three standard deviation measures ($\bar{X}$ + and $-3\sigma'$). The process that produced the 35 measurements shown in Figures 7.1 and 7.3 had a capability of 17.2 plus and minus 6.33. The random, inherent, common cause variation that exists in that process will range from 10.87 to 23.53— take it or leave it!

Our job is to apply the intermediate statistical methods to hear and understand the voice of the process—its capability. Then, we compare that capability to the standard, budget, schedule, or any other defined requirement to determine if the process is capable. As illustrated in Figure 7.6, a teaching and learning process is capable when 100 percent of its tested outcomes (as defined by the average plus and minus three sigma) all fall above the standard.

Of course, even once a process is capable, leaders cannot allow people to conclude that it's good enough. The transformation process must result in an integration of continuous improvement, a continual pursuit of higher and higher levels of average teaching and learning process performance, with less variation around those higher levels, regardless of the standard. Besides, most standards are merely minimum standards, and we certainly can't feel a sense of excellence just because we're exceeding *minimum* standards!

Summary

Throughout this chapter, I have resisted the temptation to provide specific examples of the intermediate statistical tools for two reasons. First, I did not want to go into great detail when appendix B will serve that purpose. Examples of different control charts are also provided. Second, Deming always stressed that examples without theory teach nothing! In this and the preceding chapter, however, we have been concentrating on the theory, as well as understanding the role of the intermediate statistical methods and

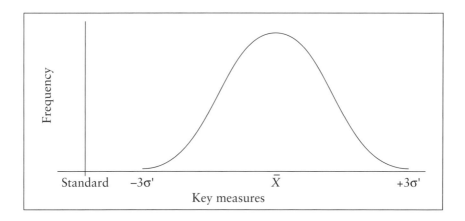

Figure 7.6. Portrait of a capable process.

concepts. Having done that, this chapter's summary will conclude with an example of a control chart applied to standardized test data. The accompanying letter serves as a review of this chapter's content. In our next chapter, we will examine where all of the basic and intermediate statistical methods fit in a basic procedure for improving a system.

Applying Intermediate Statistics to Analyze Grade 5 Standardized Test Scores

Not long ago, a director of curriculum and instruction from upstate New York mailed me his district's fifth-grade Stanford Achievement Test (SAT) scores for the previous five years. He wanted advice on how best to analyze the data using control charts, and what conclusions one should draw from the charts for purposes of planning curricular improvements. Following is my letter of response to his request, with attachments.

July 24, 1994

Dear John:

Thank you for sending me your fifth-grade SAT data for the years 1989–1993. Please forgive me for taking so long to respond with the attached summaries.

The following comments are offered as a supplement to those pages. Although the detail of the explanation may not be appropriate for you and others familiar with the tools and concepts, I do go into some detail for the benefit of others with whom you may share this feedback.

1. *Introduction.* The whole idea behind statistical process control charts—and the intermediate statistics in general—is the theory that variation is the enemy. This theory is based on the following very simple observation: Students already know or do not know

material by the time they take the SAT. The enemy is the variation and sources of variation in learning and achievement in and around the teaching and learning process. Of course, even though we may view it as the enemy, there will always be variation: between students, between teachers, between schools, between districts, and so on. The question to be addressed is, What is the variation trying to tell us?

For example, your printouts exhibit variation in SAT scores between and among four or five schools over a five-year period. Control charts are used to determine what type of variation is present: common cause variation from within the teaching and learning process or special cause variation from outside the process.

If the data plot in a random pattern over the five year period, this would indicate that the process is stable or in statistical control. In other words, the tested results would be different, but not significantly different. Such a state of stability would indicate that the process, as measured by the fifth-grade SAT, is under the influence of common causes only from within the teaching and learning process. In other words, the stable process output was produced by the curriculum design, texts and other materials, teachers and staff, students, teaching and learning methods, facilities and equipment, the test itself, and other sources of common cause (random) variation.

If the data plot in a nonrandom pattern, we would interpret this to mean that there is a special cause of variation present. In such a case, some measured results would not only be different from other results, but significantly different. Such nonrandom variation would be the result of some special cause from outside the process.

In conclusion, the purpose of applying intermediate statistics is to find out what type of variation we're dealing with: common cause or special cause variation. Another way to view the effort would be to try to determine the source of the enemy: common causes of variation from within the teaching and learning process or some special cause(s) of statistically significant variation from outside the process. Knowing what type of variation is present guides school and district leaders to select the appropriate strategy for corrective action.

In the case of common cause variation, form a team of people from the different groups involved in or affected by the process: classroom teachers, specialist(s), administrator, parent(s), and, in the case of middle or high school programs, student(s). The team would be directed to seek to identify the major causes of the low level of achievement, then return with recommendations—backed up by data—for changes we can make to our process and programs to improve achievement levels.

In the case of special cause variation, direct the specialist to aim a rifle at the specific case, then take or recommend special action to address that special case. No amount of work on the standard process or program will address it, because by its very nature special cause variation comes from outside the process.

2. *Control charts selected.* For your SAT data, I selected the p chart (for percent or proportion defective) to analyze the total reading and total math results. The p chart is particularly useful in school settings for two reasons.

First, unlike a manufacturing setting, educators can't "stack the deck" to process lots of 50 units at a time every time. Different classes have different numbers of students. However, the p chart allows one to take the data as it comes, with no need to manipulate the measurements into samples or units of equal size.

Second, the p chart automatically factors in how the same number of incidents has a very different impact as a percentage on groups of different sizes. For example, in a classroom of 10 students, if one is absent, we have a percent absenteeism rate of 10 percent. In a class of 20 students, one absence produces a percent absenteeism rate of 5 percent.

The same number of incidents has a very different impact on small classes versus large classes. This is one reason small districts live in fear when regional report cards of standardized test results are published in the media. If you're a small district, you don't need many kids to score below standard to look terrible as a percentage!

By the same token, over the five-year period reflected in your data, some schools had as many as 84 fifth-grade students, while others had as few as 41. It would be neither fair nor rational to compare such different-sized groups on a strict percentage basis. The *p* chart automatically factors in the reality of higher impacts as percentages on smaller groups.

3. *Attachments A and B.* As a first pass, I summarized the percentage of SAT scores that fell at or above average over the five-year period. Attachment A summarizes the total math results by school, and Attachment B the total reading results. The calculations for the *p* chart CL, UCL, and LCL are shown at the bottom of each summary.

4. *Attachment C.* [See Figure 7.7.] Here you'll find the *p* chart for the total math results. You'll note that the data plot in a random pattern, with no points falling outside the upper and lower limits of controlled, random variation. The five schools' levels of achievement, though different, were not significantly different. Therefore, one would conclude that the process is stable, under the influence of common causes only from within the math teaching and learning process.

Recommendation: If these results are not acceptable, charter a team of classroom teachers, a math specialist, an administrator, and a couple parents (total of six to eight team members) to (a) study the major causes of low levels of math achievement; then (b) submit recommendations—backed up by data—for changes you should make to the district's K–5 math program to improve the levels of math achievement.

5. *Attachment D.* [See Figure 7.8.] Unlike the *p* chart on Attachment C, this chart does not plot in a random pattern. School No. 5's 1993 percentage of total reading scores at or above average fell significantly low in comparison to all the other scores over the five-year period. In this case, one would want to provide special help to that school and its students. Central office resources should

be deployed to help local teachers and administrators identify the special cause, then take special action to prevent its reoccurrence.

Of course, one can't always remove a special cause. For example, one small district in the Albany region had its third-grade PEP scores fall statistically significantly low in comparison to all other districts in the same region. Resources from the Albany BOCES went out to provide special help, and it was later determined that the special cause was that a beloved third-grade teacher was tragically killed in a car accident one week before the PEP test. (Those third graders had a lot more on their minds than the test!) Clearly, one can't prevent all fatal car accidents, but in this case special action was taken by getting a counselor in with the third graders to help them cope with their loss.

6. *Attachments E and F.* On the *p* charts on Attachments C and D [Figures 7.7 and 7.8], you'll note that the central lines fall at 92.8 percent for the total math and 93.7 percent for the total reading. In other words, over the five-year period about 93 percent of your students scored at or above average on the reading and math SATs. That's an A on anyone's report card! If people draw such a (flawed) conclusion, however, that might prove to be a barrier to improvement. ("Why incur this pain? We're already at 93 percent!") Therefore, I summarized the same SAT scores over the five-year period on Attachments E and F, but this time dealt only with the percentage of SAT scores above average. Viewing the data in this form enables you to apply a higher standard to your reading and math programs and thereby avoid the trap of mediocrity if people get comfortable with results that fall at or above (norm-referenced) average.

7. *Attachment G.* [See Figure 7.9.] On this *p* chart of the total math results above average, note that two schools plotted statistically significantly high in 1989. Something special occurred that enabled their results to fall outside the system on the high side. That special cause might have been anything from a new workbook,

to cheating on the test, to a particularly good job prepping the students for the test, to an extremely effective teaching method, or any number of other candidates for the special cause.

Unfortunately, we're trying to look back five years to find a special cause! It's unlikely one can go that far back in time and capture needed details with any precision. Now that you have the process limits established, however, you can plot the 1994 scores, as well as subsequent years' test data. In that way, you'll be able to use the tool real time and will have a much higher probability of identifying and acting on future special causes.

Your total math percent SAT scores above average [plotted on Figure 7.9] illustrate an all-too-common tragedy. If we're not focused on the process (seeking to differentiate between common cause and special cause variation), opportunities for significant improvements may be missed. Here we find a case of statistically significantly good performance—something very good and very special going on—but because it's five years old we can't capture and integrate it!

On the other hand, the same scores illustrate a great opportunity for identifying and reacting to future special causes if, and only if, you continue to plot and analyze standardized test data in control chart format.

8. *Attachment H.* [See Figure 7.10.] Viewing the percentage of test scores above average over the five year period indicates that the reading process is stable. Once again, the appropriate corrective action in this case would call for a team to study the major causes of low levels of reading achievement, then identify ways to change the K–5 reading programs to accomplish improvement. Once the team submits those recommendations (backed up by data), school and district leaders accept responsibility to see that the changes are implemented.

John, thanks again for giving me the opportunity to work with and learn from your test data. Please accept again my apologies for taking too long to get back to you. I hope you find the attachments and remarks helpful as you plan improvements in your district. Of course, should any questions arise, or if you'd like additional information, don't hesitate to contact me.

Best wishes for a safe and happy balance to your summer.

Sincerely,
James F. Leonard
Consultant

Attachment A: Grade 5 SAT Scores (1989–1993)

Total math: Percentage of test scores at or above average (p)

Test date	School	No. of students tested (n)	p	$\sqrt{n}$	$\dfrac{.775}{\sqrt{n}}$	UCL	LCL
5/89	1	68	.971	8.2	.094	1.00	.834
	2	75	.973	8.7	.089	1.00	.839
	3	69	.971	8.2	.094	1.00	.834
	4	56	.946	7.5	.103	1.00	.825
5/90	1	84	.917	9.2	.084	1.00	.844
	2	83	.988	9.1	.085	1.00	.843
	3	68	.956	8.2	.094	1.00	.834
	4	58	.914	7.6	.102	1.00	.826
5/91	1	74	.892	8.6	.090	1.00	.838
	2	71	.930	8.4	.092	1.00	.836
	3	57	.930	7.5	.103	1.00	.825
	4	70	.929	8.4	.092	1.00	.836
	5	47	.851	6.9	.112	1.00	.816
5/92	1	77	.935	8.8	.088	1.00	.840
	2	80	.936	8.9	.087	1.00	.841
	3	71	.944	8.4	.092	1.00	.836
	4	78	.872	8.8	.088	1.00	.840
	5	42	.905	6.5	.119	1.00	.809
5/93	1	80	.875	8.9	.087	1.00	.841
	2	71	.901	8.4	.092	1.00	.836
	3	72	.944	8.5	.091	1.00	.837
	4	74	.959	8.6	.090	1.00	.838
	5	41	.902	6.4	.121	1.00	.807

$$\Sigma \ 21.341$$

$$CL = \bar{p} = \frac{\Sigma p}{23} = .928$$

$$\left.\begin{array}{l} UCL \\ \\ LCL \end{array}\right\} = \bar{p} + \text{ and } - \frac{3\sqrt{\bar{p}(1-\bar{p})}}{\sqrt{n}} \qquad \frac{3\sqrt{\bar{p}(1-\bar{p})}}{\sqrt{n}} = \frac{.775}{\sqrt{n}}$$

where n = sample size

Attachment B: Grade 5 SAT Scores (1989–1993)

Total reading: Percentage of test scores at or above average (p)

Test date	School	No. of students tested (n)	p	$\sqrt{n}$	$\dfrac{.729}{\sqrt{n}}$	UCL	LCL
5/89	1	68	.956	8.2	.089	1.00	.848
	2	75	.973	8.7	.084	1.00	.853
	3	69	.928	8.2	.089	1.00	.848
	4	56	.964	7.5	.097	1.00	.840
5/90	1	84	1.000	9.2	.079	1.00	.858
	2	83	.964	9.1	.080	1.00	.857
	3	68	.956	8.2	.089	1.00	.848
	4	58	.931	7.6	.096	1.00	.841
5/91	1	74	.932	8.6	.085	1.00	.852
	2	71	.972	8.4	.087	1.00	.850
	3	57	.965	7.5	.097	1.00	.840
	4	71	.930	8.4	.087	1.00	.850
	5	47	.915	6.9	.106	1.00	.831
5/92	1	77	.987	8.8	.083	1.00	.854
	2	80	.962	8.9	.082	1.00	.855
	3	72	1.000	8.5	.086	1.00	.851
	4	78	.885	8.8	.083	1.00	.854
	5	42	.881	6.5	.112	1.00	.825
5/93	1	80	.925	8.9	.082	1.00	.855
	2	71	.915	8.4	.087	1.00	.850
	3	72	.889	8.5	.086	1.00	.851
	4	74	.932	8.6	.085	1.00	.852
	5	43	.791	6.6	.110	1.00	.827
			$\overline{\Sigma\,21.553}$				

$$\text{CL} = \bar{p} = \frac{\Sigma p}{23} = .937$$

$$\left.\begin{array}{c}\text{UCL}\\[18pt]\text{LCL}\end{array}\right\} = \bar{p} + \text{ and } - \ 3\frac{\sqrt{\bar{p}(1-\bar{p})}}{\sqrt{n}} \qquad\qquad \frac{3\sqrt{\bar{p}(1-\bar{p})}}{\sqrt{n}} = \frac{.729}{\sqrt{n}}$$

where n = sample size

Attachment C

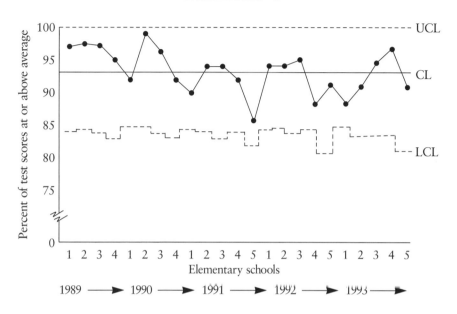

Figure 7.7. 1989–1993 total math *p* chart.

Attachment D

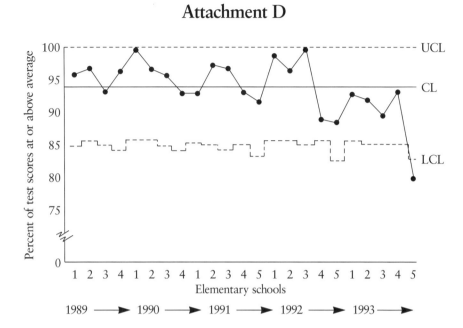

Figure 7.8. 1989–1993 total reading *p* chart.

Attachment E: Grade 5 SAT Scores (1989–1993)

Total math: Percentage of test scores above average (p)

Test date	School	No. of students tested (n)	p	$\sqrt{n}$	$\dfrac{1.42}{\sqrt{n}}$	UCL	LCL
5/89	1	68	.338	8.2	.173	.513	.167
	2	75	.600	8.7	.163	.503	.177
	3	69	.536	8.2	.173	.513	.167
	4	56	.250	7.5	.189	.529	.151
5/90	1	84	.214	9.2	.154	.494	.186
	2	83	.361	9.1	.156	.496	.184
	3	68	.382	8.2	.173	.513	.167
	4	58	.293	7.6	.187	.527	.153
5/91	1	74	.297	8.6	.165	.505	.175
	2	71	.197	8.4	.169	.509	.171
	3	57	.474	7.5	.189	.529	.151
	4	70	.500	8.1	.169	.509	.171
	5	47	.191	6.9	.206	.546	.134
5/92	1	77	.221	8.8	.161	.501	.179
	2	80	.225	8.9	.160	.500	.180
	3	71	.437	8.4	.169	.509	.171
	4	78	.333	8.8	.161	.501	.179
	5	42	.310	6.5	.218	.558	.122
5/93	1	80	.275	8.9	.160	.500	.180
	2	71	.310	8.4	.169	.509	.171
	3	72	.444	8.5	.167	.507	.173
	4	74	.392	8.6	.165	.505	.175
	5	41	.244	6.4	.222	.562	.118
			Σ 7.824				

$$CL = \bar{p} = \frac{\Sigma p}{23} = .340$$

$$\left.\begin{array}{c} UCL \\ \\ LCL \end{array}\right\} = \bar{p} + \text{ and } - \frac{3\sqrt{\bar{p}(1 - \bar{p})}}{\sqrt{n}} \qquad \frac{3\sqrt{\bar{p}(1 - \bar{p})}}{\sqrt{n}} = \frac{1.42}{\sqrt{n}}$$

where n = sample size

Attachment F: Grade 5 SAT Scores (1989–1993)

Total reading: Percentage of test scores above average (p)

Test date	School	No. of students tested (n)	p	$\sqrt{n}$	$\dfrac{1.42}{\sqrt{n}}$	UCL	LCL
5/89	1	68	.441	8.2	.173	.514	.168
	2	75	.307	8.7	.163	.504	.178
	3	69	.478	8.2	.173	.514	.168
	4	56	.321	7.5	.189	.530	.152
5/90	1	84	.393	9.2	.154	.495	.187
	2	83	.325	9.1	.156	.497	.185
	3	68	.397	8.2	.173	.514	.168
	4	58	.310	7.6	.187	.528	.154
5/91	1	74	.324	8.6	.165	.506	.176
	2	71	.310	8.4	.169	.510	.172
	3	57	.439	7.5	.189	.530	.152
	4	71	.380	8.4	.169	.510	.172
	5	47	.298	6.9	.206	.547	.135
5/92	1	77	.351	8.8	.161	.502	.180
	2	80	.313	8.9	.160	.501	.181
	3	72	.389	8.5	.169	.510	.172
	4	78	.333	8.8	.161	.502	.180
	5	42	.286	6.5	.218	.559	.123
5/93	1	80	.288	8.9	.160	.501	.181
	2	71	.338	8.4	.169	.510	.172
	3	72	.361	8.5	.167	.508	.174
	4	74	.257	8.6	.165	.505	.176
	5	43	.209	6.6	.222	.563	.119

$$\Sigma\ 7.848$$

$$CL = \bar{p} = \frac{\Sigma p}{23} = .341$$

$$\left.\begin{array}{c} UCL \\[2ex] LCL \end{array}\right\} = \bar{p} + \text{and} - \frac{3\sqrt{\bar{p}(1-\bar{p})}}{\sqrt{n}} \qquad \frac{3\sqrt{\bar{p}(1-\bar{p})}}{\sqrt{n}} = \frac{1.42}{\sqrt{n}}$$

where n = sample size

Attachment G

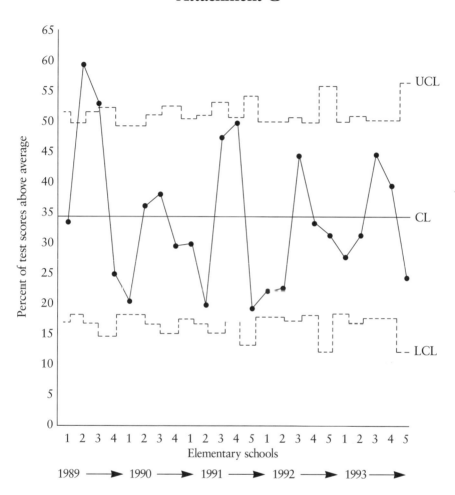

Figure 7.9. 1989–1993 total math *p* chart.

Attachment H

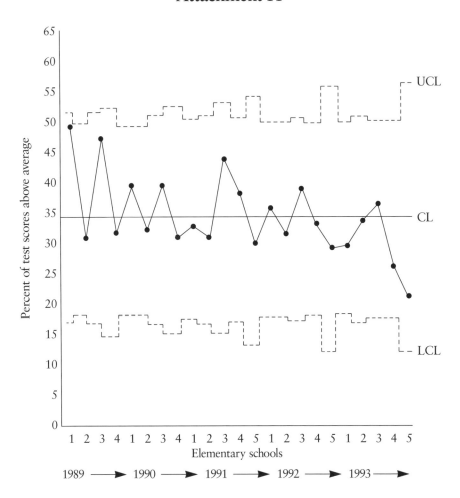

Figure 7.10. 1989–1993 total reading *p* chart.

Notes

1. B. Small, *Statistical Quality Control Handbook*, 132.
2. Wheeler and Chambers, *Understanding Statistical Process Control*, 49.
3. B. Small, *Statistical Quality Control Handbook*, 6.
4. Deming, *Out of the Crisis*, 404.
5. Ishikawa, *Guide to Quality Control*, 61–62.

Chapter Eight

Basic Procedure for Improving a System

When guided by the systems perspective, school and district leaders come to realize that systems problems by their very nature cut across various curricular and program lines, as well as grade levels, departments, schools, families, and other groups. Therefore, one strategy for systemic improvement is to select representatives from those various groups and sit them at one table. The table in this case is formed by a focused, formal, multidisciplined process improvement project. Legs of the table include training in the essential statistical methods (with great emphasis on the basic tools), clear direction and support from school and district leadership, time, and other needed resources.

Peter Scholtes suggests that the main agenda of these projects is to improve a process that leaders have identified as important to change. He adds that such project teams "are an instrument of widespread education, a purpose equally if not more important in the long run than their focus on improvement."[1]

Initially, it is this type of team that applies the procedure summarized in Figure 8.1. Eventually, people throughout the local school system will apply this basic procedure for improving a system in order to yield dramatic improvements of teaching, learning, and administrative processes on a continuous basis.

The flowchart in Figure 8.1 illustrates the typical stages through which a process improvement effort will advance over time. To the

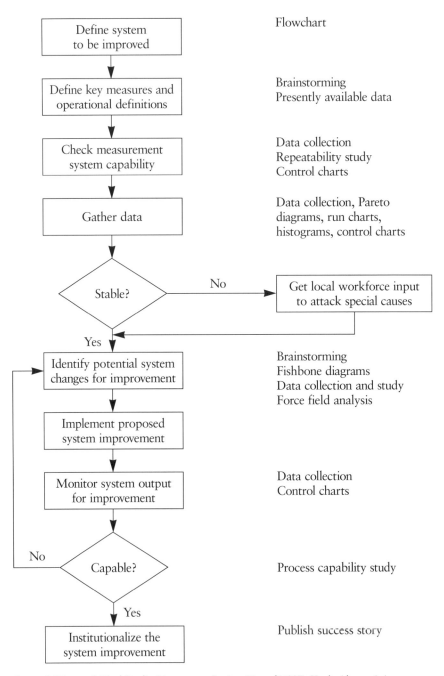

Source: J. F. Leonard, *Total Quality Management Seminar Manual* (1987). Used with permission.

Figure 8.1. Basic procedure for improving a system.

right of the flowchart are listed many of the basic and intermediate statistical methods teams employ to successfully complete each stage of the procedure.

Not all team members need be expert in the intermediate statistics. Enlightened school and district leaders will see to it that a few staff members are fully trained in those tools and concepts, then made available to help teams as they work to accomplish improvement. Following is a step-by-step description of each stage of the basic procedure for improving a system.

Step One: Define the System to Be Improved

As a first step in a process improvement project, teams will draft a flowchart of the process under study. This will yield a common, shared picture and understanding of the process. Another benefit of flowcharting is the help that basic tool provides in clearly defining customers (whoever uses the process output) and their needs.

The flowchart in Figure 8.2 was generated as a result of Ware Shoals, South Carolina Superintendent Jim McAbee's interest in defining and better understanding one key process in his district. In a letter he sent me, McAbee wrote:

> We know that the only way to improve any output is to improve the process that produces the output. In relation to school, there are at least three basic outputs.
>
> First, there are affective outputs: the attitudes, values, and beliefs that are developed. Second, there are abilities to use tools appropriately and effectively (e.g., using a dictionary, typing, and various algorithmic processes). Third, there is the intellectual product—knowledge acquired—which is much more than recitation, merely providing the right answers, and using formulas . . . .
>
> While these three do not exist in isolation, but are constantly in a state of interaction, I believe we

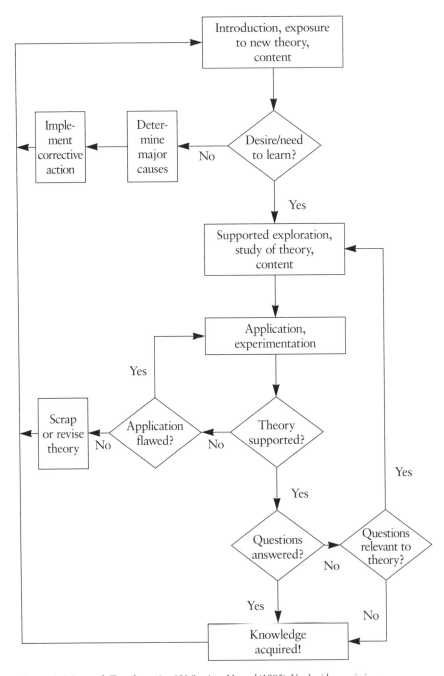

Source: J. F. Leonard, *Transformation 101 Seminar Manual* (1995). Used with permission.

Figure 8.2. Process for acquiring knowledge (versus acquiring tools or skills).

can and must isolate the latter two and draw a picture (flowchart) of the process so we can study them. Once we have done that, we can begin to identify key variables of input, [value-adding] process, and output that can be studied to generate knowledge of the process using statistical methods.

Step Two: Define Key Measures and Operational Definitions

Here the team works to clarify its understanding of customer needs and key measures of those needs. Clear operational definitions are needed so everybody understands what is meant by terms like *good, bad, late, on time, improvement, mastery, effective,* and so on.

A team in St. James-Assiniboia School Division, Winnipeg, Manitoba, was assigned to study the major causes of high school dropouts, then propose ways to reduce the current dropout rate. In its report to district leaders, the team noted, "One of the major problems in the literature respecting dropout studies is that the definition of who is a 'dropout' is not consistent from study to study."

The team recognized that without a clear definition of dropout, it too could run into problems when analyzing data or trying to reach consensus on recommendations for improvement. Therefore, very early in the project, it established the following operational definitions to guide the process study and improvement efforts.

> *Basic definition:* A dropout is any resident student of legal school age who fails to complete high school graduation.
>
> Other clarifications for our study have been established as follows:
>
> 1. Force-outs because of attendance policies, discipline, and so on are considered dropouts.

2. Resident students who attend a full-day program in private schools are not reported as dropouts, but as transfers. Students attending commercial business or similar (store-front) training programs in the community are designated as dropouts. (They have essentially dropped out of our school system.)

3. Any listed student who is still attending at least one course is considered as an active student (not a dropout).

4. Nonresident students, or students moving out of our school division before graduating, are stricken from the list of names and are not considered in the statistics. (The study is concerned with resident students only.)

5. Students transferring to another school in St. James-Assiniboia are not reported as dropouts.

After establishing clear definitions of terms, teams at this step must also define appropriate key measures. Below is a five-step procedure for defining key measures.

1. *Select a process.* Picture a pipe coming down at an angle from where the wall meets the ceiling to desktop height. On the side of the pipe, stencil the name of the process selected for analysis (for example, "Elementary schools' reading instruction process").

2. *List the outputs.* List what comes directly out of the pipe or process. For example, high test scores do not flow directly out of an instructional process. Rather, instruction process outputs include skills, knowledge, methods, materials, and so on.

3. *List users of the outputs (or customers of the process).* List who or what groups use the outputs of the process. In the case of processes with multiple customers, pick one of those customers and proceed to the next step.

4. *List the customers' needs.* Needs will often include terms like, *good, timely, user-friendly, interesting, effective, cost-effective, applicable,* and so on.

5. *List key measures.* Here teams are trying to determine how best they can put a number on the customers' needs. For example, if customers of a staff development planning process need timely outputs, a key measure could be the variance (in hours, days, or weeks) between scheduled and actual issuance of the development plan.

These metrics become the key measures for the process. They are used later in the basic procedure for improving a system to drive people back up into the process pipeline to study the process, change the process, and improve the process. They will also indicate if process improvement efforts have an appropriate effect; in other words, key measures move up or down over time.

Again, key measures are used to drive process improvement efforts—not merely to determine good or bad, and not to sort or filter defective outputs. Guided by the systems perspective, key measures derived at step two of the procedure are *never* used for grading, ranking, sorting, grouping, or tracking students! To do so is to fall prey to the *person = output* model from the age of mythology, confounding students with all the other variables in a process.

Step Three: Check the
Measurement System Capability

Having identified key measures in step two of the procedure, teams next move on to consider what is currently known about those metrics. It may be necessary to set up new data collection systems to get data on key measures that are not now available.

Teams will also challenge themselves with the question, "What right do we have to trust our measurements?" For example, a school in Elmira, New York, collected data on student disciplinary referrals and summarized its data on a Pareto diagram. The diagram showed the number of disciplinary referrals by reason for the referral. By far, the top reason for referrals was "inappropriate behavior," but nobody seemed to know what inappropriate behavior really meant!

That team had gone too far too fast. It had collected data before having established clear operational definitions; it had skipped step two! Therefore, it had no right to trust the data. In the absence of clear operational definitions, it also ended up in a situation in which it was unable to follow Ishikawa's third reminder for collecting data; it could take no action according to the data.

Step Four: Gather Data

Many teaching, learning, and administrative processes yield very slowly evolving data. Therefore, teams will initially post their measurements using check sheets, run charts, Pareto diagrams, and other basic tools. Once they have sufficient data, and if it's appropriate for the team's project, the measures or counts will be transferred to an appropriate control chart format.

Step Five: Is the Process Stable?

Upon review of the control chart, teams will apply appropriate tests for nonrandom, special cause variation. (Those tests are described in appendix B.) If special causes are evident, the team or administration will seek input from the local workforce. This step is based on what Deming referred to as "responsibilities for improvement," derived from the theory and knowledge of variation.

As noted previously, in the absence of understanding what type of variation is present, any discussion of accountability is a burlesque. This is because different types of variation require different types of corrective action for which different people will be accountable. The criteria for determining responsibility for corrective action are

1. If a process is in statistical control, it is under the influence of common causes of variation from within the process. Since only management has broad control over a process, management is responsible for improving stable processes whose outputs are not satisfactory.

2. If a process is not in statistical control, it is under the influence of some special, local, assignable cause(s) of nonrandom variation from outside the process. In this case, local workforce personnel are responsible for identifying the special cause and initiating corrective action. In this regard, Deming wrote, "The discovery of a special cause of variation, and its removal, are usually the responsibility of someone who is connected directly with some operation. It is his job to find the cause, and to remove it."[2]

Figure 8.3 illustrates these criteria in the form of Deming's responsibility assignments. When reviewing this matrix, one might ask, "Who is local workforce? Who is management?" My sister, Pat, the lawyer would respond, "It depends!" It depends on the process under study.

In his seminars, Deming provided wonderful operational definitions of what he meant by the terms *local workforce* and *management*. In the context of the systems perspective and knowledge of the theory of variation, my notes included the following definitions.

| | | Is the process stable? | |
		Yes	No
Are the outcomes satisfactory?	Yes	No action needed now; i.e., slow, gradual improvement acceptable	Local workforce must find the special causes and initiate corrective action
	No	Management must change the system	Local workforce must find the special causes and initiate corrective action

Figure 8.3. Deming's responsibility assignments.

Local workforce personnel are those people who work in a process, but lack the authority to change it. David Audette is the principal of Van Buren Moody Elementary School in Middletown, Connecticut. To the staff and students of that school, on a day-in, day-out basis Audette is management. But in Middletown's districtwide, annual budgeting process, what is Audette? In that process, he's local workforce. He's a part of the process, and he may have some great ideas for improving it; but on his own, he lacks the authority to change the overall budgeting process.

Management includes those people who supervise or are a part of the process and have the authority and wherewithal to change those parts of the process under their control. Clearly, Audette and other building administrators will fall under this definition in most cases.

Now, picture a nonexempt school employee who works in the maintenance department. Right now, he or she may be out in the building, working on some repair or preventive maintenance activity. In that setting, maintenance employees will sometimes (not often, but sometimes) find themselves in a position where they do have the brains, experience, wherewithal, and *authority* to change those parts of the repair or preventive maintenance process under their control. Thus, in certain process settings, nonexempt maintenance employees—people we might usually view as local workforce personnel—will fulfill the operational definition of management.

In the classroom, a teacher may assign a science project to teams of middle school students. In those settings, students will sometimes find themselves falling within this definition of management. They have the wherewithal and the teacher has provided authority to change parts of that science project under their control!

Recall the defined roles of the student (in chapter 3): customer of the system, worker in the system, and interdependent self-manager we want to see emerge from the system. If we agree that interdependent self-managers should graduate from our high schools, and in the context of the systems perspective, we should observe in high schools an exponential increase in opportunities for students to fulfill this definition of management.

Step Six: Identify Potential Systems Changes for Improvement

At this step of the basic procedure for improving a system, the team employs the basic tools to generate creative ideas for improving stable processes. (Since by this step the process is stable—under the influence of common causes only—improvements must come from changing the process.) Through data collection and study, and by applying the Pareto principle, teams assign values to the alternatives. As a common, shared view begins to emerge, consensus is reached on what appear to be the best ways to improve the process under study.

Step Seven: Implement the Proposed System Improvement

If I have observed one difference in my work with educators versus my work with businesspeople, it is this: It seems educators never do anything on a small scale! One district decides to adopt a new strategic planning model and *BAM!*—it's rolled out and applied to all schools, involving a huge number of people and focus groups. Another district decides to introduce site-based decision making and *BAM!*—site teams are set up in all schools at the same time. The result is that people are overloaded and buried, and the interventions may collapse.

At this seventh step of the basic procedure for improving a system, often system improvements should be introduced on a small scale or pilot basis. For example, a new report card for elementary school students—one that shifts emphasis away from measuring and ranking students and toward helping them via suggestions for improvement—may be implemented in only one school or one grade level.

Later, as lessons are learned from the pilot effort, the initiative may be expanded into other schools and areas of the district. Another advantage of initially taking this step on a small scale is that, should mistakes be made, their damage is limited. Pilot efforts may also uncover obstacles and resistance that were not anticipated, and plans for expanding the improvement can be refined to address those unanticipated obstacles.

Step Eight: Monitor the System Output for Improvement

Via continued data collection and study, teams and leaders at this step try to determine if the changes implemented at step seven had the desired effect. In other words, people try to answer the questions, "Did what we did on purpose to improve the process have an effect? Where's the data?"

Borgers and Thompson suggest that, even prior to this step, teams should have a plan to monitor and assess process changes. They add, "This would be an excellent place to [use] control charts to track such statistics."[3] Statistics to monitor improvement will include the key measures that the team defined back in step two of the procedure.

How will we know improvement has occurred? We'll see those key measures move up or down, depending on what direction is better for the process outputs. Where appropriate, the use of control charts at this step will help teams determine whether measures are moving not merely up or down, but significantly up or down. Significant changes in the patterns of key measures indicate that the process had indeed changed (hopefully, for the better!). If the patterns remain random, this would indicate that the process was not changed or improved, or that changes and improvements have not had a significant effect on outcomes.

In the case of a new report card format, control charts would probably not be an appropriate tool to monitor the effects of the change. Rather, a team may survey parents for their feedback and reactions to the change. Perhaps the school will send out both the old report card and the new report card at the same time. Survey data, often summarized in the form of a Pareto diagram, and seeking additional suggestions for improvement will occur at this eighth step of the procedure.

Step Nine: Is the Process Capable?

At this point, teams compare data collected at step eight to current requirements (standards, schedules, planned outcomes, budgets, and so on). If the process capability does not meet those requirements, the team will have to return to step six to generate new ideas for improvement.

If the process is not capable, the return loop to step six may lead to seeking ideas from people outside the team. Where appropriate, advanced tools like designed experiments will be applied. After identifying additional or new ideas for improving the system, the team will move again through steps seven, eight, and nine.

In some project settings, districts at step nine are determining not so much if the process is capable of meeting requirements, but if their system is capable of taking on the change. Do they have the time, staff, funding, and other resources to implement the change? For example, one district, on a pilot basis, introduced a new report card format. Though it reported to parents how their children were doing in the school's programs, it emphasized suggestions for improvement. Those suggestions were directed to the students and parents, and self-directed to the teacher.

At step eight of the procedure, parent survey data indicated that the parents *loved* the new report card. Overwhelmingly, the feedback applauded the team and reported that the new format was a definite improvement over the old A-B-C-D-F approach. At this step of the basic procedure for improving a system, however, the team determined that the district was not capable of expanding and adopting the new report card format. The team had discovered that it required almost one hour per student for teachers to fill out the new report cards! One might think, "What's the problem? Why can't teachers find a way to spend one hour per student per marking period to fill out a report card!?" Unfortunately, it was a problem; an unwieldy paperwork burden for the teachers.

But the team and district leaders were determined that the new report cards had to be implemented! They agreed that the traditional grading system was arbitrary, unjust, and destructive—not only to students' joy in learning, but also to their future academic progress. So the team had to return to step six of the procedure. It sought additional input from teachers and data to determine answers to the following questions: "What takes most of our time now? What are the major causes of wasted teacher time?" Once it had identified and eliminated some major causes of wasted time, it freed up time for teachers and was able to introduce the new report cards in all the elementary schools in the district.

Once processes are capable and/or acceptable versus current standards and other requirements, the procedure advances to its next and final step.

Step Ten: Institutionalize the System Improvement

At this step, school and district leaders do not establish a new standard. Nor do they allow any semblance of a definition of "good enough" to be applied to the stable, capable, improved system. Rather, at this last step of the basic procedure for improving a system, improvement is literally institutionalized. Since the process is capable, slow and gradual improvement is perfectly acceptable. Limited school and district resources—in the form of future process improvement project teams—must be directed toward improving processes that are not yet capable.

Improvement continues, however, and is institutionalized at step ten via training and use of the basic statistical methods by all people who work in the process. They apply these basic tools on a continuous basis to generate continuing, gradual, never-ending improvements. Here the school system and its students begin to benefit from *kaizen*.

The Japanese word *kaizen* does not translate cleanly into any English word. It refers to a situation in which literally thousands of 1-percent improvements are generated on a continuous basis. Gabor suggests that *kaizen* in Japan resulted from Japanese managers' adoption of the Deming cycle "as the principal model for establishing and carrying out quality [improvement] strategies throughout an entire organization."[4]

The Deming Cycle

Care must be taken to ensure that process improvements don't end at the tenth step of the basic procedure for improving a system. Rather, at that step, leaders must work to institutionalize improvement. They must integrate continuous improvement into the process itself.

William Scherkenbach observed that a process of continuous improvement should spiral toward fulfilling customer needs. "Improvement is possible because integral to the process is the Deming Cycle. (He calls it the Shewhart Cycle . . . .) It is in this process of continuous improvement that several important precepts of the Deming philosophy are manifested."[5]

The Deming cycle is composed of four sequential segments or stages: plan, do, study, and act. (Earlier versions of the model labeled the third stage "check.") Figure 8.4 illustrates the Deming cycle and how the process of improvement flows through the four stages.

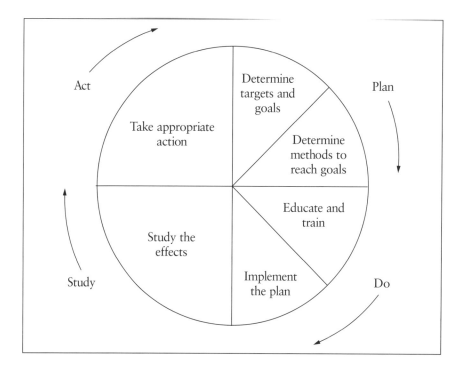

Figure 8.4. The Deming cycle.

Ishikawa refined the first two stages of the cycle. He noted that planning involves more than establishing targets and goals; we must also determine and agree on the methods to reach those goals. Doing involves more than just implementing a plan. Leaders must also provide appropriate training, education, explanation, or orientation for people who will be involved in or affected by the change.

Deming viewed the cycle as not only a helpful procedure for process improvement, but "also as a procedure for finding a special cause detected by statistical signal."[6] He went on to credit Shewhart for illustrating how the four segments of the cycle can yield improvements based on the following considerations.[7]

1. *Plan.* What could be the most important accomplishments of this team? What changes are desirable? What data are available? Are new observations needed? If yes, plan a change or test. Decide how to use the observations.

2. *Do.* Carry out the change or test decided upon, preferably on a small scale.

3. *Study.* Observe the effects of the change or test.

4. *Act.* Study the results. What did we learn? What can we predict?

5. *Repeat step 1, with knowledge accumulated.*

6. *Repeat step 2, and onward.*

The key to institutionalizing continuous improvement is the last two words of step 6: "and onward." Imagine how our children will benefit throughout the balance of their lives if they graduate with the means to do the same thing as it relates to continuous, lifelong learning.

Summary

As the essential statistical methods and the basic procedure for improving a system are learned and applied throughout the district, the main beneficiaries of the resulting continual improvements will be our children and their development.

On Figure 8.1, note the recommendation printed next to the last step of the procedure: "Publish success story." Successful system improvements must be publicized throughout the local community. This will help to celebrate the success, as well as build momentum for the transformation process. It also helps the school board and administration to continue their efforts to educate the local community about the problems of education.

Copies of the published evidence of improvement should be provided to local media and higher levels of the bureaucracy to help remove barriers to improvement and to contribute to the long-term success of the local transformation effort. In fact, a district should strive to have several such reports in local media—describing successful process improvements for the good of students' learning and development—for every one article that ranks the district based on its standardized test scores!

In conclusion, this chapter describes a basic procedure to improve any process and how statistical methods apply in that procedure. Some people may be concerned about their ability to learn and use the statistical methods, but relatively speaking, the statistical methods are easy! It's just a matter of time on task: attend a seminar, read this text, collect some data, build some charts—in time you'll get real good at it.

The hard part is the third key element of the transformation process: providing leadership to create, maintain, and strengthen a healthy environment for work and learning. Much more difficult than learning statistical methods is providing that healthy environment in which, among other things, people will use the essential statistical methods correctly, effectively, comfortably, and without fear.

Having built a foundation with the systems perspective, theory of variation, and statistical methods, it is now time to take on the hard part. In our next chapter, we'll begin to examine Deming's philosophy and principles as a model of the healthy environment for work, learning, and continuous improvement.

Notes

1. Scholtes, *The Team Handbook*, 1-17–1-18.

2. Deming, *Quality, Productivity, and Competitive Position*, 116.

3. W. Borgers and T. Thompson, *Implementing Continuous Improvement Management in the Schools* (New York: Scholastic, 1994), 130.

4. A. Gabor, *The Man Who Discovered Quality* (New York: Times Books, 1990), 56–57.

5. W. Scherkenbach, *The Deming Route to Quality and Productivity: Road Maps and Roadblocks* (Rockville, Md.: Mercury Press, 1988), 35.

6. Deming, *Out of the Crisis*, 88.

7. *Ibid.*

Chapter Nine

The Transformation Model

Figure 9.1 lists Deming's 14 points for management, followed by a restatement of those points as obligations of the school board and administration in Figure 9.2. The original listing has also been referred to as the 14 obligations for management, the Deming 14-point philosophy, or simply the 14 points. It has been available to managers in business and industry for years as a model of a healthy work environment. By the same token, the restatement of the 14 points as obligations for educational leaders can be viewed as a model of the district's work and learning environment after the transformation has occurred.

Outside the context of the systems perspective and the theory of variation, on the surface, some of the 14 points seem strange. For example, in both the original model and its restatement, several points call for the elimination of numerical goals, targets, and standards. But how does one manage an organization without numerical goals (budgets, schedules, forecasts)?

Consider the position of a school district's local business partners. Do those companies ever expect their customers to send them orders that read, "Ship it whenever you're ready"? Or do they expect those customers to continue to place on them more and more stringent, demanding requirements and *goals* for delivery performance?

1. Create constancy of purpose toward improvement of product and service.

2. Adopt the new philosophy.

3. Cease dependence on inspection to achieve quality.

4. End the practice of awarding business on the basis of price tag . . . . Move toward a single supplier for any item, in a long-term relationship of loyalty and trust.

5. Improve constantly and forever the system of production and service.

6. Institute training on the job.

7. Institute leadership.

8. Drive out fear, so that everyone may work effectively for the company.

9. Break down barriers between departments.

10. Eliminate slogans, exhortations, and targets for the work force asking for zero defects and new levels of productivity. Such exhortations only create adversarial relationships, as the bulk of the causes of low quality and low productivity belong to the system and thus lie beyond the power of the work force.

11. Eliminate work standards (quotas) on the factory floor. Eliminate management by objective. Eliminate numerical goals.

12. Remove barriers that rob the hourly worker of his right to pride of workmanship. Remove barriers that rob people in management and in engineering of their right to pride of workmanship. This means, *inter alia*, abolishment of the annual or merit rating and of management by objective.

13. Institute a vigorous program of education and self-improvement.

14. Put everybody in the company to work to accomplish the transformation.

Figure 9.1. Deming's 14 points for management.[1]

Will your school district ever find itself in a world in which the state legislature, department of education, and the local community request, "Keep us posted"? Or will the district have to exist in a world in which those various publics lay upon it ever more stringent and demanding *standards* for district, school, and student performance? Clearly, districts can expect to find themselves dealing with the latter. Therefore, how can one simply eliminate goals and standards that are imposed by the marketplace (in the business setting) and society at large (in a school setting)?

1. Create constancy of purpose toward improvement of the entire school system and its services. Think and plan for the long-term needs of the school and its students, rather than short-term requirements.

2. Adopt the new philosophy.

3. Cease dependence on tests and grades to measure quality.

4. Cease dependence on price when selecting the curriculum, texts, equipment, and supplies for the system. Make selections based on quality to result in lower costs long term for the system.

5. Improve constantly and forever every process for planning, teaching, learning, and service.

6. Institute more thorough, better job-related training.

7. Institute leadership (management of people).

8. Drive out fear.

9. Break down barriers between groups in the school system.

10. Eliminate the use of goals, targets, and slogans to encourage performance.

11. Closely examine the impact of teaching standards and the system of grading student performance.

12. Remove barriers that rob staff and administrators of pride of workmanship and rob students of the joy of learning. Abolish annual ratings of staff and the system of grading student performance.

13. Institute a vigorous program of education and self-improvement for everyone in the system. Don't forget the needs of parents.

14. Plan and take action to accomplish the transformation. Start with education for all in positions of leadership. Help them view the school system as a system.

Figure 9.2. Obligations of the school board and administration.

Indeed, taken only at face value, these and other points in Deming's model seem radical; divorced from the realities of customers' demands. When viewed in the context of the systems perspective, process thinking, and some knowledge of the theory of variation, however, these points—so goofy on the surface—are not at all radical.

In the context of the theory of variation, the intermediate statistical concepts teach us that processes will define their own capabilities, as determined by the average plus and minus three standard deviations ($\bar{X}$ + and − $3\sigma'$). In other words, processes are stupid! They do not know and do not care what might be our hopes, wishes, standards, or goals. They will provide us what they're capable of providing us; take it or leave it!

Deming was merely calling for leaders to work on improvement of processes, instead of setting numerical goals and standards. Improving processes alone will improve their capabilities and levels of performance. "A numerical goal accomplishes nothing. Only the method is important. By what method?"[2]

During one of his seminars, Deming applied this rationale to several of the Bush administration's America 2000 goals, as well as the Clinton administration's Education 2000 goals. For example, he cited the goal for American students to be number one in the world in math and science by the year 2000, then asked the not-so-rhetorical question, "By what means?" Later, he noted the goal to raise the high school graduation rate to 90 percent by the year 2000 and asked, "By what means?"

In the early sixties, faced by the threat of *Sputnik* and other Soviet advances, President Kennedy set a goal for the United States to put a man on the moon by the end of the decade. His administration—as well as those of Lyndon Johnson and Richard Nixon—provided the means to achieve that goal. An infrastructure was created with the National Aeronautics and Space Administration (NASA); huge investments were placed in research and technology development; and Cape Canaveral, the Houston Space Center, and other physical facilities were built. In the absence of such investment in means and methods, President Kennedy's goal would have remained just that: a goal.

In the absence of providing means and methods—in the absence of systemic change—the America 2000 and Education 2000 goals have remained just that: goals.

Scherkenbach adds that goals often tend to confuse people's understanding of exactly what their job is. He provided an example of such confusion that results from obsession with numerical goals and standards, as opposed to customers' needs.

One such state of confusion existed in an office full of people charged with settling customers' claims. They also were evaluated on the number of calls they processed in a day and, in fact, had a work standard of ten calls per hour. What was their job? You know exactly what it was. When a call approached six minutes in duration, they politely excused themselves and hung up, even though they hadn't met their customer's needs.[3]

What is the district's purpose? Is it to achieve high test scores, or is it to facilitate child development? What is the teachers' job? Is it to see that students achieve high test scores, or is it to identify and meet their students' development and learning needs? In any district locked in the age of mythology, in any district driven by test scores alone, what is a teacher's job? As Scherkenbach might say, "You know exactly what it is."

Pushing for Balance

Some people look at some of the 14 points and conclude that Deming must have been naive. He was not naive. More than many, he understood how many numerical goals and standards imposed by higher levels of the bureaucracy are not only destructive, but also beyond the control of those on whom the goals are imposed! Rather than exhibiting naivete, in the statement of some of his points Deming seems to have been pushing for balance.

In our age of mythology, we've gotten out of balance. More energy is put into setting goals than in providing means for improvement. The American management system also seems to have lost sight of how numerical goals and standards, though intended to encourage higher levels of performance, often end up acting as *barriers* to improved performance.

What is a human being's natural behavioral tendency upon achieving a goal? Most often, we relax and exclaim, "We did it! Where's my reward?" Too often, numerical goals have the unintended effect of defining "good enough" in the minds of people and in their subsequent behavior. Future suggestions for improvement encounter resistance: "If it ain't broke, don't fix it . . . . We're no worse than anyplace else . . . . We're meeting the standard; what's the cost-benefit ratio of getting a few percent better?" Hence, such goals end up fostering mediocrity. They were never intended to foster mediocrity, but they do.

Every state in the country has established minimum teacher certification standards. They were always intended to serve as just that: the *minimum*. In my seminars with educators, I always ask them, "What has been the effect of these minimum standards?" The reply: "They've become the maximum or at least the norm."

Those teacher certification standards were never intended to serve as a norm for good teaching. Minimum teacher certification standards were never intended to foster mediocrity in the school of education, producing graduates who barely meet minimum standards; they just do—and will continue to do so in the absence of a systems perspective and leadership for continuous improvement.

Therefore, one way to view the 14 points is as a model of management balance. As it relates to numerical goals and planning systems, the American management system has gotten out of balance. Attention to the 14 points will help leaders question these practices and provide more means and methods for improving processes, instead of America 2000 and Education 2000 goals that help no one. Once such inhibitors to improvement in the current work and learning environment are removed, the transformation can occur. Conversely, once transformation occurs, those inhibitors to improvement will no longer exist.

The Deming Philosophy

As noted earlier, some people refer to the 14 points as the Deming philosophy. Over time, however, I have determined that the 14 points are not the philosophy. They weren't even around in 1950 when Deming started teaching Japanese business leaders how to transform their organizations; how to delight their customers and capture world markets. Nor were the 14 points even appropriate in that setting. Deming reported, "The plague of barriers that rob the hourly worker of his right to pride of workmanship in American companies today was zero or at a low level in Japan."[4] Therefore, Deming was able to concentrate on helping Japanese business leaders to view their organizations from a systems perspective and learn and apply the essential statistical methods. Four years later, Juran made his first visit to Japan, and, in Deming's words, "his masterful teaching gave to Japanese management new insight into management's responsibility for improvement of quality and productivity."[5] Thus, emphasis was placed by Deming and Juran on a philosophy of management, but not on the 14 points.

Some years ago, Mat Self, president of Greenwood Mills, had the chore of introducing me at a conference in South Carolina. He did so by saying I was the author of the Deming philosophy for education. The restated 14 points as obligations of the school board and administration are *not* the philosophy. They weren't even around in draft form before the mid-1980s.

If not the 14 points, then what is the Deming philosophy? More importantly, how would one state that philosophy as a *new philosophy for education?* One could do so as follows:

> Learning and applying the system of profound knowledge in order to (1) understand the statistical nature of work and learning; and (2) view work and learning as dynamic processes; then take appropriate action to accomplish improvement because wherever children and their futures are concerned, there is and can be no such thing as good enough in our schools.

Taken in the context of this philosophy, many of the 14 points are merely descriptions of common American management beliefs and practices that act as barriers to the philosophy; barriers to leaders being able to implement the philosophy; barriers to children being able to benefit from the philosophy in our schools. For example, if the unintended effect of numerical goals, targets, and standards is to end up defining good enough, that will forever be a barrier to people's taking appropriate action to accomplish improvement. If we're not willing to question our obsession with grading, ranking, and evaluating people, that will forever be a barrier to two other critical facets of the philosophy.

• *Understanding the statistical nature of work and learning.* Recall that the question is not, "Are these students different?" The question is, "Are they significantly different?" Traditional American management practices (myths) of grading and performance appraisal pay no attention to the statistical nature of work and learning.

• *Viewing work and learning as dynamic processes.* Grading and merit rating practices are valid only if the model, *person = output,* is valid. Grading and ranking are valid only if, since $A + B + C + D + E + F = 73$, the variable F equals 73 in all cases and without exception. Since neither of these assumptions is valid, traditional grading and merit rating practices cannot be valid. Test scores are produced by teaching and learning processes, not the students alone.

Deming went so far as to call for the total elimination of grades in our schools. He wrote, "Abolish grades (A, B, C, D) in school, from toddlers on up through the university. When graded, pupils put emphasis on the grade, not on learning . . . . The greatest evil from grades is forced ranking—only (eg.) twenty percent of pupils may receive A. Ridiculous. There is no shortage of good pupils."[6]

Who can imagine schools without grades? How will we communicate student performance without grades? In the minds of many people, to simply abolish them would cause chaos; it's just too radical. Indeed, Deming's proposal was radical, but that makes it no less rational.

For example, Jacob is a high school student in your district. His final semester average is 89.9. His neighbor achieved a final average of 90.0 for the same semester. What is the difference between those two final averages?

Using that measurement scale, the difference between the 89.9 and the 90.0 is a difference of one one-thousandth, spread out over an entire academic term. From any rational point of view, one would conclude that this difference clearly is not significant. After all, a nose cold during one homework assignment could account for such an insignificant difference. Incorrectly rounding one decimal on one math exam (caused perhaps by a poor teaching method and, therefore, having nothing to do with Jacob's cognitive abilities) could account for such an insignificant, one one-thousandth difference at the end of a four-month academic semester.

In the traditional American school, however, we take that insignificant difference of one one-thousandth and we make it significant! It becomes the difference between an A and a B. It becomes the difference between whether or not Jacob is eligible for a scholarship or for a break on his auto insurance premiums.

In the age of mythology, obsessed with grading and ranking people, the difference of one one-thousandth becomes the difference between whether Jacob's called up during assembly for an honor roll certificate or not; whether or not his name is published in the local paper as an honor roll student; whether or not his parents receive a Proud-Parent-of-an-Honor-Roll-Student bumper sticker! (Whenever I'm driving behind cars with those bumper stickers, I'd like to talk to their drivers. I'd like to ask them, "What kind of a person are you? Do you mean you would not be proud of your child if he *wasn't* on the honor roll?")

As more emphasis is placed on protecting students' self-esteem, these irrational grading and ranking practices are expanded. Many schools no longer publish just one honor roll. They've added a principal's list and a high honor roll to the mix! Additional sorting occurs by diagnosing students as learning disabled, attention deficient, and other categories.

In the interest of so-called progressive education and reform, our schools are finding new and exciting ways to sort and label outcomes so students feel good, or at least better, about themselves. Unfortunately, these sorting practices do nothing to improve the process of teaching and learning. They do nothing to remove systemic barriers to higher levels of learning and achievement.

Susan Robertson, an education and learning consultant, has worked for years with learning disabled (LD) students. She reports that up to one-third of the students in public elementary schools have been labeled LD. Among those students with whom she has worked, 100 percent of those labeled LD (barring those with clear physical or mental handicap) perform at or above average after tutoring in basic reading skills. Robertson insists that these students "are not learning disabled, they are teaching disabled!"[7]

The alternative to non–value-adding filtering, or setting numerical goals and standards that help nobody, is provided by the core of the new philosophy: the system of profound knowledge. Leadership decisions and action guided by profound knowledge drive the transformation, the change in state. Transformation in turn results in continuous improvement of processes throughout the organization. Continuous improvement of processes yields higher and higher levels of performance that cannot and will not result merely by setting goals and standards for improvement.

The System of Profound Knowledge

The underlying theory of transformation is profiled by the system of profound knowledge. Appendix C provides an unpublished paper by Deming, in which he described that system. As defined by Deming, the system of profound knowledge is made up of four segments, each of which interacts with the others.

1. Appreciation for a system
2. Some knowledge of the theory of variation
3. Theory of knowledge
4. Psychology

Deming's paper in appendix C provides his explanation of these four components, as well as the overall system. Following are a few supplementary observations for applying profound knowledge in an educational setting.

Appreciation for a System

The first component of the system of profound knowledge includes all the material covered in chapters 2 through 4 of this text and more. At its core, appreciation for a system provides understanding of the interdependence among components within a system; for example, the interdependence of the K–12 components of a district's language arts curriculum.

In this regard, Senge observes that schools, businesses, and other human endeavors are systems, bound by "invisible fabrics of interrelated actions, which often take years to fully play out their effects on each other. Since we are part of the lacework ourselves, it's doubly hard to see the whole pattern of change. Instead, we tend to focus on snapshots of isolated parts of the system, and wonder why our deepest problems never seem to get solved."[8]

Senge has also described systems thinking (Deming called it appreciation for a system) as a conceptual framework that helps not only to more clearly see patterns of interaction between components, but also to see how to improve them more effectively. Earlier in this text, this challenge was oversimplified by describing the need to get the components of our engines working better together, rather than striving for perfect, individual components.

In his text, *The New Economics,* Deming described what a staggering challenge this is for public education. He wrote,

> A public school in the United States is not operated as a component of a system. Optimization is obstructed by a city superintendent, a county superintendent, a school board (elected, shifting over time, no constancy of purpose), district board, local government, county government, state board of

education, federal government, assessed by standardized tests of pupils, comparisons between districts and states.[9]

The solution to this dilemma will be found in the application of
the system of profound knowledge and its first component, appreciation for a system. (Recall that the philosophy entails learning
and applying the system of profound knowledge.) Such application
is detailed in the obligations of the school board and administration
(hereafter obligations), which serve as not only a model for the
transformation, but also as the manifestation of the system of profound knowledge itself.

Among others, two of those points help to apply appreciation
for a system. The first of the obligations reads, "Create constancy
of purpose toward improvement of the entire school system and its
services." Inherent in this point is the deployment of a clearly
defined purpose that is understood and shared by groups (components) throughout the district.

In order to deploy constancy of purpose by the various components of the local system, any barriers that exist between those
groups must be identified and removed. Thus, point 9 reads,
"Break down barriers between groups in the school system."
Chapter 10 will elaborate on these and the rest of the obligations.
For now, we'll proceed with an overview of the remaining three
components of the system of profound knowledge.

Some Knowledge of the Theory of Variation

When Deming first mailed me the paper provided in appendix C,
I was thrilled to see the short sentence at the beginning of its second
paragraph: "One need not be eminent in any part of profound
knowledge in order to understand it as a system, and to apply it."[10]
Upon reading that sentence, I thought to myself, "Thank God! I'd
never be able to become eminent in any of this stuff!"

Equally comforting is the wording of the second component of the system of profound knowledge: *some* knowledge of the theory of variation. In other words, one need not have a Ph.D. in statistics to understand and apply this component of profound knowledge. Rather, what is needed is for leaders to understand and differentiate between common cause variation (from within a process or system) and special cause variation (from outside the process or system). Such understanding guides the development of plans for appropriate corrective action.

- In the case of common cause variation, management is responsible to work to change the process.

- In the case of special cause variation, local workforce personnel are responsible for identifying the special cause and initiating corrective action.

Chapter 4 provided details regarding the theory of variation. One example of its application (or lack thereof) in a school setting was experienced by Heero Hacquebord and his six-year-old daughter. Deming reported the incident as follows:

> Need a teacher understand something about variation? Mr. Heero Hacquebord sent his six-year-old daughter to school. She came home in a few weeks with a note from the teacher with the horrible news that she had so far been given two tests, and this little girl was below average in both tests . . . . The little girl learned that she was below average in both tests. She was humiliated, inferior. Her parents put her into a school that nourishes confidence. She recovered.[11]

Fortunately, the little Hacquebord girl's story had a happy ending. How many students' stories have a sad or tragic ending because they have teachers who do not possess some knowledge of the theory of variation?

Theory of Knowledge

This is the one component of the system of profound knowledge that continues to challenge me. How can I possess sound knowledge of the theory of knowledge without some theory of knowledge on which to base my knowledge of the theory of knowledge? Since Deming passed away in December, 1993, I can no longer ask him about it! In his text, *The New Economics,* and in his paper reproduced in appendix C, he did leave us some guidelines for grasping the theory of knowledge. He wrote, for example, that any plan—however simple—requires prediction, and that prediction must be based on some theory. What's the theory?

In our schools, there remains great confusion between information and theory, and between facts and knowledge. A thesaurus provides a lot of information about words and their synonyms, but the thesaurus provides me no knowledge on how to write a good essay. An atlas will provide some facts about countries and the geographic location of their major cities, but the atlas provides no knowledge about the history or cultures of those countries.

Shewhart quoted Harvard University's C. I. Lewis: "Knowing begins and ends in experience; but it does not end in the experience in which it begins."[12] Therefore, Shewhart postulated that in the application of statistical methods, knowledge may begin and end in experimental data, but it does not end in the data in which it begins.

Shewhart presented the following theory of knowledge: "There are three important components of knowledge: (a) the data of experience in which the process of knowing begins; (b) the prediction in terms of data that one would expect to get if he were to perform certain experiments in the future; and (c) the degree of belief in the prediction based on the original data or some summary thereof as evidence."[13] He illustrated this theory with the model reproduced in Figure 9.3.

It is not uncommon in my seminars with businesspeople for someone to say, "Deming said our merit pay system was wrong. Give us an alternative to our merit pay system." Some educators

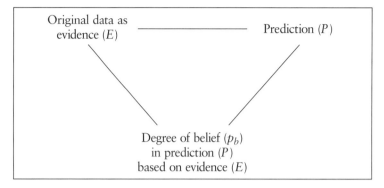

Source: W. A. Shewhart, *Statistical Method from the Viewpoint of Quality Control* (New York: Dover Publications, 1986): 86. Used with permission.

Figure 9.3. Illustration of Shewhart's theory of knowledge.

ask for an alternative to the traditional grading system that Deming insisted must be abolished.

Regarding theory of knowledge, Deming wrote, "An example is of no help in management unless studied with the aid of theory. To copy an example of success, without understanding it with the aid of theory, may lead to disaster." Therefore, he insisted that examples without theory teach nothing, and that no number of examples or case studies will teach a theory.

Due to this insight, over time I learned that the best response to requests for alternatives to merit pay and grading systems is to submit a request of my own. I now respond to such requests by asking, "If I give you an alternative to your merit pay or grading systems, do you promise me you'll implement it?" In every case, the response to my question has been *no*.

I then ask, "If I give you an alternative to your rating or grading system, what will you do with it?" The most common response: "We'll compare it to our current system."

It took me some time, but applying the theory of knowledge helped me realize that I would do those people a disservice if I gave them an alternative to their appraisal or grading system! I don't want them to compare it to what they're doing now. I want them to compare it (the alternative) *and* what they're doing now to a rational theory.

One best way to teach the rational theory is to conduct Deming's classic bead experiment, which provides knowledge based not only on appreciation for a system and variation, but also on an understanding of the destructive effects of grading and ranking on the people themselves. Because of its power for teaching the theory, chapter 11 is devoted to describing the procedure and lessons of the bead experiment.

Knowledge Versus Experience

During one of Deming's seminars, I served on a panel discussion. A member of the audience posed a question that began, "All of our experience tells us . . . ." As I started to respond to that question, Deming interrupted to declare, "Experience without theory teaches nothing!"

While other panelists added their comments, I pondered Deming's terse statement. I was confused, because I'd always heard that experience was the best teacher.

Over dinner that evening, I shared my thoughts with Deming and asked if he meant to say that *examples* without theory teach nothing. (After all, I'd finally started to figure that one out.) Deming replied, "No. I said what I meant!"

When I asked for further explanation, he asked me what nation has the most experience in manufacturing, as measured by man hours. He answered his own question by noting that the United States has the most experience. Next, he asked me, "What have we learned? Where are we now?" Glancing down at his dinner, he growled that we have become "an object of pity."

Later I thought about that conversation. Now, I often ask in my seminars how many people own a VCR and just about every hand in the audience goes up. Next, I ask them where they can buy an American-made VCR. The response: "There aren't any American-made VCRs!"

I've been told that VCR technology was invented at Iowa State University. On top of that, the United States has more experience in manufacturing than any other nation on earth. Unfortunately, in the absence of sound theory all that experience did not teach us enough to be able to make and sell VCRs at a profit. We lost the market; bad management; absence of profound knowledge.

Charles F. Desmond, who heads an initiative for gifted and talented middle and high school students in Boston, criticized the U.S. Department of Education's report, *National Excellence: A Case for Developing America's Talent*. In an article in the *Roeper Review*, Desmond observed:

> Regrettably, rather than an uplifting celebration of the progress and gains that have been made over the last twenty years, the report is a hard hitting narrative chronicling the continued decline and ongoing failure of schools to responsibly address the intellectual challenges raised by our nation's most gifted children . . . . The crisis in educating talented students is pervasive . . . affecting learners as early as kindergarten and extending well into the college years.[14]

In other words, it seems as though Desmond and other members of the gifted and talented lobby don't want to deal with facts and data that prove that our fastest students have gotten slower as a result of sorting, as opposed to education. They would much prefer to blame schools for failing the meet the needs of talented students (as if others aren't), beginning in kindergarten. But how can one determine that this five-year-old is gifted and predict that she will be a success in life? How can one determine that another five-year-old is not gifted and predict that he will be a failure? How could one possibly know?

In the absence of theory, two decades of experience in gifted and talented sorting has yielded no new knowledge. It has merely reinforced the same myth 20 times over.

Psychology

This fourth component of the system of profound knowledge helps leaders understand people, their interactions, differences, and different needs. At the center of knowledge of psychology is a leader's ability to understand and differentiate between intrinsic motivation and how it is influenced over time by extrinsic motivators.

Is the appropriate strategy, then, to try to motivate people? Or is it to remove barriers to their own motivation? Senge has written about how this dilemma exists in efforts to achieve the goal of continuous improvement, "which remains an elusive target" for many American organizations.

> *Motivate them.* From an extrinsic perspective, the only way to get continuous improvement is to find ways to continually motivate people to improve . . . . Otherwise they'll just sit there—or worse yet, slide backwards. This leads to what workers perceive as management continually raising the bar to manipulate . . . them.
>
> *Loose their motivation with information and appropriate tools.* However, from an intrinsic perspective, there is nothing mysterious at all about continuous improvement. If left to their own devices, people will naturally look for ways to do things better. What they need is adequate information and appropriate tools.[15]

Deming's philosophy for leadership is grounded in the belief that people are intrinsically motivated; naturally striving for self-dignity, pride, and joy in their work. Unfortunately, the current American management system destroys intrinsic motivation by substituting extrinsic motivators. Deming's argument is best illustrated in Figure 9.4, which he published in his text, *The New Economics*.[16]

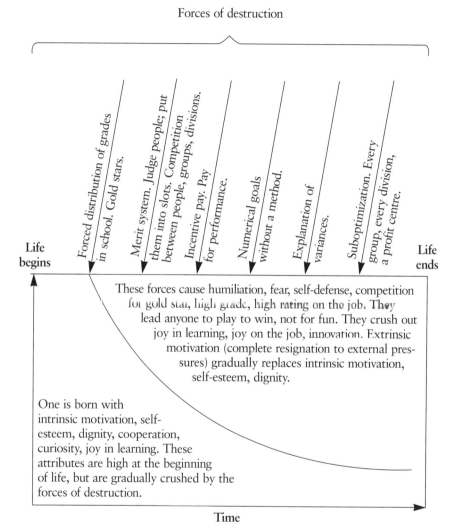

Figure 9.4. Effects of extrinsic motivators on intrinsic motivation.

The forces along the top rob people, and the nation, of innovation and applied science. We must replace these forces with management that will restore the power of the individual.

Figure 9.4. Effects of extrinsic motivators on intrinsic motivation.

Interaction of the Components

Deming insisted that the different components of the system of profound knowledge cannot be separated; they interact with each other. He described, for example, how knowledge of psychology is incomplete without knowledge of variation, just as understanding of variation will be incomplete without appreciation for a system.

Senge cited one way in which the first component (appreciation for a system) interacts with the fourth component (knowledge of psychology). He observed that, over time, people will take on the characteristics of the system of which they are a part. "The systems perspective tells us that we must look beyond individual mistakes or bad luck to understand important problems. We must look beyond personalities and events. We must look into the underlying [systemic] structures which shape individual actions."[17]

I'm grateful to Jim McAbee, superintendent of schools in Ware Shoals, South Carolina, for guiding my thinking about how the third and fourth components of the system of profound knowledge (knowledge and psychology) interact with each other. For example, Sigmund Freud and other determinists worked for the most part with the deranged; but their findings have been applied to people with healthy minds. In the absence of sound theory of knowledge, what damage might psychologists be causing?

Similarly, the work of Skinner, Watson, and other behavioral psychologists was largely with animals, but some have applied their findings to people. As McAbee asked in a letter, "How long will we continue to destroy our most important asset—our children—with grading practices based on [behavioral] sticks and carrots?"

Using extrinsic factors, behavioral psychologists demonstrated one could create a conditioned response in animals. What has that to do with children? Without guidance from theory of knowledge, experts in psychology have unleashed terrible forces of destruction as children's joy of learning is submerged by extrinsic carrots and sticks. Thus, too many students strive for grades, not knowledge. They work for rank, not joy.

Summary

Deming's 14 points have existed for years as a model of a healthy work environment in a business context. In this chapter, we introduced a restatement of that model as obligations of the school board and administration. The obligations may be viewed as a model of a district's healthy work and learning environment after transformation has occurred. However, that listing should not be viewed as the Deming philosophy.

Rather, the new philosophy for education involves learning and applying the system of profound knowledge. Doing so helps people to understand the statistical nature of work and learning, and to view the quality of work and learning as outcomes of dynamic processes. This understanding in turn enables people to take appropriate corrective action, because wherever children and their future are concerned, there is and can be no such thing as good enough.

Outside the context of this philosophy, several of Deming's 14 points, as well as their restatement for an education setting, appear to be quite strange. Viewed in the context of the system of profound knowledge, however, they are for the most part a listing of common American management beliefs and practices that act as barriers to a district being able to implement—and children being able to benefit from—the philosophy.

The system of profound knowledge is made up of four interrelated components: appreciation for a system, some knowledge of the theory of variation, theory of knowledge, and psychology. The 14 points and the obligations may be viewed as a logical extension and application of the system of profound knowledge.

The purpose of this chapter was to examine the philosophy as a model, or guide, for transformation. In doing so, we concentrated on the system of profound knowledge, the essence of that philosophy. In chapter 10, we will elaborate on the restatement of the 14 points as obligations of the school board and administration.

Notes

1. Deming, *Out of the Crisis*, 23–24.

2. Deming, *The New Economics*, 33.

3. Scherkenbach, *The Deming Route*, 86.

4. Deming, *Out of the Crisis*, 489.

5. *Ibid.*

6. Deming, *The New Economics*, 148.

7. S. Robertson, *Reading, Writing and Ripped Off* (Humble, Tex.: Higher Knowledge, 1993), videocassette.

8. Senge, *The Fifth Discipline*, 7.

9. Deming, *The New Economics*, 74.

10. Deming, "Profound Knowledge," 1.

11. Deming, *The New Economics*, 101.

12. Shewhart, *Statistical Method*, 80.

13. *Ibid.*, 85–86.

14. C. F. Desmond, "A National Tragedy: The Retreat from Excellence in America," *Roeper Review* 16 (June 1994): 224.

15. P. Senge, "Building Learning Organizations," Reprint from the *Journal for Quality and Participation*, March 1992, 3.

16. Deming, *The New Economics*, 125.

17. Senge, *The Fifth Discipline*, 42–43.

Chapter Ten

Elaboration on the 14 Obligations of the School Board and Administration

The previous chapter introduced a restatement of Deming's 14 points for management as obligations of the school board and administration. The obligations serve as a manifestation of the system of profound knowledge for schools and districts. Beyond that, they define what will exist after transformation guided by profound knowledge: a healthy environment for work, learning, and continuous improvement.

Many managements get themselves in trouble by trying to treat the 14 points or the obligations as a cafeteria plan. For example, they have no problem with working to reduce the total cost of purchased materials and services or trying to improve coordination and teamwork among different departments or groups in the organization. Therefore, great effort is invested to implement the points that address those issues. The same managements, however, decide that points 11 and 12 do not apply to their organization cultures, histories, and practices. They cling to numerical goals and appraisal practices, while at the same time working to implement others of the 14 points. The results are disappointment, confusion, and little improvement.

In American business today, one can't swing a dead cat without hitting some mission statement. They all look great on the plaque in the bank's lobby or reproduced on the back of the salesperson's business card. Most of them are concise statements of the organization's mission to serve customers and provide growth opportunities for employees. Many include statements like, "As a unified employee/management team we commit to . . . ."

Yet most of those organizations—and 85 percent of American businesses at large—cling obsessively to their individual merit reward systems. Unfortunately, those organizations cannot achieve effective teamwork (point 9) if they continue to cling to a merit system (point 12) that rewards people for keeping successful work techniques to themselves. They cannot achieve effective teamwork when individuals are rewarded for getting ahead of their teammates!

In other words, one cannot achieve the benefits of point 9 without paying attention to points 3 and 12. The obligations are not a cafeteria plan. They are intimately, intricately interwoven in a fabric of a strong, healthy and complex environment for work, learning, and continuous improvement.

Beyond our past examination of the system of profound knowledge, there's not much more to be said about the obligations as a whole. After all, they are but a logical extension and application of the philosophy. For the balance of this chapter, however, we will briefly elaborate on the individual obligations, bearing in mind that each is directly related to, and interacts with, other points in the model.

Point 1: Create Constancy of Purpose Toward Improvement of the Entire School System and Its Services

Deming taught that organizations face two sets of problems: problems of today and problems of the future. "It is easy to stay bound up in the tangled knot of the problems of today, becoming more and more efficient in them . . . [however] problems of the future command first and foremost constancy of purpose and dedication to improvement."[1]

The core essence and theme of this first of the 14 obligations addresses the need for long-term constancy of purpose or long-term thinking and behavior. Long-term thinking helps pull the school board and administration above the fray of today's concerns to put more energy into planning for the future of the district and its students. Robert Audette once shared with me his insight regarding constancy of purpose by posing the question, "What is the purpose of the district?" As noted previously, without an aim, there is no system. Without clear purpose, there can be no constancy of purpose!

Audette and Algozzine stressed the need for district leadership (point 7) to clearly define its long-term goals relative to child development needs, due to the current "lack of clarity or constancy of purpose for children. As educators we behave as though our purposes for children are clear and shared. This is a false assumption."[2] More specifically, what are the desired characteristics of the district's high school graduates? What do we want our graduates to have relative to

- Cognitive skills and abilities?
- Mastered communication skills?
- Critical thinking processes and strategies?
- Work habits?
- Attitude and value placed on continued learning?
- Choices for future direction and occupation?

In June 1991, the Department of Labor produced an important resource for districts interested in clarifying purpose for long-term learning and child development. (Though this report concentrated on needs for workplace know-how, one would be hard pressed to find that the same qualities are not important for those high school graduates who proceed directly to an institution of higher education.) Known as the SCANS report, that document listed the competencies, skills, and personal qualities that are needed for solid job performance.[3]

> COMPETENCIES—effective workers can productively use:
>
> - **Resources**—allocating time, money, materials, space, and staff;

- **Interpersonal Skills**—working on teams, teaching others, serving customers, leading, negotiating, and working well with people from culturally diverse backgrounds;

- **Information**—acquiring and evaluating data, organizing and maintaining files, interpreting and communicating, and using computers to process information;

- **Systems**—understanding social, organizational, and technological systems, monitoring and correcting performance, and designing or improving systems;

- **Technology**—selecting equipment and tools, applying technology to specific tasks, and maintaining and troubleshooting technologies.

THE FOUNDATION—competence requires:

- **Basic Skills**—reading, writing, arithmetic and mathematics, speaking, and listening;

- **Thinking Skills**—thinking creatively, making decisions, solving problems, seeing things in the mind's eye, knowing how to learn, and reasoning;

- **Personal Qualities**—individual responsibility, self-esteem, sociability, self-management, and integrity.

There is a great need for leadership (point 7) and breaking down barriers between groups in the local school system (point 9) in order to engage various constituencies in the delineation of these desired characteristics. Once they are clarified and agreed upon, work can be undertaken to design pre-K–12 teaching and learning process components that work well together to develop those characteristics in children during the 13 or 14 years they invest as students in the district. Policies and practices can then be aligned to support that purpose and to contribute to the long-term good of children.

Many organizations find the development of a solid mission statement to be important for defining their long-term purpose and direction. By mission statement I do not mean the two- or three-sentence, Mom-and-apple-pie slogans that too many organizations are publishing. Rather, I am referring to a detailed, well-thought-out statement of mission, aims, purpose, and guiding principles. Such a statement should help leaders at all levels to figure out how they and their groups fit into the overall aims of the organization. In other words, that document should serve as the definition of *purpose* in the phrase, "constancy of purpose."

Once clear purpose is defined, constancy of purpose will be impeded by numerical goals and standards (points 10 and 11) that put people into short-term, reactive modes. Other barriers will exist if grading and ranking (points 3 and 12) continue, based on past or short-term results. Besides, leadership (point 7) toward long-term objectives requires prediction and influence of the future—not merely knowing the score. As a second-grade teacher, how could I predict that Emma will be a success in life (A+ student), mediocre (C), or a failure (F)? How could I know?

Point 2: Adopt the New Philosophy

This point requires little elaboration, since the whole theme of this text is the need for transformation, change in state. The philosophy was described in some detail, with emphasis on the system of profound knowledge, in the previous chapter. In this context, Algozzine and Audette wrote:

> Embracing the new philosophy will necessitate radically changing the way that we think about school. For example, 70% is generally viewed as a measure of acceptable performance in our schools. Does 70% represent quality? Does 90% represent quality? Does any such percentage provide a useful way to consider quality? It certainly does not in most other areas of endeavor (competitive sports are the exception).[4]

Borgers and Thompson elaborated on this point by noting that the organization's management style must be transformed.

> Cooperation rather than competition among students, and between students and teachers, is the goal. The teacher must accept the new philosophy and teach it to the students. Teachers should ask students to define quality in their own terms . . . . What is a quality assignment? Why? What is quality work? Why? Students should also be encouraged to display what they consider [to be] quality work.[5]

Point 3: Cease Dependence on Tests and Grades to Measure Quality

Please note that this point does not call for the elimination of standardized tests or testing in general. After all, without assessment we will not be able to answer the critical question, "How are we doing?" Rather, this point calls for eliminating *dependence* on standardized and other tests as the sole measures of quality.

Recall that standardized tests, at best, assess child development along cognitive lines. Such assessment must continue in order to monitor development of such basic skills as reading, writing, and mathematics. At the same time, the limitations of standardized tests must be appreciated. For one thing, they provide only a once-a-year response to the question, "How are we doing?" Using those instruments alone, one would need almost 20 years of data to determine if changes to curriculum generated a significant improvement trend!

Therefore, many districts are placing greater emphasis and trust on their classroom teachers and those end-of-unit, end-of-chapter quiz scores, homework, and classwork assessments. Such instruments are more robust and can generate 10, 15, or 20 responses each term to the question, "How are we doing?"

Another danger of dependence on standardized tests is that they were never designed to assess progress in social and emotional development or in the development of interpersonal skills and other competencies cited in the SCANS report. No standardized test will ever yield the following profound insight recorded by a Ware Shoals, South Carolina, high school student in her learning log: "I will learn great thinking skills that will go with me forever, not just some grade or test score that's only on a sheet of paper anyway."

Point 3 also calls for educational leaders to recognize certain weaknesses of standardized tests, even as assessments of skills development. One fourth grader in Middletown, Connecticut, has been writing beautiful poems from scratch for two or three years. The following is one of his poems.

The Wind
The wind is a wispy tail.
The wind is a soft motion blowing in my hair.
The wind is a tornado picking up houses.

Wind is a savage monster ripping powerlines.
The wind is a singer, singing to nature.
The wind is a delightful whistler.

The wind is laughing at our mistakes.
The wind is crying at poverty and racism.
The wind blows because it wants to see the world.

The wind is a wonderful, scary
jolly, sad, happy free soul in me.

The author of this beautiful piece of creative writing tested below the remedial level in writing on the Connecticut Mastery Test. Obviously, there is a need to cease dependence on such standardized tests and to place greater emphasis on other ways to observe, assess, and cherish evidence of children's development.

On the other hand, point 3's treatment of grades is quite different. Deming did not suggest that we merely cease dependence on grades, but that we abolish them. Full explanation of this point has been provided in earlier chapters, including how the grading system blocks a statistical understanding of the nature of work and learning, as well as ignores how work and learning are dynamic processes.

I do not want this point to come across as if grades should be abolished solely in the interest of low-scoring students' self-esteem. Granted, the fourth component of the system of profound knowledge (psychology) is a factor here. The traditional grading system indeed serves as a barrier to students' joy of learning (point 12), but one must also recognize how the system of grading student performance hurts the top students, too.

During one of my seminars with educators, a high school teacher talked about one of her students who was in the running for the valedictorian award at graduation. The teacher said, "Throughout her high school career, this student has not once challenged for an AP [advanced placement] course. She can't take the chance, because she's afraid her grades will go down."

Thus, beyond all the evidence of the destructive effects of the grading system on students' self-esteem, the same system leads to a situation in which far too many top students dumb down their own learning experience! Relative to the current system, the call to abolish grades may be viewed as a radical proposal, but that makes it no less rational.

Point 4: Cease Dependence on Price When Selecting the Curriculum, Texts, Equipment, and Supplies for the School System

As in the case of standardized tests (point 3), this point stresses the need to cease dependence on price—but not ignore price. Purchase price is one variable in determining the total cost of use of purchased items, but it is only one variable. District purchasing practices must be guided by concern about total cost—including after-sale service. Though many states still mandate purchasing from the lowest bidder, most district business managers with whom I've worked seem to understand the difference between lowest bidder and lowest *qualified* bidder.

Deming shared one example of an administrator whose thinking is now guided by point 4. Sr. Jeanne Perreault, president of

Rivier College in Manchester, New Hampshire, reported, "We cannot afford to purchase equipment and buildings at the lowest price. We have to be careful."[6]

Developing partnerships with suppliers (point 9) helps to engage them in efforts to continuously improve processes throughout the district (point 5). Conversely, purchasing decisions driven by concerns for this year's budget alone may impede long-term improvements and constancy of purpose (point 1).

Point 5: Improve Constantly and Forever Every Process for Planning, Teaching, Learning, and Service

One might wonder what's the difference between point 1 and point 5. After all, both seem to be talking about the improvement of the system and its processes over the long term. Gitlow and Gitlow described how ongoing efforts to improve processes (point 5) are guided by long-term thinking (point 1).

> Making a commitment to constantly improve the system necessitates a long-term perspective. Analyzing, understanding, and improving the process are ongoing tasks that stretch out into the infinite future. Management must be able to deal with the day-to-day issues of the organization and also move toward never-ending improvement. The scope of never-ending improvement is vast and overwhelming, but Point Five offers some very tangible ways of improving the system.[7]

Those tangible ways for improving processes include the essential statistical methods (see chapters 5 and 7, as well as appendices A and B). They are applied by teams of teachers, parents, specialists, and others via the basic procedure for improving a system, which was described in chapter 8.

Obviously, learning and applying statistical methods and the basic procedure for improving a system will require training (point 6). Because the procedure is most often applied by a multi-disciplined project team of representatives from different groups throughout the district, attention must also be paid to removing barriers that may exist between those groups (point 9).

Finally, it must be stressed that the core theme of point 5 involves improvement of processes—not problem solving, not fire fighting. In this regard, Deming wrote, "Putting out fires is not improvement of the process. Neither is discovery and removal of a special cause detected by a point out of control. This only puts the process back to where it should have been in the first place."[8]

Improvement of processes, on the other hand, produces significant changes in their outcomes. Ongoing process improvement efforts yield higher and higher levels of student learning and development without need of numerical goals (points 10 and 11), which too often serve to impede improvement!

Point 6: Institute More Thorough, Better Job-Related Training

Scherkenbach suggests that part of continuous improvement (points 1 and 5) is to provide all staff members with a broad understanding of statistical thinking and statistical methods.[9] As these tools are learned and applied, they contribute to one major aim of the training: reduced variation in methods.

In every district I visit, I hear stories about some teachers whose classes are highly structured and disciplined, while other teachers in the same building allow just about anything in their classes. What are the effects on students of those mixed messages, and of that variation in classroom discipline criteria and practices?

In an elementary school, three different fourth-grade teachers may employ three different methods in teaching certain math facts. Some combination of the three fourth-grade teachers' students end up in the same fifth grade next year. What problems does this create for the fifth-grade teacher?

Therefore, point 6 addresses training in not only the essential statistical methods, but also reducing variation in other work and teaching methods. Of course, when planning for any training, leaders must keep the following formula in mind.

$$\text{Training effectiveness} = f[(\text{Quality of subject matter}) \times (\text{Probability of use})]$$

(This formula was introduced in chapter 5 under the heading, "A Word of Caution." It is so critical to addressing point 6 that it bears repeating.)

This equation states that the effectiveness of any training will be a function of the quality of the subject matter times the probability of use. Scherkenbach put it a little differently: "If training is so important, why hasn't it been effective? It hasn't been very effective because of a series of inhibitors. Because management has not changed [organization] systems to use the training, untold millions of dollars are being wasted on training."[10]

One way leaders can provide a high probability of use for the training is by placing trainees on process improvement project teams. Leaders must also pay attention to identifying and removing inhibitors to people using the new tools; among them barriers between different groups in the district (point 9) and numerical goals and standards that drive short-term thinking and fire fighting (points 10 and 11) as opposed to improvement of processes (point 5).

Please note that in this brief elaboration on the sixth obligation, reference has been made to five other points. An equal number of obligations were referenced while examining point 5. It should by now be clear that the 14 obligations are indeed intimately and intricately interwoven, as one would expect of a complex model of a dynamic, healthy environment for work and learning. As noted, the model is not and cannot be viewed as a cafeteria plan.

Point 7: Institute Leadership (Management of People)

The overall transformation is and must be guided by the system of profound knowledge. As people in positions of leadership learn and apply that system, they exhibit certain behaviors that truly lead people and organizations toward continuous improvement of processes for teaching, learning, and service (points 1 and 5). As it relates to managing people, those leadership behaviors are guided by appreciation for a system, rational theories of variation and knowledge, and an understanding of intrinsic motivation.

Unfortunately, traditional views of leadership behavior are rooted in our individualistic society, as opposed to an appropriate systemic view. Senge wrote:

> Especially in the West, leaders are heroes—great men (and occasionally women) who "rise to the fore" in times of crisis. Our prevailing leadership myths are still captured by the image of the captain of the cavalry leading the charge to rescue the settlers . . . . So long as such myths prevail, they reinforce a focus on short-term events . . . rather than on systemic forces.[11]

Thus, the prevailing style of leadership in most American organizations carries with it inherent barriers to long-term constancy of purpose (point 1), as well as the creation of heroes through short-term crisis management instead of continuous improvement (point 5).

Leaders guided by the system of profound knowledge, on the other hand, exhibit very different behaviors. In his seminars, Deming used a list headed "Attributes of a Leader." (We viewed a restatement of those general behavioral attributes as attributes of the effective leader/teacher in chapter 3.) To complete our elaboration on point 7, let's briefly examine Deming's attributes of a leader.

1. *The leader understands how the work of his or her group fits into the overall aims of the organization.* As in the case of the effective leader/teacher, we're making an assumption here that

people in top management have done their jobs. They have clearly defined the purpose and aims of the organization so leaders at all levels can figure out how they and their groups fit in. (See point 1 of the obligations.)

2. *The leader focuses on the customer, both internal and external.*

3. *The leader is coach and counsel, not a judge.* (See points 3, 6, and 12 of the obligations.) District leaders must examine their current systems for coaching and developing staff members. What systems and practices currently exist that help supervisors coach, counsel, and develop members of their staffs? What systems and practices currently exist that require those supervisors to pass judgment? Any of the latter will interfere with the former. Trying to do both sends mixed and confusing signals to staff members (or to students in the classroom).

4. *The leader removes barriers to joy in work.* (See points 8 and 12 of the obligations.) Deming long insisted that the most important measures facing American managers are unknown and unknowable. In the business context, he used to pose the following questions.

- How much business does a happy customer bring in to you? Nobody knows. What is the value of the satisfied customer? Nobody knows.

- What is the cost of the dissatisfied customer? Nobody knows. How much business does the dissatisfied customer drive away? Nobody knows.

How many readers have heard the saying, "If you can't measure it, you can't manage it"? I heard that mantra again and again in the graduate business school. I continue to hear it from advocates of outcomes-based education and from consultants (Deming called them hacks) trying to get schools to use control charts. The hacks teach, "After all, we need control charts to effectively manage our processes; but before building a control chart you must measure something. Therefore, if you can't measure it, you can't manage it."

Welcome to the age of mythology. Despite what they teach in business school, the most important measures facing leaders in education are indeed unknown and unknowable. They can't be measured, but they must be managed.

Many district leaders are concerned about costs and budgets. What, then, is the cost to the district of the untrained staff member, working in fear? Let's agree that cost is staggering, but it's unknown and unknowable. It can't be measured, but it must be managed.

What is the value of the satisfied parent? What is the value to the district of the support provided by parents who are at this weekend's Little League practice, bragging to their neighbors about the quality of their child's learning experience in your classrooms? Let's agree that value is priceless, but it's unknown and unknowable. It can't be measured, but it must be managed.

As soon as one starts talking about joy in work or joy of learning, many people fear they're getting into the touchy-feely swamp of the behavioral sciences or into affective, values-oriented areas that people may feel have nothing to do with academics. However, this fourth attribute of a leader deals with a very real, very concrete factor in any work environment, and it's based on a very simple premise: It is a joy to work with people who enjoy their work.

Readers can think about their own experience at work. Have you ever worked with people who really enjoyed their work? What was it like? (Great, energizing, fun, contagious.) Have you ever worked with people who did not enjoy their work? What was that like? (Draining, stressful, not fun, infectious.)

If a local company's workers are suffering barriers to their right to joy in work, it is lowering the productivity and efficiency of that organization; and it doesn't have a thing to do with labor utilization versus internal standard, or with equipment utilization versus internal standard, or with any other numbers managers look at when concerned about productivity and efficiency. But if workers in that organization are experiencing obstacles to their right to joy in work, the company is losing productivity and efficiency every hour of every work day.

This is one of the few areas where I see a significant difference in terms of impact when applying Deming's principles to schools, as opposed to businesses. After all, in our schools the stakes are much higher than merely lost productivity or machine hours. In schools we're dealing with fragile, raw human potential.

Readers may reflect back on their experience as students in the classroom. Did you ever have a teacher who really enjoyed teaching? What was it like? (Great, fun, energizing, learned a lot.) Beyond that, many people tell me they went into education in the first place because of those teachers who enjoyed teaching. When you were students, did you ever have a teacher who did not enjoy teaching? What was it like? (Thought the bell would never ring, boring, endless, didn't learn very much.)

I realize that bringing up joy of learning and joy in work sounds touchy-feely. I used to feel the same way. However, we are talking here about a very real, very concrete factor that affects our children's development. If teachers in your local district are suffering barriers to their right to joy in work, it is retarding the learning and development of children throughout your community, and it doesn't have a thing to do with the district's ranking on that last state audit; it doesn't have a thing to do with the latest round of standardized test scores (point 3); and it doesn't have a thing to do with any other numbers school boards look at out of concern for child development and learning. But if your teachers are experiencing barriers to their right to joy in work, it is retarding your children. The cost is staggering, though unknown and unknowable. Leaders who understand and behaviorally exhibit this fourth attribute of a leader do not always need numbers to manage; they have profound knowledge, so they understand intrinsic motivation.

5. *The leader understands variation.* (See chapter 6, "Theory of Variation," as well as points 10, 11, and 12 of the obligations.) The leader understands that if I were to take any 10 people out into the parking lot to run a 40-yard dash, five of those people will come

out equal to or above average, and five will come out equal to or below average. That's normal. The leader understands that.

The leader also understands how to use systems thinking, statistical thinking, and statistical methods to determine who, if anyone, is outside the system and in need of special help. In such a case, the leader provides special help to those who need it. If, after providing the special help, that person still doesn't fall in the group that constitutes a system, the leader must find a less demanding or more appropriate placement.

Some knowledge of the theory of variation enables the leader to differentiate between that which is different and that which is significantly different. Therefore, the leader does not rank people who fall into a group that constitutes a system. Their levels of performance or achievement may be different, but they are not significantly different!

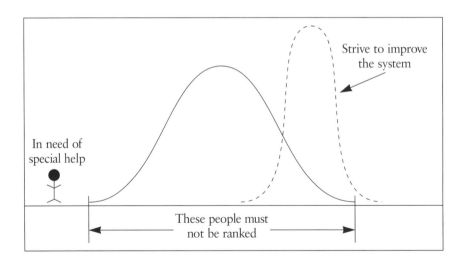

6. *The leader works to improve the system in which he or she and his or her people work.* (See point 5 of the obligations.)

7. *The leader creates trust.* (See points 8 and 9.)

8. *The leader forgives a mistake.* (See point 8.)

9. *The leader listens and learns.* (See point 13.)

A quick review of the attributes of a leader (point 7) will indicate reference to *eight* other obligations. In other words, we cannot talk about point 7 without at the same time talking about eight of the other 13 points. Once again, this is because the model is not a cafeteria plan; its points are indeed interdependent.

Point 8: Drive Out Fear

Audette and Algozzine elaborated on this point by observing, "In most of our schools, faculty, students and parents are afraid to speak out or take risks. Fear of 'being wrong' or 'rocking the boat' has prevented many seminal ideas from being fully developed. Fear of ridicule, reprimand, and retribution has kept many solutions to our problems from ever being considered. Fear is essential to supervisors' power in the traditional school."[12]

Borgers and Thompson add that the "single most fear-producing system used in schools is grades. Reduce the reliance on grades for motivating students. Successful learning occurs when the activities are . . . intrinsically rewarding."[13]

One will note that, in addressing point 8 of the obligations, these authorities made reference to points 3, 5, 7, 9, and 12.

Point 9: Break Down Barriers Between Groups in the School System

I have no more disheartening an experience in my seminars than to have high school teachers come up to me and complain about the lack of skills they see in the students who come from their own district's elementary and middle schools. I can't help but wonder, Why are they talking to me? Indeed, lack of communication and program coordination across school lines are problems we can no longer afford to tolerate. Multidisciplined project teams that include teachers from the elementary, middle, and high schools are one means for breaking down the traditional barriers between those components. Inclusion of parents and central office personnel on the same teams provides even greater opportunities.

Audette and Algozzine elaborated on point 9 as follows:

> The boundaries between regular education and special education are heavily fortified with processes which do not address the needs of children but rather categorize the children themselves. For all of its good intent and its attempts at precision in the design of Individual Education Plans (IEP's), special education is a separate system disassociated from the (unclear) purposes, goals, and outcome benefits envisioned for other children in our schools.[14]

Finally, one could not write about point 9 in this day and age without some comment regarding the tension between the so-called progressive educators and the so-called religious right. One zealous and eloquent spokesman for the religious right is the Rev. Pat Robertson, who wrote,

> The classic meaning of education was to train the *minds* and *morals* of students. Education by common definition existed to impart to the young the moral and intellectual heritage of a nation, a culture, or a civilization . . . [however] the theories of modern education can be summed up as a basic denial of the value of Western tradition and a repudiation of the role of religion in the welfare of the community. Modern educators are moved not only by a denial of the existence of God, but militant hostility to any form of Judeo-Christian theism.[15]

In recent years, I've been amazed at the number of administrators and teachers I've met who share Rev. Robertson's concerns! But they express frustration that "the other side" is exaggerating the situation, or at least blaming the wrong people. During one of my seminars, a district superintendent offered her assessment: "Some parents in our community want us to put prayer back in schools. I agree with them—from a personal point of view, I'd love to open each school day with a prayer. But I don't sit on the Supreme Court, nor do I control the U.S. Congress."

In other words, many educators are as frustrated by the current system as the religious right and other activists. They're also frustrated when attacked for pushing outcomes-based-education (OBE), when in fact many planned changes (such as block scheduling) have nothing to do with OBE.

Of course, exaggeration occurs on both sides. For example, in early March 1993, a consultant visited a district in the Bronx. Not long before that visit, the New York City School Board had voted not to renew the contract of Superintendent Joseph Fernandez, the author of that city's Rainbow Curriculum, which had produced a storm of controversy because many people believed it placed too much emphasis on diversity, sexuality, and political correctness, as opposed to academic issues.

During the meeting that week, an administrator commented on the Fernandez dismissal and added, "This is why administrators need tenure. They cut Fernandez off at the knees before he had a chance to follow through" (introduce the new curriculum).

The consultant replied that it seemed that many parents of school children in the Bronx had three priorities: learn to read, learn to write, and come home alive—and not necessarily in that order! Next, the consultant challenged that administrator to describe *anything* in the Rainbow Curriculum that adequately addressed those parents' top three priorities. He was unable to do so.

Unfortunately, educators across the country continue to suffer the after-effects of that Rainbow Curriculum. OBE has become synonymous with values programming; Christian parents and others are in fear for their children's morals; and generalizations are made that all educators (to use Robertson's words) "are moved by . . . hostility to any form of Judeo-Christian theism."

To close this elaboration on point 9 and barriers between educators and the so-called religious right, below are excerpts from my correspondence with a Christian parent activist in one district with which I've had the honor of working. A letter she mailed me read, in part,

> I would also like to give you the gift of sharing moments of shocked joy you gave me during your presentation to our Board. You gave the Bible credit for being an authority . . . . Anyone with less prestige would have been shut up immediately or had everything they said past, present and future negated.

In response to her letter I wrote:

> I certainly hope that in my remarks I did not come across as "preachy." My duty is not to pass judgment on people because of their beliefs (or lack thereof), but rather to try to help them learn a system for better management in education . . . . I view the current battle in education between the so-called "religious right" and so-called "progressives" as but a symptom of a greater problem. That greater problem is a core lack of trust and communication.
>
> We'll not be able to eliminate that core problem until we get "all the components of our engine" working better together. Many arguments between the above groups have descended into accusations and judgments passed on "the other side." I must wonder, "Who's talking about kids?"
>
> To keep from losing my mind, I can only reflect on a remark Mother Theresa of Calcutta made at the National Prayer Breakfast last year: "If we're

busy judging people, we'll have no time left to love them.". . . . Because of your kind feedback, I'll be able the next time I'm in [your community] to check my balance between judging and loving, between criticizing and helping.

Point 10: Eliminate the Use of Goals, Targets, and Slogans to Encourage Performance

Point 11: Closely Examine the Impact of Teaching Standards and the System of Grading Student Performance

The first half of chapter 9 dealt with these two points in some detail. Having used that much space to elaborate on points 10 and 11, I'll offer no more of my own observations.

Instead, I offer the following profound insights written by Audette and Algozzine. Regarding traditional academic standards, they noted that scores of 70 percent yield passing grades (success) in education, but

> Most of us would not be satisfied with appliances or cars which work 70% or even 90% of the time. Undoubtedly, a 70% recovery rate is not a satisfactory standard for successful gall bladder surgery. A hotel that maintains accurate reservation records only 70% of the time would not stay in business very long . . . . [Many students] merely do what is necessary to get by (70%) in classes because quality is not apparent to them in their schoolwork. Likewise, these same students will make extraordinary efforts in another class (frequently a non-academic class) where quality is perceived to be valued.[16]

Point 12: Remove Barriers That Rob Staff and Administrators of Pride of Workmanship and Rob Students of the Joy of Learning

Elaboration on this point was provided under points 2, 3, and 5 through 11. The essence of this point calls for the elimination of annual ratings for staff and abolishing the system of grading student performance.

This is not to suggest that leaders no longer provide feedback and help to staff members and students; quite the opposite. However, traditional rating and grading practices fail to provide helpful feedback. After all, what is a grade? Almost four decades ago, Michigan State University's Paul Dresser defined it as follows: "A grade is an inadequate report of an inaccurate judgment by a biased and variable judge of the extent to which a student has attained an undefined level of mastery of an unknown proportion of an indefinite amount of material."[17]

Once again, this point does not call for the elimination of assessment; only that leaders recognize that test scores and other outcomes are produced by work and learning processes—not the people alone. Hence, when conducting reviews with workers, emphasis must be placed on planning and development for the future, as opposed to just grading or evaluating past performance.

Many administrators are saddled with state-mandated systems that emphasize teacher appraisal and ranking, often to the detriment of coaching and development. Such practices often prove to be barriers to staff members feeling good about themselves and their work. Instead of solid plans for training and development (points 6 and 13), traditional appraisal practices generate fear (point 8). Later, when the appraisals are employed to drive recognition and reward systems, teamwork suffers (point 9).

Leaders in the short term can shift their staff reviews from a mode of appraising past performance to one of coaching and planning for future development. Even with current systems designed for ranking, during review discussions leaders can seek and take action on answers to the following questions.[18]

- Do I know what this person must do in order to succeed in this job?
  - Who are the users (customers) of the results of this job?
  - What do the customers need in order to best use the results of this job?
  - Who supplies the inputs to this job? Are those inputs suitable for use?
- Have I discussed the above with this employee so that there is a clear understanding of what he or she needs to do?
- Have I provided this employee the necessary resources to do this job well? (tools, training, time, equipment, information, good materials, and so on)
- What does this person see as the major barriers to doing this job well? What have I done to remove those barriers?
- Have I asked what this employee needs from me to do this job well?
- Do I know this person's needs as an individual?
- Am I acting as a coach and a teacher in this review, as opposed to simply grading past performance?
- Have I provided opportunities for in-depth discussion with this person about this job and its objectives?

With minor editing, these questions could be restated as questions to ponder when coaching students (and their parents). Action based on the answers to these questions will provide much greater development of the organization's human resources than any grading or appraisal system ever could.

In closing, consider the following entry in a student's learning log at the high school in Ware Shoals, South Carolina: "The work required is our best, so when we give it, we pass. I truly like that.

Because sometimes our best is not always so good. We are able to concentrate on learning and teamwork without thinking of grades and the competition that goes along with them."

Point 13: Institute a Vigorous Program of Education and Self-Improvement for Everyone in the System; Don't Forget the Needs of Parents

In a business context, Deming elaborated on the need for continuing education and self-improvement as follows:

> Students in schools of business in America are taught that there is a profession of management; that they are ready to step into top jobs. This is a cruel hoax. Most students have had no experience in production or in sales. To work on the factory floor with pay equal to half what he hoped to get upon receipt of the MBA, just to get the experience, is a horrible thought to an MBA, not the American way of life. As a consequence, he struggles on, unaware of his limitations, or unable to face the need to fill in the gaps. The results are obvious.[19]

How many graduates of the teachers' college find themselves in the same position as the employee Deming described? Too often, they emerge from the school of education ill-prepared to be successful in the classroom. In the absence of a vigorous program for staff development and continuing education, teaching staff will struggle on, "unaware of [their] limitations, or unable to face the need to fill in the gaps."

Point 13 addresses this critical issue in the healthy environment for work and learning. Attention to this point leads to the provision of opportunities and encouragement for people throughout the local school system to keep learning and growing.

Thus, point 13 is different from point 6. Point 6 referred to training in work (and learning) methods that one should later observe in the person's behavior; whereas point 13 deals with continuing education and gaining new knowledge. As it relates to the needs of parents, district leaders may pursue several paths, all interrelated.

First, ongoing efforts to educate the local community about the problems of education lead to a broader understanding of the scope of those problems, as well as a greater appreciation for the complexity of education. Second, many districts offer evening courses in adult literacy, parenting skills, and other topics. Finally, parents involved in multidisciplined project teams for improving processes (point 5) and site-based management teams are provided not only training in the statistical methods (point 6), but also greater knowledge of the education system and child development in general.

Point 14: Plan and Take Action to Accomplish the Transformation

To effectively address this last of the obligations, districts should start by providing education for all in positions of leadership. The initial education should include exposure to the system of profound knowledge, with great emphasis on helping those leaders to view the school system as a system. Chapter 12 provides more specific guidelines for getting started on the transformation.

Algozzine and Audette paraphrased their understanding of Deming's steps for planning and carrying out the transformation as follows:[20]

1. The school board and superintendent must examine all of the first 13 points, agree on the direction to take, and agree to implement the new philosophy.

2. The school board and superintendent must feel dissatisfaction with past procedures and muster the courage to change them. They must experience a burning desire to transform their management strategies. (This argues for much more importance being attributed to the election of school board members. There is a need for much more than one-issue candidates.)

3. The school board and superintendent must explain to a critical mass of school personnel, students, parents, and community participants through presentations, inservice training, and other means, why change is necessary, and that the change will eventually involve everyone. There must be enough people in the district and in each school who know the *what* and the *how* of the transformation.

4. Every job and role in the district is part of a process that can be improved. Everyone belongs to a team and has a part in dealing with one or more of the issues at hand (for example, constancy of purpose or working to improve a specific process).

Summary

The 14 obligations of the school board and administration serve as a manifestation, or a logical extension, of the system of profound knowledge applied to schools and districts. They also provide a model of the healthy environment for work and learning that will be in place after a process of transformation that's guided by profound knowledge.

The obligations cannot be viewed as a cafeteria plan. That is, they are intricately interwoven and interdependent. That complex relationship between and among the 14 points was obvious in the above elaboration on each point of the model. One finds it impossible to talk about one of the points without at the same time making reference to several others.

Finally, the fourteenth obligation—planning and taking action to accomplish the transformation—must begin with education for all in positions of leadership. The education should provide a sound introduction and initial understanding of the system of profound knowledge. That system, described in earlier chapters, then guides leadership decisions and action to accomplish the transformation.

Before examining a process for getting started on the transformation, the next chapter will describe the procedure and lessons of the bead experiment. That experiment provides an excellent review of the four components of the system of profound knowledge, as well as a number of the 14 points.

Notes

1. Deming, *Out of the Crisis,* 23–25.

2. From "Free and Appropriate Education for All Students: Total Quality and the Transformation of Public Education" by R. Audette and R. Algozzine, Nov. 1992, *Remedial and Special Education,* Vol. 13, No. 6, pp. 8–18. Copyright (1992) by PRO-ED, Inc. Reprinted by permission.

3. L. Martin et al., U.S. Department of Labor, *What Work Requires of Schools: A SCANS Report for America 2000,* Secretary's Commission on Achieving Necessary Skills (SCANS) (Washington, D.C.: GPO, 1991); vii.

4. Audette and Algozzine, "Free and Appropriate Education."

5. W. Borgers and T. Thompson, *Implementing Continuous Improvement Management in the Schools* (New York: Scholastic, 1994), 215.

6. Deming, *Out of the Crisis,* 33.

7. H. Gitlow and S. Gitlow, *The Deming Guide to Quality and Competitive Position* (Englewood Cliffs, N.J.: Prentice-Hall, 1987), 77.

8. Deming, *Out of the Crisis,* 51.

9. Scherkenbach, *The Deming Route,* 95.

10. *Ibid.,* 91.

11. Senge, *The Fifth Discipline,* 340.

12. Audette and Algozzine, "Free and Appropriate Education."

13. Borgers and Thompson, *Implementing Management,* 218.

14. Audette and Algozzine, "Free and Appropriate Education."

15. P. Robertson, *The Turning Tide: The Fall of Liberalism and the Rise of Common Sense* (Dallas: Word Publishing, 1993), 213, 231.

16. Audette and Algozzine, "Free and Appropriate Education."

17. P. Dresser in *Basic College Quarterly* (winter 1957): 6.

18. Derived from "Deming's Point Seven: Adopt and Institute Leadership," *Commentaries on Deming's Fourteen Points*, (Piqua, Ohio: Ohio Quality and Productivity Forum, 1989), 4–5.

19. Deming, *Out of the Crisis*, 130.

20. Audette and Algozzine, "Free and Appropriate Education."

Chapter Eleven

The Bead Experiment

To demonstrate the character of systems and variation, in his seminars Deming used to conduct an experiment using beads. Referred to as the bead experiment or the red bead experiment, this demonstration used the following materials.

- Two plastic containers
- Four thousand small beads (3200 white beads and 800 red beads)
- A paddle with 50 depressions used to scoop beads out of the container (50 beads at a time)

To conduct the experiment, Deming would have six volunteers from the audience pour the beads from one container into the other, then insert the paddle to withdraw 50 beads. They were urged not to draw out any red beads because red beads were considered to be defective. Inspectors would count and record the number of red beads in the paddle after each drawing. The data (number of red beads) would be recorded for each volunteer over a simulated four-day period.

This procedure would yield 24 subgroups of data (number of red beads "produced" by the six people over the four "days"). Deming would then use these data to commend and reward the people who produced the lowest number of red beads and to ridicule those who produced the highest number of defective beads.

Gabor explained the purpose of the bead experiment as follows:

> [With the] red bead experiment, Deming illustrates a "typical" production scenario to show two things: first, that the performance of individual workers can be no better than the system (as defined by management) allows; second, that the performance of any system is by nature variable, and therefore differences between the performance of two different workers are a matter of chance and thus frequently utterly meaningless.[1]

In my own seminars, I also conduct a bead experiment. My materials and procedure differ from those used by Deming, but the lessons of the experiment remain the same. The balance of this chapter will describe the procedure and lessons to be learned from the bead experiment.

The Procedure

Rather than using loose beads, two containers, and a paddle, my process has just one machine: the bead box. Illustrated in Figure 11.1, the bead box measures 19 centimeters long, 3.5 centimeters high, and 10 centimeters deep. Inside the box are 1000 white, yellow, purple, red, green, and blue beads. Out of the total of 1000 beads, 100 are blue. The top and bottom of the box are covered with plexiglass, to keep the beads in the box.

On the end of the bead box is a lever, which, when pressed, allows beads to fall down into a plastic sheet of 100 holes at the bottom of the box. Releasing the lever traps those 100 beads. By turning the bead box over and pressing the lever again, the holes at the bottom are cleared.

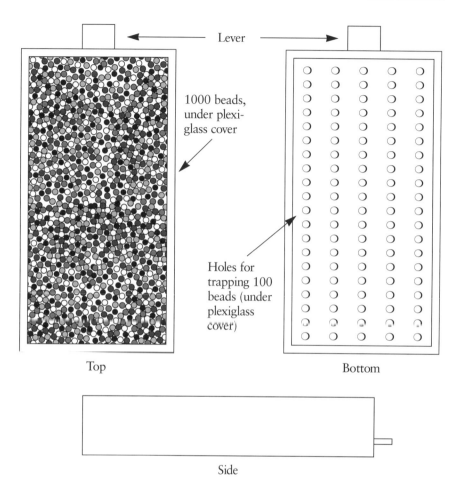

Figure 11.1. Illustration of the bead box.

To conduct the experiment, four volunteers are selected from the seminar participants. Before proceeding, the four volunteers are asked if they're interested in quality. If they respond yes, they are designated "willing workers" and allowed to proceed. If a volunteer asks what is meant by quality, he or she is dismissed and another volunteer is selected. (Stupid questions and bad attitudes are not allowed among willing workers.)

Next, the four volunteers are asked to sign a pledge showing their commitment to quality and customer satisfaction. The pledge reads

> I hereby pledge to be a QUALITY WORKER, to produce only the HIGHEST QUALITY work, and to do my utmost to achieve ZERO DEFECTS.
>
> Signed,
>
> _____
>
> _____
>
> _____
>
> Beads, Inc.

If any worker hesitates to sign the pledge, he or she is dismissed. Another volunteer is selected—one willing to commit to quality without hesitation. Additionally, since there are only three spaces for signatures, the fourth volunteer usually signs somewhere else on the form. When they do so, such volunteers are commended for their initiative.

A fifth volunteer is selected to play the role of the local manager. This volunteer need not be interested in quality nor sign the pledge. Since the fifth volunteer plays the role of manager, all that's necessary is that he or she knows how to count.

The four willing workers are provided training in how to operate the bead box, according to the following standard operating procedure (SOP). The SOP reads:

1. Do not shake the box.

2. Hold the box at waist level with the top facing up and the bottom facing down.

3. Push in the lever and hold it in throughout step 4.

4. Slightly tilt the box from side to side four times. (A gentle tilt is called a *doink*. The workers are cautioned not to tilt the box too far, because that would be a *schwaunk*. They are to doink the box, not schwaunk it.)

5. Release the lever, in doing so trapping 100 beads in the holes at the bottom of the box.

6. Pass the bead box to the manager.

The workers are urged not to produce any blue beads. Blue beads are defective. It's all right to end up with white, yellow, green, purple, or red beads—but no blue beads.

The manager's job is to count the number of blue beads in the holes, record that number, and report it to top management. (The rest of the seminar audience plays the role of the school board and senior administrators.) Because top management support is so critical for good quality outcomes, throughout the experiment they chant, "Be a quality worker! Be a quality worker!"

The manager counts the number of blue beads produced by each worker, then records those results each day over a simulated five-day period. The bead box is then passed to the next worker, who clears the holes and repeats the procedure. Day by day, and run after run, the manager builds the record for the week's work. Figure 11.2 shows the final results of this experiment in a recent seminar.

Supervisory Practices from the Age of Mythology

Upon viewing the workers' results on Monday, top management was dismayed. None of the four workers achieved the goal (zero

Operators	Number of defective (blue) beads					
	Mon	Tue	Wed	Thu	Fri	Totals
1. Jacob	9	7	16	6	7	45
2. Molly	19	15	19	10	15	78
3. Justin	13	11	16	12	17	69
4. Maryanna	21	11	21	16	18	87
					Total	279

Figure 11.2. Final record of recent bead experiment.

defects). It was noted, however, that Jacob did considerably better work than his coworkers, producing less than half as many defective beads as either Molly or Maryanna. Therefore, it was announced that management was considering the introduction of a merit pay system. After all, it wouldn't be fair to reward Maryanna and Molly the same as Jacob, who had produced less than half as many defective beads as they had. A merit pay system would empower Jacob's supervisor to reward him for his superior work.

On Tuesday, all four workers improved their performance. Obviously, the possibility of earning large merit increases motivated them, and they had also learned from Monday's experience. Supervisors could look forward to continuing improvement.

Wednesday's results were a great disappointment. All four workers produced more defective beads than they had the previous day. Even Jacob more than doubled his number of defectives in comparison to Tuesday. Supervisors held a meeting and listed all their activities to date.

- They had worked on the workers' attitudes, making sure they were interested in quality.

- They had provided the workers good training in how to operate the bead box.

- They had given the workers a clear goal (zero defects).

- They had provided the workers with immediate feedback each day regarding their performance.

The supervisors noted, however, that they had failed to give the workers an incentive! Therefore, at the beginning of the workers' shift on Thursday, it was announced that whoever produced the lowest number of defective beads that week would receive a free trip to Disney World for that worker and a guest. Having provided an incentive, the supervisors were confident that their workers would get better. After all, workers will not apply themselves to their tasks without some external motivation to do so. Besides, competition among the workers for the free trip would drive everyone to get better.

The supervisors' faith in the power of incentives was rewarded on Thursday. All four workers produced fewer defectives than the day before. Jacob set a record for the week for fewest number of blue beads, and even Molly cut her number of blue beads by almost half.

Friday's results produced still more disappointment, as everyone's level of performance dropped. Jacob's increase in number of defective beads produced on Friday was very small, however, and his low number of blue beads for the week won the trip to Disney World.

A closer look at the week's totals led the supervisors to the following conclusions.

- Jacob produced only 45 defective beads.

- Maryanna produced 87 blue beads—more than 93 percent more defectives than Jacob.

- All four workers produced a total of 279 defective beads, for an average of 69.75 blue beads per worker.

- Finally, it was noted that half of the workers (Jacob and Justin) produced below the average number of defective beads, and half of the workers (Molly and Maryanna) produced above the average number of defective beads.

If the bead results were measures of academic achievement, one would note that Jacob and Justin produced between them an average of only 57 defectives, whereas Molly and Maryanna averaged more than 82 defectives. Clearly, there exists a gender bias in our process that makes it more difficult for girls to achieve than boys. The district should be directed to review all of its programs for sources of gender bias, then submit to the state department of education a detailed strategy for eliminating the obvious gender bias.

Rewarding Performance

Many people in management find it totally unacceptable when half of their workers are below average. Therefore, they adopt merit pay, grading, recognition, and other practices to reward above-average performers and to withhold rewards from workers who demonstrate below-average performance.

In the case of our bead business, management established a 5 percent merit budget. Based on their performance, the four workers were given the following pay increases.

- Jacob performed well above average, so the supervisors voted him a 9 percent pay increase.

- Justin performed slightly better than average, so he got a 6 percent raise.

- Molly did worse than average, so she received a 4 percent pay increase.

- Maryanna, who produced over 93 percent more defective beads than Jacob, was given only a 1 percent raise. (Her supervisor would have given her no raise at all, but he didn't want to have to explain it to Personnel!)

Note how merit pay and similar practices empower supervisors to reward above-average performers and withhold reward from below-average performers. If Molly and Maryanna want bigger raises, they'll work to perform better than average. As long as they continue to perform below average levels, however, they will continue to receive below-average rewards.

This practice is fair and consistent with everything we ever learned and believed as good supervisors and good Americans. After all, this country was built by above-average people, dragging below-average people along on their coattails. During my seminars, I always insist that rewarding our four workers the way we did was fair.

To justify our reward decisions, one need only refer to the run chart in Figure 11.3. The arrows pointing to the highest number of defective beads indicate Maryanna's performance. The arrows pointing to the lowest numbers of blue beads indicate Jacob's results.

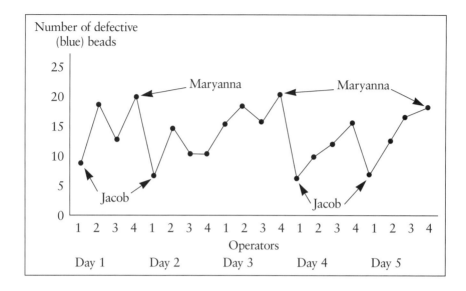

Figure 11.3. Run chart of the bead experiment results.

Some of my seminar participants will occasionally claim that it's not fair to give Jacob a 9 percent raise, Justin 6 percent, Molly 4 percent, and Maryanna 1 percent. They claim that the bead experiment is a lottery and that half the workers will always come out above average, while the other half will always be below average. Therefore, they claim it's not fair to differentiate the rewards given to the workers based on whether workers are above or below average.

To counter such ridiculous claims, I suggest that the results of our experiment are no longer beads, but test results (number of incorrect responses). Then, I review with those participants what we do in America's classrooms. We label Jacob gifted and talented, we give Justin a B, we give Molly a C, and we reserve for Maryanna a seat on the short bus with the seat belts.

The traditional grading system does to students exactly what I did to the bead workers. Above-average students get As and Bs. Below-average students get Ds and Fs. We would never do to children that which was not fair. Therefore, because they're based on the results achieved by workers and students, merit pay and grading systems are not only fair, but also consistent with everything we ever learned and believed as good supervisors, good teachers, and good Americans.

The Missing Ingredients

After discussing the above issues with my seminar audiences, I always ask them the following question: What was missing from my bead business? One thing that was missing was a systems perspective!

Throughout the bead experiment, we reacted to the workers' daily outcomes as discrete events. On Monday, Jacob produced less than half as many defective beads as Maryanna or Molly. Based on this discrete event, we started considering merit pay. Then, on Tuesday, all four workers' performance got better. Based on this discrete event, we concluded that the mention of merit pay had an effect. After viewing Wednesday's (discrete) results, we announced the contest for the free trip to Disney World. When all four workers' performance improved on Thursday, we concluded that the incentive was working.

In other words, throughout the week we reacted to all daily results as discrete events, as opposed to stepping back and trying to understand all of the outcomes—high and low, good and bad—as the output of some system. In the absence of a systems perspective, however, we have no choice but to assign all of the outcomes to the workers alone; then rank, grade, reward, and punish accordingly.

Frederick Taylor's factory model included the idea of piecework incentive pay for production workers. Taylor lacked a systems perspective; therefore, he had no choice but to assign all the outputs from a machine to the machine operator alone—then rank, grade, reward, and punish accordingly with piecework incentive pay.

Nobody knows who did it; nobody knows exactly when it occurred. But whoever proposed the traditional grading system and whenever that system was adopted in America's schools, we obviously lacked a systems perspective. In the absence of a systems perspective, we have no choice but to assign test scores to the students alone—then rank, grade, sort, group, track, label, reward, and punish accordingly!

Also missing from my bead business was any understanding of the theory of variation. That theory would teach me that half of my workers will and must be above average, and half my workers will and must be below average. I distributed rewards (and punishments) because my workers' performance was different, but I did not determine if they were significantly different.

Absent knowledge of the theory of variation, I ended up punishing half my workers for doing the best they could do; punishing them when perhaps they could do no better. Because the performance of a system is by its very nature variable, all of my workers were constrained by the system itself.

What was missing from my bead business? The missing ingredients were the systems perspective and sound theory of variation. In the absence of a systems perspective and some knowledge of variation, we have no choice but to continue to apply merit pay, grades, and other destructive practices from the age of mythology.

Applying the Systems Perspective and Knowledge of Variation

To add the missing ingredients to our bead business, one need only convert the run chart in Figure 11.3 to a control chart. Control charts help supervisors to understand variation; to determine whether measured outcomes are different or if they're significantly different. Deming noted, "The Shewhart control charts do a good job in a wide range of conditions. No one has yet wrought improvement."[2]

The outcomes of our bead production process were measured using attributes data. Such data can fall into only one of two categories: good or bad; on time or late; on or off; above or below standard; and so on. Since every run of the bead experiment had the same area of opportunity for defectives (we produced 100 beads at a time), the type of control chart we should use to analyze our process is the *np* chart. The formulae for the *np* chart are as follows:

Central line $=$ CL $= n\bar{p}$, where $n =$ sample size

$$\text{and } \bar{p} = \frac{\text{total number of defectives}}{\text{total number of samples}}$$

$$\left. \begin{array}{l} \text{Upper control limit } = \text{ UCL} \\ \text{Lower control limit } = \text{ LCL} \end{array} \right\} = n\bar{p} + \text{ and } - 3\sqrt{n\bar{p}(1 - \bar{p})}$$

In our bead experiment, the sample size (*n*) was 100, since every run produced 100 beads. Throughout the simulated five days of work, the four workers produced a total of 2000 beads (100 beads per run times 20 runs). Over the five-day period, our workers produced a total of 279 defective (blue) beads. Plugging these values into the above formulae yield the following statistics:

$$\text{CL} = n\bar{p} \qquad\qquad n = 100$$

$$= 100(.1395) \quad \bar{p} = \frac{279 \text{ defective beads}}{2000 \text{ beads produced}} = .1395$$

$$\text{CL} = 14.0 \text{ (rounded to nearest tenth)}$$

$$\left. \begin{array}{l} \text{UCL} \\ \text{LCL} \end{array} \right\} = n\bar{p} + \text{ and } - 3\sqrt{n\bar{p}(1 - \bar{p})}$$

$$= 14.0 + \text{ and } - 3\sqrt{14(1 - .14)}$$

$$= 14.0 + \text{ and } - 3\sqrt{12.04}$$

$$= 14.0 + \text{ and } - 10.4$$

$$\text{UCL} = 24.4$$

$$\text{LCL} = 3.6$$

Imposing these statistics on the run chart yields the control chart in Figure 11.4. Upon review of the pattern of the data in

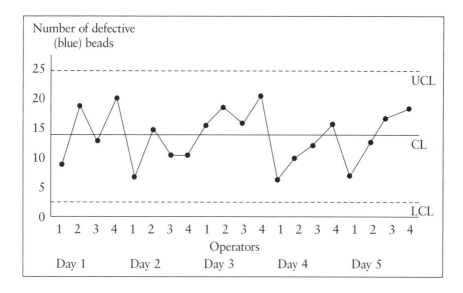

Figure 11.4 *np* chart of bead experiment results.

comparison to the CL and control limits, one guided by some knowledge of the theory of variation would conclude

1. The process is stable, or in statistical control.

2. The variation is the result of common causes only from within the process.

3. There is no evidence of special cause variation from outside the process.

4. The measured outputs, though different, are not significantly different.

5. If one is not happy with the outputs, one must change the process. If we do not change the process that's producing these defectives, we will forever experience the defective outcomes, falling at random somewhere between 3.6 and 24.4, with an average of 14.0.

As it relates to traditional practices of grading and ranking, the fourth conclusion above is perhaps the most difficult to swallow.

After all, Maryanna produced over 93 percent more defectives than Jacob; but the theory of variation indicates that this difference is not significant! The systems perspective would add that Jacob alone did not produce the low number of defectives, nor did Maryanna alone produce the high number of blue beads.

Rather, the same system—of which Jacob, Molly, Justin, and Maryanna were only a part—produced all of the defective beads, and those workers could perform no better than the system allowed. Therefore, differences in the performance of the workers were the result of a lottery, and comparisons between them would be meaningless.[3]

Lessons of the Bead Experiment

1. As noted, the process was stable, in statistical control.

2. All of the variation—as measured by the number of blue beads produced by the workers—was the result of common causes only, from within the process. Sources of the common cause variation included not only the workers, but also the materials, methods, machine (bead box), and measurement system.

3. Therefore, we assigned to the workers alone the outcomes that, in fact, were produced by the system. About this lesson of the bead experiment, Deming wrote:

> All the variation—differences between willing work-
> ers in the production of [defective] beads, and the
> variation day to day of any willing worker—came
> entirely from the process itself. There was no evi-
> dence that any one worker was better than the other.[4]

4. The workers' outcomes, though different, were not signifi-cantly different. They occurred at random and as the result of chance.

5. Because the workers' outcomes were not significantly dif-ferent, we were wrong to differentiate their rewards. All should

have received the same raise. (Of course, if any worker had produced a significantly high or low number of blue beads, he or she should be rewarded differently.)

6. If the chart in Figure 11.4 was of midterm test scores among 20 students, the capability of the process is such that it would produce at random raw scores between 76 and 96. Those test scores, though different, would not be significantly different. Since they'd be produced by the teaching and learning process, and not the students alone, issuing different grades for those scores would be no different from the way we (arbitrarily) rewarded and punished the workers in the bead experiment!

7. Recall that out of the total of 1000 beads, 100 of them were blue. Therefore, one might expect that over time the process will produce an average of 10 defective beads for every 100 produced. Since 10 percent of all the beads are blue, many would conclude that, on the average, 10 percent of the beads will come out blue (10 out of 100). Such thinking guides the analysis of norm-referenced standardized test results in many districts.

One lesson of the bead experiment is that such thinking is flawed. Even in the closed-loop system of our bead box, there are common causes of variation at work.

- Different-sized holes, into which the beads are trapped
- Variation in the size, weight, and density of the 1000 beads
- Different size, weight, and density of the blue beads
- Effects of static electricity on the plastic beads from the plexiglass cover, shaking of the box by workers, humidity in the room, and carpeting

Therefore, we have no right to expect an average of 10 blue beads! We have a right to expect—in the absence of special causes or changing the process—outcomes that fall at random between 3.6 and 24.4 blue beads, with an average of 14.0.

8. If we're not happy with these outcomes, management must fulfill its responsibility to change and improve the process. The

workers' performance will be no better than the system allows it to be, and management defines the system.

9. Management's goal (zero defects) was beyond the capability of the system it had provided for the workers. Because the lower control limit of random, controlled, common cause variation fell at 3.6, neither the process nor the workers were capable of achieving the goal of zero defects.

10. The best any one worker could perform on any given day would not be 3.6 defective beads, even though that was the lower control limit. Systems are by their very nature variable; there will always be variation. Therefore, the best any one of our workers can do on any given day will be somewhere between 3.6 and 24.4, with an average of 14.0. That's the best they can do—they can do no better!

Summary

In American government, business, and education, why do we persist in punishing people like Maryanna when they do the best they can do; when they're constrained by the system? Why do we persist in issuing low raises to workers? Why do we continue to issue low grades to students when it's the system that's failing?

If students in the school of education do not have an opportunity to ponder the lessons of the bead experiment—early and often in their undergraduate and graduate studies—they emerge with the power to destroy children. Today, teachers are wielding that power without mercy throughout America's school districts. Without appreciation for a system and absent some understanding of the theory of variation, educators will continue to wield that power without mercy, because they wield it without knowledge.

We do not need education reform. We do not need to continue to find ways to improve current systems of grading and ranking children. America's school districts need not reform nor restructuring, but transformation.

As an early step in the transformation process, education must be provided for leaders at all levels of the district, including classroom leaders (teachers). The goal of the education should be to help them understand the system of profound knowledge, including appreciation for a system and some knowledge of the theory of variation—the key lessons of the bead experiment. In our next chapter, we'll examine a process for beginning the transformation.

Notes

1. Gabor, *The Man Who Discovered Quality*, 59.

2. Deming, *The New Economics*, 180.

3. Gabor, *The Man Who Discovered Quality*.

4. Deming, *The New Economics*, 172.

Chapter Twelve

Getting Started on the Transformation

In his text, *Out of the Crisis,* Deming provided the following suggestions (among others) for getting started on the transformation.[1]

- Management in authority will struggle over every one of the [14 points] . . . . They will agree on their meaning and on the direction to take. They will agree to carry out the new philosophy.

- Management in authority will take pride in their adoption of the new philosophy and in their new responsibilities. They will have courage to break with tradition, even to the point of exile among their peers.

- Management in authority will explain by seminars and other means to a critical mass of people why change is necessary, and that the change will involve everybody.

- Start as soon as possible to construct with deliberate speed an organization to guide continual improvement of quality . . . .

- Everyone can take part in a team. The aim of a team is to improve the input and the output of any stage [of a process]. A team may well be composed of people from different areas . . . .

These recommendations have been factored into the flow diagram in Figure 12.1. It lists a sequence of events for initiating the transformation process at a school or district level. Next to the events are listed types of assistance districts may seek from consultants, professional organizations, business partners, and other external resources.

Because every district is unique, these events and their sequence may vary. They are offered as general planning guidelines. The balance of this chapter will provide a few more details and expansion on the general guidelines for getting started on the transformation process.

Event 1: Provide Leadership with an Introduction to the Transformation Process

This first event may involve a general orientation session or executive overview for school and district leaders. The target audience for this event includes senior administrators, board members, and teacher union leaders, as well as representatives from parent groups, staff, teachers, and the community. It may take the form of a one-day workshop that covers the key elements of the transformation process, as well as a general description of how a school or district may proceed from that point.

If a school or district does not have staff development funds available to sponsor such a workshop, other approaches can be taken. For example, members of a district's administrative council and/or board could be provided a copy of this or another relevant text. Members may commit to read two or three chapters a week and make notes in response to the following questions.

- What did I learn?

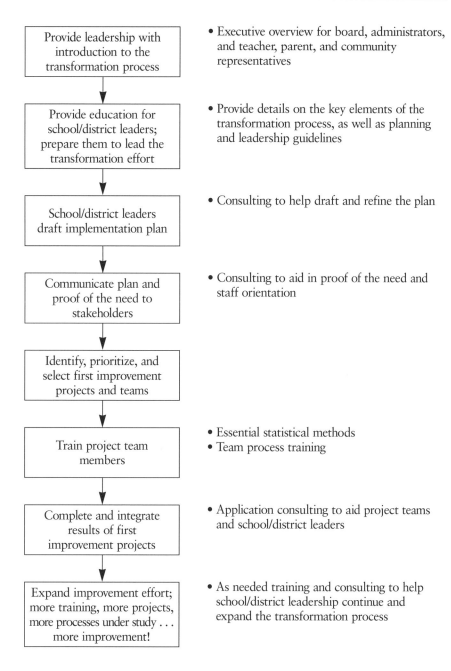

Source: J. F. Leonard, *Introduction to a Deming Road Map for Transforming America's Schools*, workshop materials (1995). Used with permission.

Figure 12.1. Process for getting started on the transformation.

- How does it fit current plans and programs?

- What questions do I have?

At the end of each board or council meeting, members may discuss their answers to these questions. Week after week, the group can build its own introduction to Deming's concepts, the transformation model, and how they appear to fit the local situation.

No matter what approach is taken (group workshop or self-study), the objective of this first event in the process is not to train people; nor is it to change their leadership behavior. Rather, the goal is to put school and district leaders in a position to make a decision: Do we want to move forward and learn more about this model or not?

Event 2: Provide Education for School and District Leaders

If the decision on the part of school and district leaders is to move forward, the next event in the process is to provide them with more formal education. In doing so, leaders will prepare themselves to lead the transformation effort at a local level. Those receiving such training should include board representatives, administrators from both central office and building levels, site-based decision-making team members, as well as teacher union and parent representatives. If possible, representatives of other components of the local community should also be included, such as local business partners, administrators or professors from higher education (two- or four-year institutions), and local government officials.

The education provided at this stage of the process should include, at a minimum, details on each of the key elements of the transformation process. The information described in the first 11 chapters of this book provides a good summary of the scope and sequence of the education needed for school and district leaders. Beyond that, some districts may desire greater detail on the essential statistical methods, such as that provided in appendices A and B.

Of course, frequent opportunities should be provided during the education program for trainees to apply the concepts to their own local concerns and issues. This can be accomplished via

- Application of the basic tools (brainstorming, cause-and-effect analysis, and so on) to specific concerns such as student motivation, parent involvement, communications, or barriers between programs or groups

- Use of school or district data (for example, test scores, disciplinary referrals, survey results) in any intermediate statistical methods taught in the training program

Finally, some guidelines—including an opportunity to apply them—should be provided for helping school and district leaders draft their plan for proceeding with the overall implementation effort. Such guidelines should address the establishment of specific and feasible action steps for completing the next five events in the process.

Event 3: Draft Implementation Plan

Recall Deming's suggestion to "construct with deliberate speed an organization to guide continual improvement."[2] In many districts, this organization will take the form of steering committees at both district and site levels. Figure 12.2 shows a typical infrastructure for guiding the transformation effort.

At the central office level, a district council will be formed with the charter to plan and provide direction for the implementation of the new philosophy throughout the district. Members will typically include the superintendent, one or two central office administrators, a board member, representatives from site steering committees, and a local business partner. Beyond its planning and leadership responsibilities, the district council will form and charter project teams to tackle issues that cut across school and program lines. In Deming's view, the aim of such teams is to improve processes. Among the projects guided by this group will be teams working on staff development, budgeting, broad

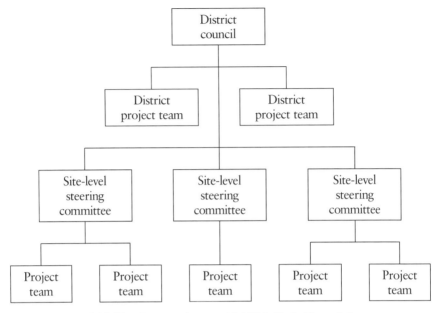

Source: J. F. Leonard, *The Team Process* seminar materials (1995). Used with permission.

Figure 12.2. Organization for guiding continual improvement.

community relations and business partnerships, or other dis-trictwide issues. Finally, district councils must ensure that learning and improvements accomplished by individual sites are shared with other schools and groups throughout the district.

At a school level, steering committees will be formed with the charter to plan and direct the transformation process within that site. These committees will form teams to tackle intraschool issues derived from local concerns and priorities. For example, one school may be more concerned right now about student discipline than others. Therefore, that steering committee will form a team to deal with that issue. Another school may be more concerned about school-to-home communication or about reading achievement levels than others. Therefore, that steering committee will form teams to study causes of those problems and to recommend process changes to improve the situation. Since these project teams deal with systems issues—either at a site or district level—steering committees will ensure that multidisciplined groups are formed with representation from teachers, specialists, parents, and other groups that are involved in or affected by the process under study.

Of course, before forming any teams and before taking on any specific projects, district and school leaders must draft their overall implementation plan. In the absence of a solid plan, future steps could cause confusion and frustration among stakeholders. That's because such action may come across as isolated events, as opposed to logical steps in a well-thought-out plan for accomplishing the transformation.

Just as there is no one right way to accomplish the transformation, so also there is no one right format for the implementation plan. Many schools and districts have used a strategic planning process, and the same approach may be applicable for building initial implementation plans.

Most organizations will see little progress in implementing their plans unless the following are clearly delineated in the plan.

1. Specific, feasible, clearly defined action steps

2. Clearly defined responsibilities (champions) for each action step

3. Checkpoints (or target dates) for completing or reviewing progress of each agreed-upon action step

The general goals or areas of emphasis provided by many strategic plans are not sufficient in this third event for getting started on the transformation. Rather, what is required is a sound plan that provides specific answers to the question, *"Who* is going to do *what* and *when?"*

At both a district and site level, initial implementation plans should address such topics as customer and community relations, training, projects and teams, supplier relations, communication, and measurement. Examples of specific action steps for the implementation plan are listed under just two of these general categories: training and projects and teams.

Plan topic: Training

Action steps	*Champion*	*Target date*
Complete initial training for key leaders		
Select training coordinator		
Select potential in-house resources (future trainers, facilitators, in-house statisticians)		

Provide statistical methods training for
- Initial project teams
- Other staff members, others

Provide team process training for
- Initial project teams
- Other staff members, others

Draft schoolwide training plan

Train in-house resources in
- Statistical methods
- Team process
- Advanced tools

Implement staff training in
- Job skills
- Work methods
- Appropriate statistical methods

Plan topic: Projects and teams

Action steps	*Champion*	*Target date*
List potential projects		
Select and define initial project(s)		
Select team members and provide training		

Action steps   *Champion*   *Target date*

Draft procedure for selecting,
defining, and managing future
project teams

Complete and integrate results
of first project(s)

Implement process for reviewing
and nurturing future project teams

Establish system to communicate
teams' progress and results

Initiate more projects

Event 4: Communicate the Plan and Proof of the Need to All Stakeholders

This event is designed to address Deming's advice that leaders explain to people why the transformation is necessary in the first place. Deming's contemporary and fellow consultant, Joseph M. Juran, taught a sequence for breakthrough, which was a project-by-project approach to improving quality. Juran defined *breakthrough* as the organized creation of beneficial change.[3]

As an early step in Juran's sequence, middle managers and staff members may have to prove the need to higher levels of management to charter an improvement project. Such proof of the need may be provided by quality cost figures, awareness of new forces that have an impact on quality, legislative issues, and other sources.[4]

In this fourth event of our process for getting started on the transformation, we use the same phrase—proof of the need—but in a much broader context. Here we are talking about a very carefully designed, highly controlled communication and orientation effort for staff members and stakeholders throughout the district. The goal of the orientation is to prove the need to incur the pain of transformation! In essence, school and district leadership tries to very clearly communicate the following:

- The need to change the system in order not just to survive, but to thrive as a viable educational community

- School and district leadership's resolve and commitment to accomplish the required transformation

The primary vehicle for providing meaningful proof of the need is a well-planned series of information meetings. Guidelines for planning such meetings include

- Meeting led by board chair, superintendent, or other senior administrator

- Sharing examples of some of the dramatic changes underway in schools and districts where quality and improvement have become the primary focus

- Description of major opportunities for improvement that may exist in the school or district (for example, local employer demands, community concerns, dropout rate, assessment data, disciplinary incidents)

- Brief overview of the Deming philosophy

- Review of school or district mission statement and what it means

- Review of what the board, administration, and others have done to date (for example, time spent in training, steering committee meetings, planning, surveys)

- Overview of school and district leaders' plan for future activity

Steering committee members may look forward to two positive outcomes of the proof of the need effort. First, they begin to educate the staff and local community about the problems of education. Second, they are able to gauge staff, parent, and community openness to the transformation, based on feedback after the orientation and information meetings.

In the wake of their proof of the need meetings, school and district leaders should keep their eyes open for what I sometimes refer to as the crazy people. These are staff members, administrators, and parents who approach leaders after the orientation sessions and say, "I'd like to learn more about it!" Such indications of interest help steering committees to identify potential team members for initial improvement projects.

Event 5: Identify, Prioritize, and Select the First Improvement Projects and Teams

In the infrastructure illustrated in Figure 12.2, the multidisciplined project team serves as the vehicle for improving teaching, learning, and administrative processes throughout the district. Juran observed that as one moves away from a small, self-contained department, mobilizing for improvement becomes more complex.[5] Therefore, teams and knowledge from several different groups or perspectives are needed to adequately address systems problems and opportunities for systemic improvement.

The fifth event in the process for getting started on the transformation involves selecting just the first one or two—never more than three—projects for multidisciplined teams. After all, leaders must keep the airplane flying while transforming it to a starship. Therefore, it is recommended that districts start on a small scale, learn from the first few project applications, then expand the effort.

Deming wrote about the Shewhart cycle for learning and improvement. (That model was described earlier in this text under its more common name, the Deming cycle). In the second stage of the cycle, teams carry out a change or test planned in the first stage, *preferably on a small scale*[6] (emphasis added). Next, teams summarize what was learned, then take appropriate action to adopt the change, hold gains, or to run through the cycle again. (For more details on the Deming cycle, see pages 165–166 in chapter 8.)

Candidates for initial improvement projects will be found in survey and test data, strategic plans, staff suggestions, annual reports, and other sources. Another excellent source for first projects may be to review the status of current teams and committees. (Maybe the last thing the district needs is another team!) A current team or project may be pulled under the umbrella of the steering committee and guided through the basic procedure for improving a system that was outlined in chapter 8.

Based on what they learned from their first round of projects in Knoxville, Iowa, district leaders drafted their process for forming and managing future teams. Figure 5.1 in chapter 5 shows the flowchart of that process. Some school and district leaders may find the Knoxville design to be helpful when forming their first project teams in this fifth event of the process for getting started on the transformation.

Event 6: Train Project Team Members

In accordance with the plan developed back in the third event for getting started on the transformation, school and district leaders ensure that appropriate training is provided for members of their first project teams. At a minimum, training must be provided in appropriate statistical methods with great emphasis on the basic tools. Teamwork or team process skills training may also be needed.

Recall that the effectiveness of any training will be a function of the quality of the subject matter times the probability of use. After training in the statistical methods is provided, quick assignment to multidisciplined project teams provides a high probability of use. Conversely, people should not be assigned to project teams without training in the tools and methods they'll need to be successful.

Seldom have I worked with a school or district that has had to pay a dime for the training of their initial project teams. For example, Dickinson Independent School District outside Houston was able to draw on trainers from Oxy Petrochemicals, a local business partner that had adopted the Deming system. School District 51 in Ware Shoals, South Carolina, received training help from Greenwood Mills. The school district in Rock Hill, South Carolina, was able to use trainers and materials from Bowater Paper Company and a local Hoechst-Celanese plant.

In these and other cases, the districts were able to provide training as well as facilitation help for their first teams by using internal trainers and resources from local business partners. However, even though school and district leaders did not have to pay for the training programs, that does not mean they were free. There was still the expense of staff members' time in the training sessions and team meetings.

District leaders are also cautioned to make sure they provide some coaching to local business people who help out in their initial training. Special emphasis must be placed on the appropriate vocabulary and context for the material presented. When training professional teachers and staff, if a trainer from business refers to our children as raw materials or products, the trainer is dead—and so is the district's training effort!

During the training of their first project teams, school and district leaders should be looking ahead to becoming self-sufficient in the future expansion of the education. Therefore, leaders must try to identify current staff members who seem to have strong potential for serving down the road as internal trainers, facilitators for future project teams, and in-house statisticians. The in-house statisticians will be people to whom others can turn for help in analyzing test scores, disciplinary referrals, and other key measures of value-adding process outputs.

These potential in-house resource personnel should be scheduled for training in the statistical methods, team process skills, and other tools provided for the first project team members. In this manner, their development will commence so in the future the district can expand the training effort without dependence on external resources.

Event 7: Complete and Integrate the Results of the First Improvement Projects

As the initial project teams develop recommendations for improving processes, school and district leaders accept responsibility for seeing that those changes are implemented. Once improvements occur, steering committees are able to use them to build momentum for the expansion of the system. (After all, nothing sells like success!)

Though work early in the process for starting the transformation generates success stories for building momentum, a more important outcome from the first successful projects is additional learning. School and district leaders learn what's involved in leading a successful systems improvement effort. Based on what they learn, plans can be revised for expanding the effort and continuing the transformation.

Event 8: Expand the Improvement Effort

Learning that occurs during the first seven events of the process provides a strong foundation for proceeding with the overall transformation. Beginning with this eighth event, the effort is expanded to involve more people, form new project teams, and study more processes. All of this activity leads to more and continuing improvements.

Leadership guided by the system of profound knowledge not only expands process improvement efforts, but also succeeds in building the healthy environment for work, learning, and continuous improvement. Never-ending efforts to maintain and strengthen that healthy environment eventually lead the district and its schools to a new state, in which they no longer have the concerns they once had; in which all children experience enrichment and ultimately achieve the status of interdependent self-managers, capable of and excited by the pursuit of continuous, lifelong learning.

Summary

Training alone will not accomplish the required transformation of America's school districts. Beyond initial training and education, leadership action is needed. The purpose of this chapter was to provide some general guidelines for planning and taking action to get started on the transformation.

The next and final chapter of this text will be quite short. In it, a few of Deming's remarks will be offered as a final word.

Notes

1. Deming, *Out of the Crisis*, 87–90.

2. *Ibid.*, 88.

3. A. Endres, *Quality Improvement for Services* (Wilton, Conn.: Juran Institute, 1986), 2-9.

4. *Ibid.*, 3-7.

5. Juran, *Managerial Breakthrough*, 67.

6. Deming, *The New Economics*, 135.

Chapter Thirteen

A Final Word

Upon reading the texts and papers written by Deming, one finds that he was profoundly influenced by the theories and teaching of Shewhart. Not only did he cite Shewhart as the source of many of his principles, but he also left a clear record of how impressed he was with the Bell Labs physicist. On one occasion, Deming wrote, "Even if only ten percent of the listeners absorb part of Dr. Shewhart's teachings, the number may in time bring about change in the style of Western management."[1]

A cursory review of the material in this text will find that I hold Deming in just as high esteem as he held Shewhart. It would not be an exaggeration for me to say that Deming, his philosophy, and his teaching have had a profound influence on both my personal and professional lives. Therefore, I will conclude this text by giving Deming the last word.

In the mid-eighties, the Encyclopaedia Britannica Educational Corporation produced a videotape of a conversation with Deming. In it, he described certain American management practices that act as detriments to continuous improvement and competitive position. These activities include appraisal of employee performance, mobility of management, lack of constancy of purpose, and other deadly diseases. (Throughout this text, we have referred to the same practices as myths.)

At the end of the video, Deming summarized in his rambling, unique style the dangers these myths pose to American competitive position in world markets and to our nation at large. That summary was both profound and chilling, and his closing remarks are provided below as a final word for this text.[2]

> And you ask me about this country:
>
> - With a storehouse of unemployed people, some willing to work, a lot of them willing to work; with skills, knowledge, willingness to work;
>
> - And people in management unable to work, through the merit system, annual review of performance, not able to deliver what they're capable of delivering.
>
> When you think of all the underuse, abuse, and misuse of the people of this country, this may be the world's most underdeveloped nation. Number one! We did it again. We're number one!
>
> For underdevelopment.
>
> Our people not used, mismanaged, misused, abused, and underused by a management that worships sacred cows; a style of management that was never right, but built good fortune for this country between 1950 and 1968; because the rest of the world, so much of it, was devastated. You couldn't go wrong no matter what you did. Well, those days are over, and they've been over for a long time.
>
> *It's about time for American management to wake up!*

Notes

1. C. Kilian, *The World of Deming*, 58.

2. *Management's Five Deadly Diseases: A Conversation with Dr. W. Edwards Deming* (Lake Orion, Mich.: Encyclopaedia Britannica Educational Corporation, 1984), videocassette.

Appendix A

The Basic Statistical Methods: Some Procedures and Examples

Basic statistical methods are sometimes referred to as the simple tools. This is because they do not require a calculator, and people often think they have to use a calculator in order to do statistics. As we shall see, the basic tools are not merely simple—they're essential. Use of these tools (eventually) by everyone in the local school system will put us in a position to enjoy literally thousands of 1-percent improvements on a continuous basis. Beyond the benefits of process improvements, the application of these methods also contributes to solid teamwork, cooperation, and synergy among different groups in the system.

Flowcharts

Deming defined a system as "a series of functions or activities (subprocesses, stages, etc.), linear or parallel, within an organization that work together for the aim of the organization." He added that the flowchart (or flow diagram) is helpful toward understanding a system.

When a team of people from different groups (departments, buildings, committees, grade levels, and so on) is pulled together to improve a system, the first step should be to develop a flowchart of the system or process under study. In its simplest form, the flowchart lists the value-adding steps (or components) of a process, in sequence.

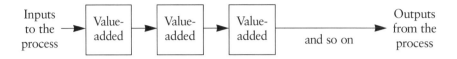

Flowcharts don't have to be highly detailed in order to reveal measurement points, problem areas, bottlenecks, unnecessary or redundant steps, and where simplification of the process may be possible. Constructing the flowchart also gets a team talking and working to clarify definitions and understanding of its processes.

Examples of flowcharts in various forms appear throughout this text. The reader is encouraged to review the diagrams illustrated in the following figures.

Figure 2.2.   Basic systems model.

Figure 2.3.   Education as a system for skill and knowledge development.

Figure 5.1.   Process for forming and managing project teams.

Figure 8.1.   Basic procedure for improving a system.

Figure 8.2.   Process for acquiring knowledge.

Figure 12.1. Process for getting started on the transformation.

Figure B.8.   Process for selecting the appropriate control chart.

Brainstorming

Brainstorming is a process by which a group of people creates a "storm" of ideas by voicing opinions openly and without criticism or evaluation. One use of brainstorming is to list as many possible causes of a problem as possible as a first step to creative problem solving. The purpose of brainstorming is to

- Generate a large number of creative ideas
- Stimulate creativity
- Learn and benefit from divergent thinking

Procedure for Brainstorming

1. State and post topic or question.

2. Provide a couple minutes for silent writing.

3. Give ideas, one-by-one, in turn.

    • No interruptions, no comments, no discussion, no questions

    • Group members may pass

4. Record ideas on flip chart exactly as they are stated.

5. Finish when all group members pass on the same turn.

Fishbone Diagrams
(Cause-and-Effect Diagrams)

Fishbone diagrams provide an orderly form for organizing brainstorming ideas, showing the relationship between a problem (effect) and its possible causes. Perceived causes should be validated (via data collection) prior to initiating solutions. The purpose of fishbone diagrams is to

• Reinforce systems and process thinking

• Summarize the group's ideas in a clearly organized form that has a lot more eye appeal than several flip chart pages full of brainstorming ideas

• Give the team a chance for self-inspection before spending any more time collecting data and/or further analyzing the problem

Procedure for Constructing a Fishbone Diagram

1. Write the problem or issue under discussion in a box on the right side of the page. This is the effect.

2. Draw an arrow from the left side of the page to the right side.

3. Review brainstorming ideas. Identify common themes or categories of ideas.

4. Write the main categories of possible causes, directing a branch arrow from each category to the main arrow.

5. Onto each branch arrow, write the relevant ideas that were generated during the brainstorming session. These will look like twigs on the main branches.

6. Onto each twig, write in even more detailed items from the brainstorming, making smaller twigs.

7. Check to ensure that all possible causes are included in the diagram. If appropriate, use brainstorming to generate additional ideas.

An example of a fishbone diagram is provided in Figure A.1.

Data Collection

As educators work to apply the statistical methods, the importance of using data often comes across as nothing new. In our schools, we already have reams of data. Some examples include test scores, per-pupil spending figures, student-teacher ratios, instructional time, and disciplinary referrals.

Data collection in the context of transformation differs in several ways from traditional practices. In his text, *Guide to Quality Control,* Ishikawa illustrates this difference with the following reminders for collecting data.[1]

1. Clarify the purpose for collecting the data.

2. Collect data efficiently.

3. Take action according to the data.

For example, what is the purpose of collecting standardized test data? In the traditional school, the purpose is often to measure student achievement. Educators guided by the systems perspective realize that this can't be done! It is impossible to measure student achievement separate from other components of the system.

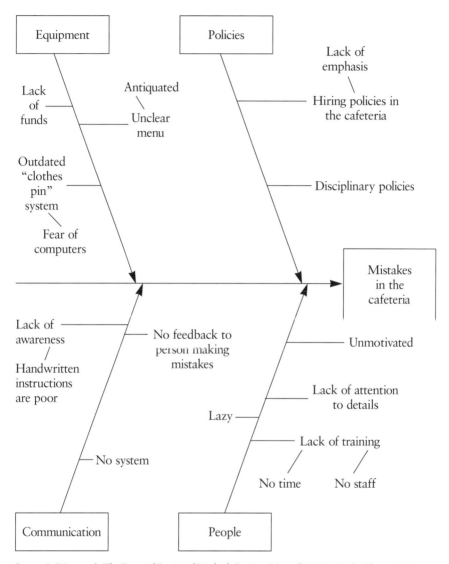

Source: J. F. Leonard, *The Essential Statistical Methods Seminar Manual* (1995). Used with permission.

Figure A.1. Fishbone diagram of causes of mistakes in the cafeteria.

Using test data to measure students too often leads to ineffective action. That is, some schools will likely use it to sort students into remedial programs, gifted and talented groups, and learning tracks. But tracking, remedial programs, and sorting practices do nothing to improve teaching and learning processes!

When guided by the system of profound knowledge, school and district leaders use test data to drive people back up into the teaching and learning process pipeline, then study the process, change the process, and continuously improve the process—not sort students, rank students, grade students, or remediate students.

In conclusion, Ishikawa offered the following guidance on the importance and role of effective data collection in efforts to improve quality.[2]

- The word *statistical* implies data, and data reflect facts.

- For a situation to be correctly analyzed and control to be realized, data must be collected carefully and accurately.

- The intent and purpose for which the data are collected must be clearly stated.

- Action should be taken when definite causes and effects become known.

Pareto Diagrams

Pareto diagrams are a form of bar graph used to rank items measured in descending order of priority. They are used to sort out the vital few from the trivial many issues. The Pareto principle is particularly key to the educator because he or she will forever have limited time, limited funding, limited people, and limited resources. It is essential that those limited resources be applied to areas that will provide the greatest return for the effort expended. Pareto diagrams are used to

- Assist in analysis of problems. Arranging data in Pareto format will often highlight something that might otherwise have gone unnoticed.

- Enhance communication with a display of data that can be commonly understood and interpreted.

- Focus attention on problems in priority order; to put first things first.

Procedure for Constructing a Pareto Diagram

1. Agree on the classification of items to be recorded (for example, kinds of mistakes, number of accidents, classrooms or grade levels, size, and costs).

    - If data records are not classified or itemized using a common scale, a Pareto diagram can't be constructed.

    - Revise data sheets so data can be organized and recorded correctly.

2. Decide on the period of time to be illustrated (for example, semester, week, or month).

    - For some situations, the time period may be days or even hours.

    - The important thing is to keep the time period for all related graphs the same so they can be compared later.

3. Total the frequency of occurrences for each classification or item for the defined time period. The total for each item will be the length of the bar on the diagram.

4. Draw horizontal and vertical axes on graph paper and mark the axes in the proper units.

5. Draw in the bars.

An example of a Pareto diagram is provided in Figure A.2. For more information and examples of Pareto diagrams, see pages 93–97 and the following figures.

Figure 5.4.   Illustration of the Pareto principle.

Figure 5.5.   Pareto diagram of 255 high school males' greatest concerns.

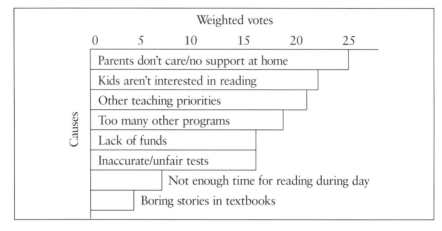

Source: J. F. Leonard, *Transformation 101 Seminar Manual* (1995). Used with permission.

Figure A.2. Pareto diagram of causes of poor reading test scores.

Figure 5.6.   Pareto diagram of 569 high school students' greatest needs.

In some cases, a team may find it's not in a position to use actual data to summarize and prioritize its ideas. In such a case, teams can employ a voting and ranking method to assign values and priorities to ideas. Each team member has one vote on each item. Votes and totals are based on the following scale.

Major cause = 5

Cause   = 3

Minor cause = 1

In fact, the Pareto diagram in Figure A.2 was prepared using the voting and ranking method. The five educators who prepared the summary then had to recognize that all they had produced was a Pareto model of their opinions—not necessarily facts. They then faced the challenge of working to validate that model with data.

Force-Field Analysis

Force-field analysis is a technique for predicting how a particular proposal, plan, or course of action may be received by those who will be affected by it. It is a way to illustrate and analyze helping forces and obstacle forces that may work for or against the proposed course of action. An example is provided in Figure A.3. Using force-field analysis will help a team to

- Illustrate the relative pros and cons of a solution or intended action

- Represent the pros and cons as helping or obstacle forces

- Help develop a strategy for dealing with anticipated forces and/or to amend the planned course of action

- Benefit from a convergent technique for problem solving

Procedure for Using Force-Field Analysis

1. Using brainstorming, generate a list of all possible forces you may encounter for or against the intended plan or course of action.

2. After the brainstorming, label each force as a helping force or an obstacle force.

3. Via voting and ranking, determine the relative strengths of both the helping forces and the obstacle forces.

4. Post the helping forces and obstacle forces, using arrows whose lengths represent the relative strength of each force.

5. The cumulative lengths of helping forces' arrows should equal the cumulative lengths of the obstacle forces' arrows.

6. Upon review of the final diagram, list strategies for strengthening helping forces, weakening obstacle forces, or both. Such strategies will help to move the plan ahead.

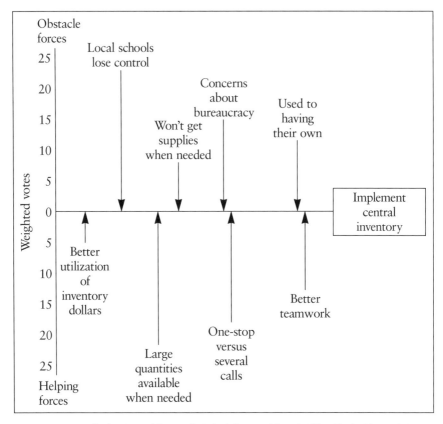

Source: J. F. Leonard, *The Essential Statistical Methods Seminar Manual* (1995). Used with permission.

Figure A.3. Force-field analysis of proposal to implement central inventory.

Scatter Diagrams

Also known as correlation charts, scatter diagrams display the relationship between two variables. The pattern of the plots shows the level of influence that one factor may have on the other. When applicable, scatter diagrams can help educators identify critical process variables that, with more care and attention, may have a significant and positive influence on outcomes.

Scatter diagrams can also help educators to avoid overreacting to insignificant variables. For example, study may show that there is no positive or significant relationship between a placement test and subsequent performance. This will help educators avoid destructive tracking of students in levels below their true capability and potential.

Scholtes et al. note that, whereas run charts and other basic tools allow one to look at only one process characteristic at a time, a scatter diagram lets one look at the relationship between two characteristics. The shape of the scatter of points indicates if the two factors are related.[3]

The following are typical patterns one may find on scatter diagrams.

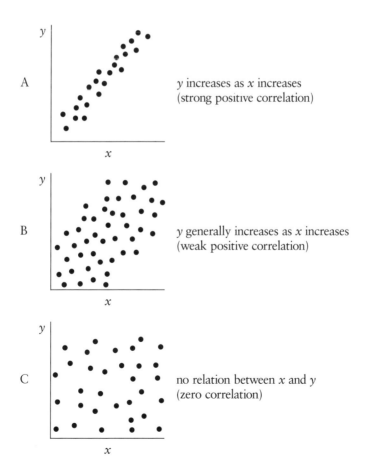

A   *y* increases as *x* increases
     (strong positive correlation)

B   *y* generally increases as *x* increases
     (weak positive correlation)

C   no relation between *x* and *y*
     (zero correlation)

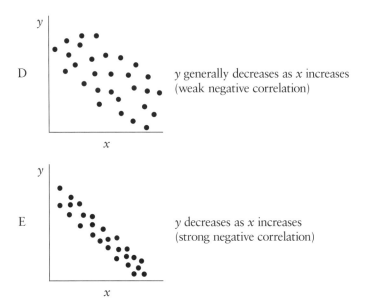

D   *y* generally decreases as *x* increases
(weak negative correlation)

E   *y* decreases as *x* increases
(strong negative correlation)

Run Charts

Run charts are used to visually represent data over time. They are useful for monitoring a system to see whether or not trends or shifts occur over time. Run charts plot the behavior (up and down) of one variable over time.

One danger in using the run chart—or in interpreting data in any form—is the tendency to consider every variation as being significant. Many educators spend much of their time trying to explain random variation! For example,

- "This week we had six eighth graders put on detention. That's the highest total we've had in five weeks! What is going on over there?"

- "Computer processing costs are skyrocketing! This is the third month in a row that they've gone up. Put together an action plan for cutting back."

The theory of variation teaches us that the question is not, "Are these outcomes different?" The question is, "Are they significantly different?" Intermediate statistical tools provide several ways to determine if variation is significant or not. (The intermediate statistical methods are presented in appendix B.) Run charts are nonetheless useful for gaining an initial understanding (or picture) of the variation in process outcomes.

Example: The Problem of Student Discipline

The administration of a small middle school was concerned about student discipline. The discipline policy had three formal steps: (1) Written warning to the student with a copy to his or her parents; (2) Detention after three written warnings or for a serious infraction; and (3) Suspension for very serious or repeated infractions.

Table A.1 lists the number of disciplinary steps (incidents) that occurred in that school over an 18-week period. That listing is followed by a run chart of the data, illustrated in Figure A.4.

Other examples of run charts will be found in the following figures.

Figure 6.1.   Run chart of grade 5 math Stanford Achievement Test scores.

Figure 11.3. Run chart of the bead experiment results.

Table A.1. Number of disciplinary incidents by week.

Week	No. of incidents	Week	No. of incidents
1	22	10	34
2	32	11	28
3	21	12	26
4	27	13	25
5	23	14	26
6	30	15	23
7	24	16	24
8	25	17	20
9	24	18	19
	Total number of disciplinary incidents: 453		

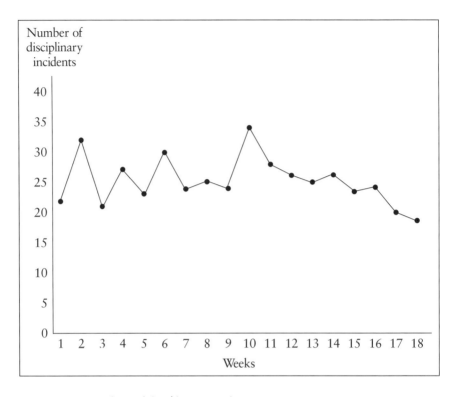

Figure A.4. Run chart of disciplinary incidents.

Histograms

Any system will produce some distribution. As noted repeatedly throughout this text, there will always be variation. For example, one person's system for driving to work will produce a distribution of different trip lengths. Not all trips to work take exactly the same amount of time. (See Figure A.5.)

Histograms, or frequency distributions, provide a picture of variation around one key measure. They're very important because they illustrate the pattern of variation in a process output and are the first step toward understanding that variation.

Unlike run charts, which illustrate the pattern of variation over time, histograms summarize all of the measurements and indicate how much variation occurred in a given period of time.

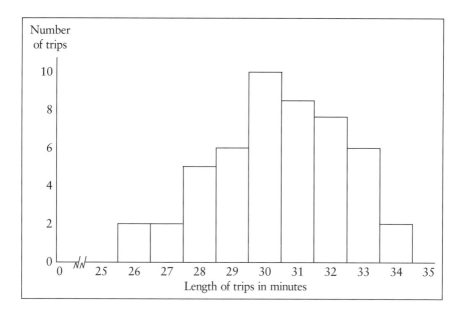

Figure A.5. Histogram of length of trips to work (in minutes).

There are special terms used when constructing histograms. They are

Class (k)   A single category or bar on the graph.

Class interval (h)   The width of a class. In Figure A.5, the class interval is one minute.

Class boundaries   The beginning and ending of a class.

Range (R)   The difference between the largest value and smallest value in the distribution.

$$R = X_{max} - X_{min}$$

Procedure for Constructing a Histogram

1. Calculate the range of all the data. (*Range = R = X_{max} − X_{min}*)

2. Determine the number of classes (number of intervals for the frequency distribution; number of bars for the histogram) as follows:

Number of data	Approximate number of classes (k)
30–50	7–10
50–100	10–15
100–250	15–20
more than 250	20–25

3. Calculate h, the class interval (width of the bar).

$$h = \frac{\text{Range}}{\text{Number of classes}} = \frac{R}{k}$$

Round h to a convenient number.

4. Determine class boundaries.

5. Tally points falling into each class.

6. Construct the histogram.

The main purpose of the histogram (or frequency distribution) is to provide a picture of the variation in the process. Many computer programs are available that will be helpful in building histograms.

Example: The Problem of Handling Phone Calls

The volume of phone calls coming into the central office had become a problem. Parents, taxpayers, teachers, building administrators, and others were complaining about either getting a busy signal or being on hold for an annoying length of time. In order to gain some insight into what was happening, five sample measurements of length of phone calls, expressed in minutes, were collected on 19 consecutive work days. Those data are listed in Table A.2.

If one were to use these data to construct a histogram, it would look like Figure A.6.

Table A.2. Measurements of length of phone calls coming into central office.

Subgroups (days)	Measurements (minutes)				
	X_1	X_2	X_3	X_4	X_5
1	6	4	5	6	5
2	3	6	4	6	6
3	7	4	7	7	6
4	3	5	4	5	6
5	7	5	4	4	6
6	4	6	4	6	6
7	6	3	4	3	6
8	4	7	6	7	6
9	7	4	6	6	7
10	6	5	2	7	8
11	4	0	4	4	8
12	7	6	4	5	4
13	5	3	5	5	6
14	5	7	7	6	5
15	6	4	5	5	4
16	2	6	4	5	5
17	8	6	5	5	6
18	5	5	3	6	3
19	6	4	7	7	7

Summary

Run charts and histograms—the last of the basic statistical methods—are key first steps to picturing and understanding variation. The histogram provides a great snapshot of the process, but it does not show how the process performs over time. The run chart does show process performance over time, but it does not have an alarm signal to identify significant events or patterns in the data. In appendix B, we will move on to the next level of the essential statistical methods: intermediate statistical tools. It is this set of tools we apply to key measures of teaching, learning, and administrative process outcomes in order to determine if those outcomes are different or if they're significantly different.

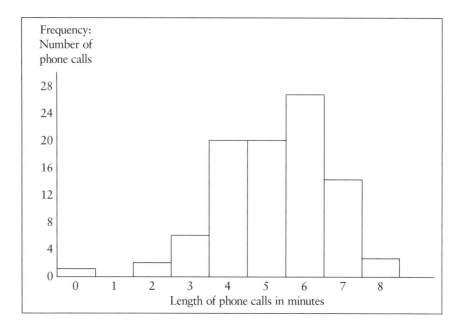

Figure A.6. Histogram of length of phone calls coming into the central office.

Notes

1. Ishikawa, *Guide to Quality Control*, 4.

2. *Ibid.*, 30.

3. Scholtes et al., *The Team Handbook*, 2-36.

Appendix B

Intermediate Statistical Methods: Some Procedures, Formulae, and Examples

In the intermediate statistical methods is a set of tools called control charts. Control charts are used to monitor a process to see whether it is in statistical control. Points on the charts that fall beyond the limits of random, controlled variation or that fall into nonrandom patterns indicate the presence of a special cause of variation.[1] In other words, control charts help to determine whether plotted outcomes are merely different or if they're significantly different.

The purpose of this appendix is not to teach intermediate statistics, but merely to describe the most common statistical process control charts. Before reading the following pages, readers are encouraged to review the material presented earlier in chapter 6, "Theory of Variation," and chapter 7, "Applying Intermediate Statistical Methods and Concepts." Before trying to apply the charts and formulae in their organizations, readers are encouraged to engage trusted local business partners, consultants, or other specialists for guidance. There is a wide selection of statistical process control software available for performing all the calculations listed in this appendix.

Types of Data

Before deciding what kind of control chart to use to analyze a process, we must first decide what kind of data is being used to measure the process output. There are three major types of data: variables data, attributes data, and counts data.

Type of data	Teaching and learning process examples	Administrative process examples
Variables data	• Teacher planning time • Average test scores • Elapsed time (homework, projects, and so on)	• Costs • Response time • Budget, schedule variance
Attributes data	• Number of incorrect responses • Percent of students scoring below standard • Number of projects completed on time or late	• Late deliveries from vendors • Missed deadlines • Percent favorable survey responses
Counts data	• Number of mistakes • Number of errors • Rate of mistakes, errors	• Number of data entry errors • Number of disciplinary incidents • Number of grievances

First, we will consider common control charts for analyzing the variation in processes that generate variables data, or measurements. Later in this appendix, we will address control charts designed for use with attributes and counts data.

The Central Limit Theorem

As noted in chapter 7, all control charts have three things in common:

- Upper control limit (UCL) of random, common cause variation

- Lower control limit (LCL) of random, common cause variation

- Central line (CL), which falls at the process average

Control charts for variables data are based on the normal distribution, so the UCL and LCL will be defined by plus and minus three standard deviations from the average ($\overline{X}$ + and $-$ $3\sigma'$). In order to calculate and use the standard deviation in this fashion, however, one must have a process output with a distribution that follows the normal distribution, and not all variables data will follow the normal distribution. For example, you cannot reach into a purse and pull out negative two dollars! You can pull out zero dollars or any amount above zero, but the distribution of raw data on spending will hit zero, then cut off.

The same is true when dealing with raw measures of time. No matter how much pressure you put on the maintenance department, it cannot finish a repair project yesterday! Like spending, raw measures of time will hit zero and cut off.

```
           X
           X X X
  Frequency   X X X X
           X X X X X X
           X X X X X X X
           X X X X X X X X
           X X X X X X X X
           X X X X X X X X X X   X
  ─────────────────────────────────────
     0
              Individual measures of time or money
```

Note that this distribution isn't normal. It doesn't have the familiar bell shape. And since it isn't normal, a calculator will give us a measure of the standard deviation—we just can't use it to determine the process limits!

If, however, we pull small *subgroups* of measurements of time or money and plot a histogram of the *averages* of the sample subgroups, the distribution of subgroup averages will approximate a normal distribution. This being the case, we can determine the UCL and LCL (+ and − $3\sigma'$ limits) of that process to determine the type of variation present (common cause versus special cause).

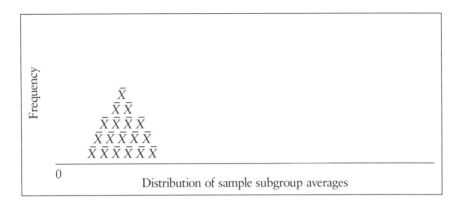

Distribution of sample subgroup averages

This phenomenon is referred to as the *central limit theorem.* The central limit theorem holds that by drawing small sample subgroups of measurements from a process generating variables data, then plotting a distribution of the sample subgroup averages, the distribution of averages will vary less than the distribution of the individuals. The distribution will also approximate a normal, bell-shaped distribution. As Box, Hunter, and Hunter noted, "The sample average tends to be normally distributed, even though the individual observations on which it is based are not."[2] This means we can calculate the standard deviation, and use control charts to learn about the process (in other words, to determine whether the process is under the influence of common causes of variation from within the process or special causes of nonrandom variation from outside the process).

Because of the power of the central limit theorem, the most common control charts used on processes generating variables data are *X*-bar and *R* charts.

X-Bar and R Charts

One requirement for using *X*-bar and *R* charts is that our data be organized into small sample subgroups. This enables us to monitor the process output in terms of its average (or location) and dispersion (range). The X-bar chart plots the subgroup averages, thereby keeping an eye on the process average (location), while the R chart plots the subgroup ranges, thereby keeping an eye on the process dispersion (variability).

A second requirement for data plotted on the X-bar and R chart (in fact, a requirement for all control charts) is that data records keep track of the run number order. We are interested in observing dynamic process outputs over time. Preserving the order of the measurements will enable us to detect significant shifts or trends that require special attention.

X-bar and R Chart Formulae

To calculate the central line and control limits for X-bar and R charts, we will use the following formulae.

X-bar chart

$$CL = \bar{\bar{X}} = \frac{\Sigma \bar{X}}{n}, \text{ where } n = \text{number of subgroups}$$

$$UCL = \bar{\bar{X}} + A_2 \bar{R}$$

$A_2 \bar{R}$ provides an estimate of three standard deviations ($3\sigma'$). See Table B.1 for values of A_2.

$$LCL = \bar{\bar{X}} - A_2 \bar{R}$$

R chart

$$CL = \bar{R} = \frac{\Sigma R}{n}, \text{ where } n = \text{number of subgroups}$$

$$UCL = D_4 \bar{R}$$

See Table B.1 for values of D_4.

$$LCL = D_3 \bar{R}$$

See Table B.1 for values of D_3.

Table B.1. Factors for X-bar and R charts.

n^*	A_2	d_2	D_3	D_4
2	1.88	1.13	0	3.27
3	1.02	1.69	0	2.58
4	0.73	2.06	0	2.28
5	0.58	2.33	0	2.12
7	0.42	2.70	0.08	1.92
10	0.31	3.08	0.22	1.78

$^*n$ = subgroup size

Example: The Problem of Handling Phone Calls

In appendix A, we looked at some data on length of phone calls at the central office during a review of histograms. Table A.2 on page 271 listed 95 individual measurements taken over a period of 19 consecutive work days (five measurements per day). We can consider each day to be a subgroup of size n = 5. Calculating the averages ($\overline{X}$) and ranges (R) for those data, then applying the above formulae, yields the following statistics.

Subgroup (day)	$\overline{X}$	R	X-bar chart
1	5.2	2.0	$\text{CL} = \overline{\overline{X}} = \dfrac{\Sigma\overline{X}}{n} = \dfrac{99.0}{19}$
2	5.0	3.0	
3	6.2	3.0	
4	4.4	2.0	CL = 5.21 minutes
5	5.2	3.0	
6	5.2	2.0	$\text{UCL} = \overline{\overline{X}} + A_2\overline{R}$
7	4.4	3.0	$= 5.21 + (.58)(3.21)$
8	6.0	3.0	UCL = 5.21 + 1.86 = 7.07
9	6.0	3.0	
10	5.6	6.0	$\text{LCL} = \overline{\overline{X}} - A_2\overline{R} = 3.35$
11	4.0	8.0	
12	5.2	3.0	
13	4.8	3.0	R chart
14	6.0	2.0	
15	4.8	2.0	$\text{CL} = \overline{R} = \dfrac{\Sigma R}{n} = \dfrac{61.0}{19} = 3.21$
16	4.4	4.0	

Subgroup (day)	$\bar{X}$	R		
17	6.0	3.0	UCL $= D_4\bar{R} =$ (2.12)(3.21)	
18	4.4	3.0	UCL $= 6.81$	
19	6.2	3.0	LCL $= D_3\bar{R} =$ (0)(3.21) $= 0$	
	Σ99.0	Σ61.0		

Transferring the control limits, subgroup averages, and subgroup ranges into X-Bar and R chart format yields the graphs illustrated in Figure B.1.

Interpreting the Language of Control Charts

The data and information plotted on a control chart can be viewed as the voice of the process. The language of a process is expressed in the patterns of data plotted on a control chart. A process is telling us that it is stable when

- All points plot on the chart in a random pattern.
- The points are clustered around the CL.
- No points fall outside the UCL or LCL of controlled, random, common cause variation.

What does it mean when we say that a process is stable? A stable process tells us that

- The process producing the outputs is in statistical control.
- All of the variation—good and bad, acceptable and unacceptable—is resulting from common causes only (from within the process).
- There is no special cause variation present (from outside the process).

If the outcomes of a stable process are not acceptable, it is the responsibility of school and district leadership to correct the system (change the process). Any adjustment to a stable process will make things worse over time; it is tampering, not improvement.

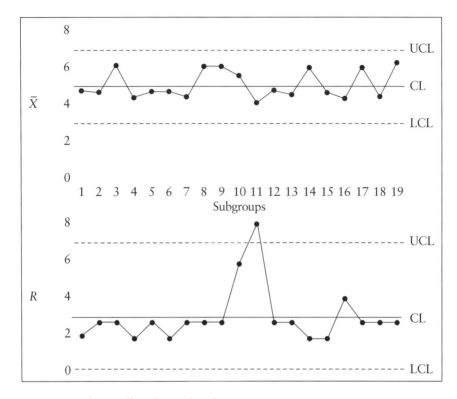

Figure B.1. Phone calls $\overline{X}$-bar and R charts.

In the case of process stability, if we do not change the process that's producing the unacceptable outcomes, it will forever produce those unacceptable outcomes. The only appropriate strategy for improvement is to study the process, change the process, and improve the process.

Tests for Nonrandom, Special Cause Variation

Sometimes the language of the process will indicate that the process is out of statistical control; it is not stable, not predictable. This will indicate that the process is under the influence of some special cause(s) of variation from outside the process. The appropriate corrective strategy is to find, remove, and prevent the reoccurrence of the special cause. Eliminating special causes will get the process back into a stable, predictable state.

In the case of the phone calls, the R chart illustrated in Figure B.1 indicates the presence of a special cause. The measured range of subgroup 11 plotted above the upper limit of controlled, random variation. That outcome was not only different from the other data plotted on the chart—it was significantly different. This would indicate the presence of some special cause from outside the normal telephone communications process.

In the actual case, closer study of the data indicated that one of the five measures taken that day was recorded as a zero; someone believed that a phone call lasted no time at all! Further investigation isolated the special cause in this case as being twofold.

1. The check sheet for initially recording the data had extremely small spaces. Someone may have squeezed a 6, an 8, or a 9 into the small space, but it was interpreted as a zero.

2. The control charts were maintained by the secretary of an administrator who worked outside the area and process under study. When she thought she saw a zero, she did not think to question it.

Corrective action in this case included shredding the old data collection sheets and replacing them with check sheets that had plenty of space for recording measurements. Beyond that, people working in the process took over the maintenance of their own charts. The secretary outside the area was no longer required to do so.

Having identified and removed the special causes of the non-random variation, the team was able to discard the five measurements taken on the 11th day of the study and recalculate the process limits with the remaining 18 subgroups of data. This provided a clear understanding of the limits of their stable process, as well as a baseline for continuous improvement in service.

Figure B.2 lists four simple tests that can be applied to most control charts to detect nonrandom, special cause variation. Again, any time these patterns or conditions emerge on a process control chart, special action is needed to identify the special cause and initiate corrective action.

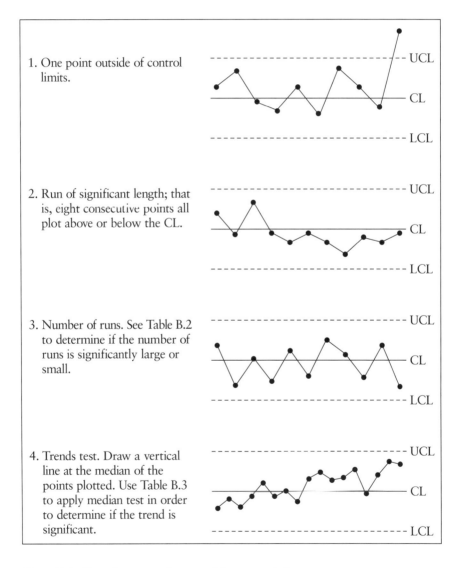

Figure B.2. Tests for nonrandom, special cause variation.

Table B.2. Test for number of runs.[3]

Number of runs = number of times the line graph crosses the central line, plus one

Nonrandom, special cause variation is evident if the number of runs is equal to or less than the value in column B, or equal to or greater than the value in column C.

Column A Number of points on the run chart	Column B Significantly small number of runs	Column C Significantly large number of runs
10–11	2	9
12–13	2	11
14–15	3	12
16–17	4	13
18–19	4	15
20–21	5	16
22–23	6	17
24–25	7	18
26–27	7	20
28–29	8	21
30–31	9	22
32–33	10	23
34–35	10	25
36–37	11	26
38–39	12	27
40–41	13	28
42–43	14	29
44–45	14	31
46–47	15	32
48–49	16	33
50–59	17	34
60–69	21	40
70–79	25	46
80–89	30	51
90–99	34	57
100–109	38	63
110–119	43	68
120–129	47	74

Table B.3. Median test for nonrandom variation.[4]

1. Drawing the vertical line at the median of the points plotted will divide your chart into four quadrants, defined by the intersection of the median line and CL.	
2. Beginning with the upper right-hand quadrant, label them I through IV (clockwise).	
3. Without counting any points that fall on the median line or CL, count the number of points in the diagonal quadrants with the fewer number of points.	
4. Conclude there is a significant (nonrandom) trend if the count is equal to or less than the critical value listed here.	

Number of points on run chart	Critical value
7 or less	no test
8–11	0
12–14	1
15–17	2
18–20	3
21–23	4
24–25	5
26–28	6
29–31	7
32–33	8
34–36	9
37–38	10
39–41	11
42–43	12
44–46	13
47–48	14
49–51	15
52–53	16
54–56	17
57–58	18
59–60	19

Limitations of X-bar and R Charts

The major limitation of X-bar and R charts is that they require a lot of data. Typically, in order for the charts to provide sufficient information about a process, one would need about 20 subgroups of data. If the subgroup size is three to five measurements, that means we would need between 60 and 100 measurements before we can comfortably calculate and analyze the process control limits.

A related limitation of X-bar and R charts is that it may take a long time to collect sufficient data. Many changes could occur in a process before one is even in a position to determine the process control limits.

In many administrative, teaching, and learning processes, we find ourselves in a situation that provides very slowly evolving data. In such a situation, the X-bar and R charts aren't helpful. Either we don't have enough data to calculate valid control limits, or we don't have time to wait for enough data to be available!

In processes that provide slowly evolving measurements, three alternatives to X-bar and R charts are available: run charts, individual and moving range charts, and moving average/moving range charts.

Run Charts

Three out of the four tests for nonrandomness (see Figure B.2) do not require control limits. They can be applied to a run chart. Therefore, the first step in evaluating processes that provide slowly evolving measurements is to plot the data as it comes; that is, to plot the measurements on a run chart, then apply the appropriate tests for nonrandomness.

For example, a certain school district spends considerable time forecasting its spending. Administrators are required to forecast four months in advance and then justify any budget variances as time goes by. After the forecasting comes the reporting. Administrators must report why they missed their forecasts. Table B.4 lists for the past 18 months the forecasts of spending (in millions of dollars). Also shown are the actual spending for the month and the budget variances (actual spending minus forecast). A run chart of the 18 monthly budget variances is illustrated in Figure B.3.

Run charts provide a simple but powerful way to determine if something special is influencing the process, particularly significant process shifts or trends. The reader can apply tests 2 through 4 from Figure B.2 for nonrandom, special cause variation to the run

Table B.4. Budget forecast and actual spending data.

Month	Forecast	Actual spending	Budget variance
1	8.3	8.0	−.3
2	8.1	8.2	+.1
3	9.6	9.5	−.1
4	7.8	7.9	+.1
5	7.8	7.6	−.2
6	9.0	8.5	−.5
7	8.4	8.4	0
8	9.5	9.2	−.3
9	10.3	10.7	+.4
10	11.4	11.2	−.2
11	11.8	11.6	−.2
12	10.4	10.5	+.1
13	11.8	11.4	−.4
14	12.4	12.0	−.4
15	10.9	11.5	+.6
16	9.5	9.5	0
17	8.2	9.0	+.8
18	10.3	10.0	−.3
		Total	−.8 million dollars
		$\overline{X} =$	−.04 million dollars

chart in Figure B.3 and will find no evidence that the variation is anything other than random.

However, run charts do not provide a means for knowing if a single point is in control or not. Since they lack control limits, run charts cannot indicate if apparent high points are significantly high, nor if low points on the chart are significantly low. If the ability to know about single points is important, we can calculate and impose control limits on the run chart by converting it to an individuals chart.

Individuals and Moving Range Charts

When moving ahead to add control limits to a run chart, two key points must be kept in mind.

1. One cannot simply calculate the standard deviation (σ') from the individual measures on the run chart, then use it to add

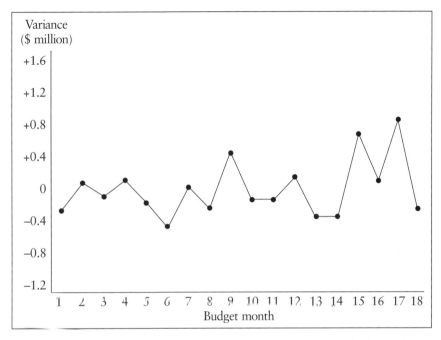

Source: J. F. Leonard, *The Essential Statistical Methods Seminar Manual* (1995). Used with permission.

Figure B.3. Run chart of monthly budget variances.

process control limits (at plus and minus $3\sigma'$). In the case of our forecasting study, only 18 measures were plotted. That is not enough data for generating trustworthy statistics.

2. The individuals chart should only be used when the histogram of individual measures approximates the shape of a normal distribution. Any heavy skewness in the shape of the histogram would suggest that the third alternative to X-bar and R charts be employed—the moving average and moving range charts.

The source of the control limits on an individuals chart is the average moving range (mR-bar) of adjacent values on the run chart. The first moving range (mR) will be the difference between the first and second values; the second moving range will be the difference between the second and third values; and so on. For our forecasting study, Table B.5 lists the moving ranges (*mR*) needed to calculate control limits for the individuals and moving range charts.

Note that in the 17 moving ranges, 34 measurements are represented. (Each moving range used two measurements.) This is sufficient data in order to calculate and impose control limits on the chart of individual values. For the individuals chart and accompanying moving range chart, use the following formulae to calculate the control limits. Below each of the standard formulae are the calculations for the above forecasting data.

Individuals chart

$$\text{CL} = \bar{X} = \frac{\Sigma X}{n}, \text{ where } n = \text{ number of measurements}$$

$$= \frac{-0.8}{18} = -.04$$

Table B.5. Budget forecasting process variance and moving ranges.

Month	Variance	mR		
1	−.3	—		
2	+.1	.4		
3	−.1	.2		
4	+.1	.2	$\bar{X} = \dfrac{\Sigma X}{n} = \dfrac{-0.8}{18} = -.04$	
5	−.2	.3		
6	−.5	.3		
7	0	.5		
8	−.3	.3		
9	+.4	.7		
10	−.2	.6		
11	−.2	0	$\bar{mR} = \dfrac{\Sigma mR}{n} = \dfrac{7.8}{17} = .46$	
12	+.1	.3		
13	−.4	.5		
14	−.4	0		
15	+.6	1.0		
16	0	.6		
17	+.8	.8		
18	−.3	1.1		

UCL $= \bar{X} + A_2 m\bar{R}$ For individuals charts, $A_2 = 2.66$

$= -.04 + (2.66)(.46) = 1.18$

LCL $= \bar{X} - A_2 m\bar{R}$

$= -.04 - (2.66)(.46) = -1.26$

Moving range chart

CL $= m\bar{R} = \dfrac{\Sigma mR}{n}$, where n = number of moving ranges

$= \dfrac{7.8}{17} = .46$

UCL $= D_4 m\bar{R}$ See Table B.1 for values of D_4.

$= (3.27)(.46) = 1.50$

LCL $= D_3 m\bar{R}$ See Table B.1 for values of D_3.

$= (0)(.46) = 0$

The resulting individuals chart and moving range chart for the forecasting process are shown in Figure B.4.

Moving Average and Moving Range Charts

The third and most statistically valid alternative to X-bar and R charts are the moving average and moving range charts. The calculations used to determine the control limits for these charts are exactly the same as the ones used for the X-bar and R charts. The difference is in how the subgroups are created.

Remember, we are considering these alternatives to X-bar and R charts only in situations where our processes provide us with slowly evolving data. For example, the business manager gets only one measure of monthly costs per month. He does not get 30 measures for building a histogram, nor does he get 20 subgroups of five measures each of monthly costs. He gets one measure per month (take it or leave it!).

Even though we can't always get our data in subgroups, we'd still like to find ways to generate subgroups as quickly as possible

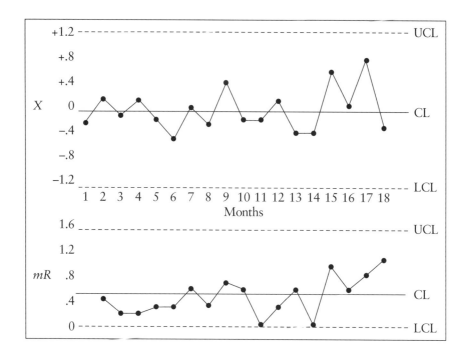

Figure B.4. Individuals and moving range charts for forecasting process.

and still maintain statistical validity. Moving average and moving range charts do this for us, using much the same approach we used to calculate moving ranges for use with the individuals chart.

Example: The Problem of the Monthly Report

A district office staff spends considerable time preparing a monthly report for the superintendent and board of education. The report covers budget variances, project status updates, test results, grievances, dropouts from the high school, and a wide range of other administrative issues. As a first step to improving their reporting process, the staff collected some data. Table B.6 lists for the past 24 months the time spent (expressed in hours) to prepare the monthly report.

Let's say we decided to place these slowly developing measures into subgroups of size $n = 3$. If we did so as we'd do for the X-bar

Table B.6. Time spend (in hours) to prepare reports by month.

Month	Preparation time	Month	Preparation time
1	10.3	13	9.9
2	11.1	14	8.3
3	8.7	15	9.9
4	9.0	16	10.0
5	12.6	17	9.8
6	8.0	18	9.8
7	8.7	19	9.5
8	10.2	20	10.8
9	9.0	21	10.7
10	11.4	22	10.7
11	10.7	23	10.5
12	10.0	24	10.5

and R charts, we'd yield only eight subgroups. However, if we use a moving average and a moving range, these same 24 monthly measurements will yield 22 subgroups, representing a total of 66 measurements, in the same amount of time. Here's how it works.

We use the first three measures to form the first subgroup, then calculate the average and the range.

$$X \quad m\overline{X} \quad mR$$

1. 10.3
2. 11.1
3.   8.7   10.03   2.4

We then drop the first measure and add the fourth measure to calculate a second set of averages and ranges for the second, third, and fourth measures.

$$X \quad m\overline{X} \quad mR$$

1. 10.3
2. 11.1
3.   8.7   10.03   2.4
4.   9.0   9.60   2.4

Continue this pattern through the whole set of 24 monthly measurements to end up with 22 moving averages and 22 moving ranges. Using the formulae on page 277, calculate the control limits for moving average and moving range charts for the monthly reporting process. (When using Table B.1, recall that our subgroup size, n, equals 3.) The resulting control charts are shown in Figure B.5.

Back to the Run Chart

Because they use moving subgroups, averages, and ranges, the moving average and moving range charts may mask nonrandom

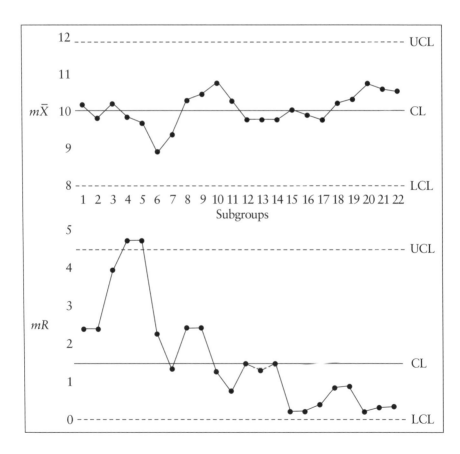

Figure B.5. Moving average and moving range charts for the monthly reports.

trends or process shifts. Therefore, it is recommended that a run chart of the individual values be plotted on occasion and that all four tests for nonrandom, special cause variation be applied.

Calculating Process Capability

During our initial exploration of variation in chapters 6 and 7, we addressed the key concept of process capability. Literally defined, the capability of a process is the random, inherent, common cause variation we observe in a process. A system's capability looks like this:

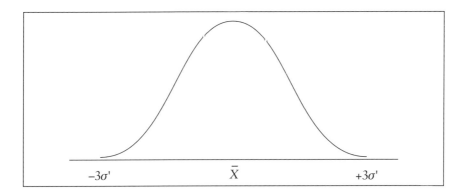

Note that a key phrase in the definition is "common cause variation." Therefore, we can only determine the capability of a process that is in a state of statistical control (stable).

Once we eliminate special cause variation, thereby achieving statistical control, we can calculate the capability of the process. Putting a number on the capability of a process enables educators to clearly communicate the extent of the variation present. To do so, one must determine the average of the distribution, plus and minus three standard deviations ($\bar{X}$ + and − $3\sigma'$).

Example: The Problem of Handling Phone Calls

Recall that the original R chart for this process (see Figure B.1) plotted out of statistical control. Therefore, one would not even bother trying to calculate the process capability. Why? Because an out-of-control process has no capability! (*Capability* is defined as the random, inherent, *common cause* variation we observe.)

After identifying, removing, and preventing the reoccurrence of the special cause indicated in subgroup 11, one could use the remaining subgroups to recalculate the control limits (CL, UCL, and LCL) for the X-bar and R charts. The revised control limits for the stable process are

X-bar chart: R chart:

$\quad$ CL $= \bar{\bar{X}} = 5.29$ $\qquad$ CL $= \bar{R} = 3.00$

$\quad$ UCL $= 7.03$ $\qquad$ UCL $= 6.36$

$\quad$ LCL $= 3.55$ $\qquad$ LCL $= 0$

In order to calculate the capability of this process, we will use the following formulae.

Process capability $= \bar{X} +$ and $- 3\sigma'$

From our X-bar and R charts,

$$\bar{X} = CL_{\bar{X}} = \bar{\bar{X}} = 5.29$$

$$\sigma' = \frac{\bar{R}}{d_2} \qquad \text{See Table B.1 for values of } d_2.$$

$$= \frac{3.00}{2.33} = 1.29$$

$$\bar{X} + \text{and} - 3\sigma' = 5.29 + \text{and} - 3(1.29)$$

What does all this mean? It means that, given the capability of the current process, nothing special has to happen for the next phone call to last as long as 9 minutes and 10 seconds. (A call of that length can be produced by the same process that may produce a call of only about one and a half minutes.) If the potential for

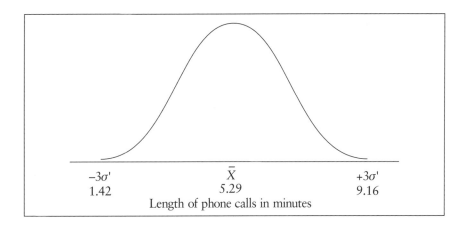

$-3\sigma'$	$\bar{X}$	$+3\sigma'$
1.42	5.29	9.16

Length of phone calls in minutes

holding other calls that long is not acceptable, office management must change the process.

Another Set of Control Charts

Throughout this appendix, we have been exploring different types of intermediate statistical methods for variables data, or measurements. These tools are applicable for analyzing processes that generate measurements, or continuous data. Many teaching, learning, and administrative processes are measured using counts instead of measures. Examples of such counts are the number of incorrect responses on a multiple choice test; the number of test scores above or below standard; and the number of disciplinary referrals in a given time period.

For reasons beyond the scope of this text, counts data behave differently from variables data (or measurements). Suffice it to say that counts data are not normal! Rather, they follow the properties of the binomial distribution or Poisson distribution.

Therefore, if we are going to control chart such data, we must select from a set of charts that differs from those presented in the previous pages of this appendix. This set of control charts includes attributes data charts, because they reflect attributes, and counts data charts, because they reflect counts of outcomes from processes under study.

Distinguishing Between Defectives *and* Defects

The first requirement for selecting the correct control chart is the ability to distinguish between *defectives* and *defects*. No matter how you may have used these words in the past, you must adopt new definitions to avoid confusion when using this different set of control chart options.

• *Defectives.* We are dealing with defectives whenever we are evaluating an outcome and deciding to which of only two categories it belongs: good or bad; on time or late; above or below standard; correct or incorrect; and so on. In other words, the outcome is binomial, and we have a clear-cut, two-option choice. For defectives, or attributes data, we will select the *np* chart or the *p* chart.

• *Defects.* We are dealing with data on defects whenever we are counting mistakes, omissions, errors, discrepancies, grievances, complaints, disciplinary referrals, and similar counts. A car may have many defects, but we wouldn't necessarily consider the whole car to be defective. A term paper may have a few errors, but we wouldn't consider the entire paper to be defective. For defects, or counts data, we will apply either the *c* chart or the *u* chart.

np Charts and *p* Charts

np charts and *p* charts are appropriate for analyzing variation in processes that produce outcomes measured with attributes data. Which one of these charts we employ depends on whether or not the area of opportunity for defectives to occur is held constant.

1. *Area of opportunity is held constant.* When studying defectives, there are two alternatives. One provides an area of opportunity for defectives to occur that is held constant. For example, on a quiz of 100 multiple-choice questions, the area of opportunity is limited to 100 correct or incorrect responses. In such a case, the *np* chart would be the appropriate control chart.

2. *Area of opportunity is not held constant.* A second alternative involves an area of opportunity for defectives that is not constant,

or different areas of opportunity. For example, standardized test results may be provided for classes with different numbers of students. In a case like this, the *p* chart would be the appropriate control chart.

np *Chart Formulae*

$CL = n\bar{p}$, where n = sample size

$$\text{and } \bar{p} = \frac{\text{total number of defectives}}{\text{total number of samples}}$$

$$UCL = n\bar{p} + 3\sqrt{n\bar{p}(1 - \bar{p})}$$

$$LCL = n\bar{p} - 3\sqrt{n\bar{p}(1 - \bar{p})}$$

For an example of an *np* chart, see the data and explanation provided in chapter 11. The calculations are shown on page 230, and the final *np* chart is illustrated in Figure 11.4 on page 231.

Reminders for Using the np *Chart*

In order for the *np* chart to have statistical validity, the data must be collected in sample sizes such that $n\bar{p}$ is greater than five. (*Note:* 5 is a minimum, not a target.) If $n\bar{p}$ is less than five, we would be trying to apply symmetric control limits to a distribution that is not symmetrical!

Other reminders for using the *np* chart.

1. You are dealing with attributes data, not measurements.

2. You are counting defectives, not defects.

3. The area of opportunity (sample size) is constant.

4. The sample size is large enough so that $n\bar{p}$ is greater than 5.

p Charts

In complex, dynamic administrative, teaching, and learning processes, we don't always have the luxury of constant sample sizes. (Recall that one condition for using *np* charts is a constant area of opportunity, or sample size.) Fortunately, this condition is not an absolute. If the sample size varies only a small amount, we can still use the *np* chart. As a rule of thumb, as long as the sample size (*n*) varies no more than 10 percent from the average, we can with validity use the *np* chart.

Some teaching, learning, and administrative processes may produce data in samples that vary a great deal. For example, suppose the maintenance department wanted to control chart late responses to repair requests, but the number of repair requests varies from 15 to 50 per day. Any time we hold a time period constant (defectives per day, week, term, and so on), the area of opportunity may vary a great deal. When the sample size (*n*) varies a lot, we will use the *p* chart.

The *p* chart doesn't plot the number of defectives. Rather, it plots the percentage or proportion defective. This percentage *p* is calculated by dividing the number of defectives by the number of samples (or repair requests, or students tested, and so on).

p *Chart Formulae*

$$\text{CL} = \bar{p} = \frac{\text{total number of defectives}}{\text{total number of samples}}$$

$$\text{UCL} = \bar{p} + \frac{3\sqrt{\bar{p}(1 - \bar{p})}}{\sqrt{n}}, \text{ where } n = \text{ sample size}$$

$$\text{LCL} = \bar{p} - \frac{3\sqrt{\bar{p}(1 - \bar{p})}}{\sqrt{n}}, \text{ where } n = \text{ sample size}$$

Examples of *p* charts are provided in chapter 7. On pages 136–137 an explanation of the use and properties of the *p* chart is provided. The calculations of central lines and control limits are found on pages 141–142 and 145–146. The actual *p* charts are illustrated in Figures 7.7 through 7.10.

Reminders for Using the p *Chart*

Recall that in order for the *np* chart to be valid, $n\bar{p}$ must be greater than 5. A similar rule of thumb applies to the *p* chart; one must collect data in samples of a sufficient size so that the lowest number of defectives in any subgroup is not less than 5.

Other reminders for using *p* charts.

1. You're using counts of attributes, not measurements.

2. You're counting defectives, not defects.

3. The area of opportunity (subgroup size, or *n*) is not constant.

4. No counts of defectives in any sample subgroup are less than 5.

c Charts and *u* Charts

The last set of intermediate statistical control charts to consider are those applied to processes that generate counts data. Recall that defectives, or attributes data, plotted on *np* charts and *p* charts can fall into one of only two categories: good or bad; on time or late; above or below standard; correct or incorrect; and so on.

c charts and *u* charts, on the other hand, are used to analyze processes that generate defects data. We are dealing with data on defects whenever we are counting mistakes, omissions, errors, complaints, and similar counts. The *c* chart is quite simple, but can be used only when the area of opportunity for defects is held constant. If this condition cannot be met, then the more complicated *u* chart must be employed.

c *Chart Formulae*

On page 267 in appendix A, Table A.1 listed the number of disciplinary incidents over an 18-week period. The run chart of those data was illustrated in Figure A.4 on page 268. Following are the standard formulae for the *c* chart's central line and control limits.

Also shown are the calculations for the disciplinary incidents. The resulting c chart is illustrated in Figure B.6.

$$CL = \bar{c} = \frac{\text{total number of defectives}}{\text{total number of samples}}$$

$$= \frac{453}{18} = 25.2 \text{ incidents}$$

$$UCL = \bar{c} + 3\sqrt{\bar{c}} = 25.2 + 3\sqrt{25.2} = 40.2$$

$$LCL = \bar{c} - 3\sqrt{\bar{c}} = 25.2 - 3\sqrt{25.2} = 10.2$$

Reminders for Using the c Chart

Teaching, learning, and administrative processes will provide many opportunities for using c charts. It is important to remember the

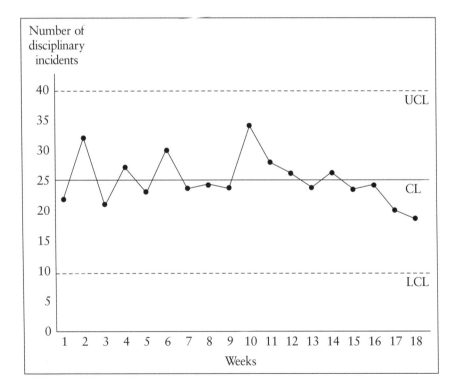

Figure B.6. c chart of disciplinary incidents.

conditions under which the *c* chart is appropriate and statistically valid.

1. You're counting, not measuring.
2. You're counting defects, not defectives.
3. The area of opportunity for defects is held constant.
4. The data averages at least 10 counts (or defects) per area of opportunity (or subgroup).

u *Charts*

Sometimes we'll be working with counts data, but may discover that the third condition above cannot be satisfied. For example, some assignments to a class of data processing students may require many entries, while others may require only a few. The area of opportunity for defects isn't constant. In such a case, it makes sense to hold time constant and let the area of opportunity vary. Then we can still develop a valid control chart of the counts data, but it will be a *u* chart (for rate of defects) instead of a *c* chart (for count of defects).

Example: The Problem of the Mechanical Drawings

A mechanical drawing class worked on drawings each day. One key measure was the number of mistakes students discovered when reviewing the completed drawings. Over a period of 10 days, the class collected the following data. (*Note:* In an actual application of control charts, we would need more data than are listed—perhaps 10 more subgroups. We will work with just these 10 days' data to demonstrate how to set up the *u* chart.)

If we tried to chart the mistakes data on a *c* chart, we'd be treating the number of mistakes on the fourth day—when the students produced 14 drawings—just like the number of mistakes on the sixth day—when the students produced only seven drawings. Common sense would indicate that we'd be mixing apples and oranges.

Subgroup (day)	Number of drawings	Number of mistakes
1	13	44
2	9	23
3	11	31
4	14	37
5	8	34
6	7	17
7	10	45
8	10	33
9	12	35
10	11	29
Totals	105	328

If we convert the data to the number of mistakes per drawing per day, we'd establish a constant area of opportunity—one drawing. We would, however, violate the requirement for counts data to average at least 10 defects per subgroup.

To set up a *u* chart, we would calculate the rate of mistakes per day, but not based on just one drawing. We need to enlarge the area of opportunity so that the rate of mistakes is at least 10 per some standard area of opportunity, or standard unit.

The first step would be to calculate the rate of mistakes per drawing so we can determine what the standard unit, or standard area of opportunity, should be.

$$\text{Rate of mistakes per drawing } = \frac{\text{total number of mistakes}}{\text{total number of drawings}} = \frac{328}{105}$$

$$= 3.12 \text{ mistakes per drawing}$$

This would indicate that our standard area of opportunity must be at least four drawings, since $4 \times 3.12 = 12.5$, and 12.5 is greater than 10. Therefore, we'll choose four drawings as our standard area of opportunity, or standard unit. (Note that we must go through some extra pain when preparing to use the *u* chart. Just like the *p* chart, we must take extra steps and precautions to put the data in a form that makes the chart a valid indicator of the type of variation exhibited in the data.)

Next, we need to express each day's data as a rate of defects per standard unit of four drawings. We can do so by organizing the data on a table like Table B.7.

The values in column E are the *u* values, the data we plot on the *u* chart. Consider what they represent. They are the rate of mistakes (or defects)—rates based on a standard area of opportunity, which we set at four drawings. For example, look at the *u* value for the fifth day: 17.00. This indicates that on day five, the class generated mistakes at a rate of 17 mistakes for every standard unit of four drawings.

The *u* chart views subgroup-to-subgroup rates of defects to determine if any are significantly different. Using this unit of measurement, we can determine what type of variation is present in the mechanical drawing class data.

- Common causes of variation from within the teaching and learning process, in which case the appropriate corrective strategy is to change the process

or

Table B.7. Table of data for *u* chart of mechanical drawing class mistakes.

A	B	C = $\frac{B}{4}$	D	E = $\frac{D}{C}$
Day	Number of drawings	Number of standard units (*n*)	Number of mistakes	Mistakes per standard unit (*u*)
1	13	3.25	44	13.54
2	9	2.25	23	10.22
3	11	2.75	31	11.27
4	14	3.50	37	10.57
5	8	2.00	34	17.00
6	7	1.75	17	9.71
7	10	2.50	45	18.00
8	10	2.50	33	13.20
9	12	3.00	35	11.67
10	11	2.75	29	10.55

- Special causes of nonrandom variation in rates of mistakes from outside the process, in which case the appropriate corrective strategy is to find, remove, and prevent the reoccurrence of that special cause, or to provide special help to students who need it

u *Chart Formulae*

Control limits on u charts are similar to those on p charts. That is, they will expand and contract as the area of opportunity for defects opens and closes. Days with a lower number of standard units (n) will have wider control limits than days with a larger n. For u charts, we use the following formulae.

$$CL = \bar{u} = \frac{\text{total number of defects}}{\text{total number of standard units}}$$

$$UCL = \bar{u} + \frac{3\sqrt{\bar{u}}}{\sqrt{n}}$$

where n = number of standard units in the subgroup

$$LCL = \bar{u} - \frac{3\sqrt{\bar{u}}}{\sqrt{n}}$$

For the mechanical drawing class data

$$CL = \bar{u} = \frac{328 \text{ mistakes}}{26.25 \text{ standard units}}$$

$$CL = 12.5 \text{ mistakes per standard unit}$$

For the first day, on which 3.25 standard units of drawings were produced, the control limits would be

$$UCL = 12.5 + \frac{3\sqrt{12.5}}{\sqrt{3.25}} = 12.5 + \frac{10.6}{1.8} = 12.5 + 5.9 = 18.4$$

$$LCL = 12.5 - \frac{3\sqrt{12.5}}{\sqrt{3.25}} = 12.5 - 5.9 = 6.6$$

Just like the p chart, the square root of the number of standard units (n) must be divided into $3\sqrt{\bar{u}}$ for every subgroup. Setting up a table like Table B.8 can prove helpful for calculating the rest of the control limits in this example.

The chart of these data is provided in Figure B.7. As noted previously, we would need more data (perhaps 10 more subgroups) before we could draw any valid conclusions about the stability and capability of this process.

Reminders for Using the u *Chart*

1. You're working with counts, not measurements.

2. You're counting defects, not defectives.

3. The area of opportunity for defects is not constant.

4. The rate of defects is 10 or more per standard unit.

Summary

The purpose of this appendix was to provide a summary of—or an initial orientation to—several types of statistical process control charts. Before deciding what type of control chart to use, we must

Table B.8. Data for u chart control limits.

Day	Number of standard units (n)	Mistakes per standard unit (u)	$\sqrt{n}$	$\bar{u}$ + and − $\dfrac{3\sqrt{\bar{u}}}{\sqrt{n}}$ UCL	LCL
1	3.25	13.54	1.8	18.4	6.6
2	2.25	10.22	1.5	19.6	5.4
3	2.75	11.27	1.7	18.7	6.3
4	3.50	10.57	1.9	18.1	6.9
5	2.00	17.00	1.4	20.1	4.9
6	1.75	9.71	1.3	20.7	4.3
7	2.50	18.00	1.6	19.1	5.9
8	2.50	13.20	1.6	19.1	5.9
9	3.00	11.67	1.7	18.7	6.3
10	2.75	10.55	1.7	18.7	6.3

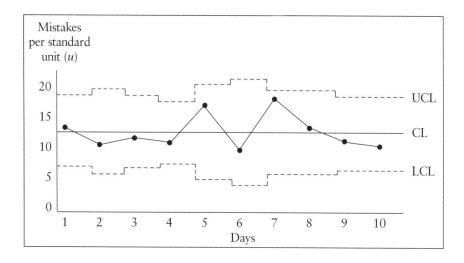

Figure B.7. Partial *u* chart: rate of mistakes on mechanical drawings.

first determine what kind of data is being used to measure the process outputs. On the next two pages, Figure B.8 illustrates a procedure for selecting the appropriate control chart. This flow-chart serves as a summary and conclusion for all of the material presented in appendix B.

Notes

1. Scholtes et al., *The Team Handbook*, 2-33.

2. G. Box, W. G. Hunter and J. S. Hunter, *Statistics for Experimenters* (New York: John Wiley & Sons, 1978), 46.

3. S. Swed and C. Eisenhart, "Tables for Testing Randomness of Sampling in a Sequence of Alternatives," *Annals of Mathematical Statistics* XIV (1943): 66–87.

4. Ishikawa, *Guide to Quality Control*, 217.

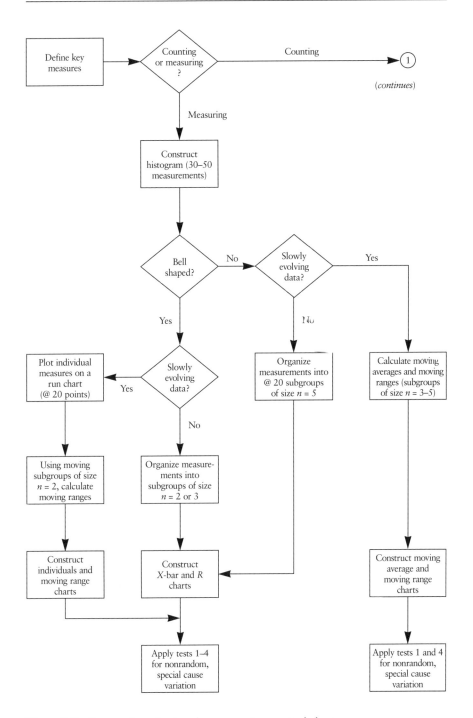

Figure B.8. Process for selecting the appropriate control chart.

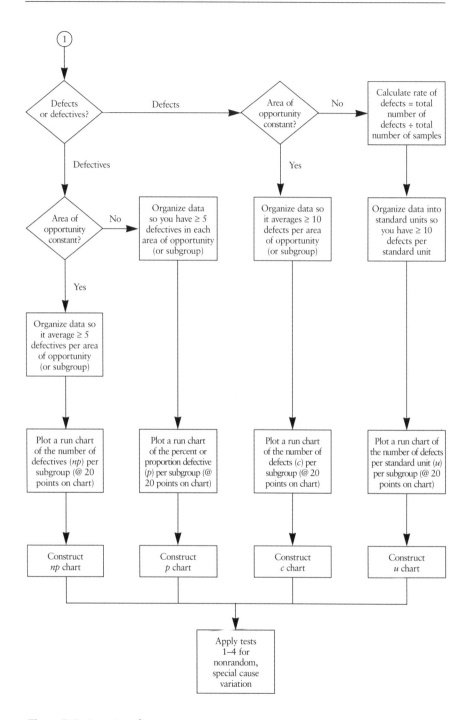

Figure B.8. (*continued*).

Appendix C

A System of Profound Knowledge

W. Edwards Deming
Consultant in Statistical Studies

The system of profound knowledge appears here in four parts, all related to each other:

A. Appreciation for a system

B. Some knowledge of the theory of variation

C. Theory of knowledge

D. Psychology

One need not be eminent in any part of profound knowledge in order to understand it as a system, and to apply it. The 14 Points for management in industry, education, and government follow naturally as application of the system of profound knowledge.

The various segments of the system of profound knowledge can not be separated. They interact with each other. Thus, knowledge of psychology is incomplete without knowledge of variation. If psychologists understood variation, as learned in the experiment on the Red Beads, they could no longer participate in continual refinements of instruments for rating people.

If statisticians understood a system, if they understood some theory of knowledge and something about psychology, they could no longer teach tests of significance, test of hypothesis, chi-square.

This is an early draft of material published in *The New Economics for Industry, Government, Education*, published in 1993 by MIT Center for Advanced Educational Services. Reprinted by permission of the W. Edwards Deming Institute.

The theory of knowledge helps us to understand that management in any form is prediction. The simplest plan—how I may go home tonight—requires prediction that my automobile will start and run, or that the bus will come, or the train. Management acts on a causal system, and on changes in the causes. Grades and ranks relate to past performance, but are used without justification for prediction of future performance in another course or job. Likewise, appraisal of employees is used without justification as prediction of future performance.

Theory of variation can play a vital part in optimization of a system. Statistical theory is helpful for understanding differences between people, and interactions between people, interactions between people and the system they work in, or learn in.

Theory of variation is helpful for most enumerative studies, and for efficiency of tests and experiments in medicine, pharmacology, chemical industry, agriculture, forestry, and in any other industry.

Statistical theory, used cautiously, with the help of the theory of knowledge, can be useful in the interpretation of the results of tests and experiments. The interpretation of the results of tests and experiments for future use: prediction.

A. A System

1. *What is a system?* It is a series of functions or activities (subprocesses, stages—hereafter components), linear or parallel, within an organization that work together for the aim of the organization. The mechanical and electrical parts that work together to make an automobile or a vacuum cleaner form a system.

There is in almost any system interdependence between the components thereof. The components need not all be clearly defined and documented; people may merely do what needs to be done. All the people that work within a system can contribute to improvement, and thus enhance their joy in work. Management of a system therefore requires knowledge of the inter-relationships between all the components within the system and of the people that work in it.

The aim of the system must be stated by the management thereof. Without an aim, there is no system. The components of a system are necessary but not sufficient of themselves to accomplish the aim. They must be managed.

The aim proposed here for management is for everybody to gain—stockholders, employees, suppliers, customers, community, the environment—over the long term. The organization will require someone in the position of aid to the president, to teach and facilitate profound knowledge.

The performance of any component is to be evaluated in terms of its contribution to the aim of the system, not for its individual production or profit, nor for any other competitive measure. Some components may operate at a loss to themselves, for optimization of the whole system, including the components to take a loss.

A flow diagram is helpful toward understanding a system. By understanding a system, one may be able to trace the consequences of a proposed change.

If the aim, size, or boundary of the organization changes, then the function of the components will for optimization of the new system change. Time will bring changes that must be managed for optimization.

The greater the interdependence between components, the greater the need for communication and cooperation between them.

2. *Optimization.* Management's job is to optimize the total system. Without management of the system as a whole, sub-optimization is sure to take place. Sub-optimization causes loss. An additional responsibility of management is to be ready to change the boundary of a system for better service and profit.

An example of a system, well optimized, is a good orchestra. The players are not there to play solos as prima donnas, to catch the ear of the listener. They are there to support each other. They need not be the best players in the country.

Bowling team		Orchestra	Business
------ X ----------------------------------- X ---------- X -----			
Low			High
	Degree of interdependence		

An automobile is not merely several thousand pieces and sub-assemblies, all individually of top quality. It is several thousand pieces and sub-assemblies that are designed to work together.

It would be poor management, for example, to purchase materials and service at lowest price, or to maximize sales, or to minimize cost of manufacture, or design of product or of service, or to minimize cost of incoming supplies, to the exclusion of the effect on other stages of production and sales. All these would be sub-optimization, causing loss. All these activities should be coordinated to optimize the whole system.

Any system that results in a win-lose structure is sub-optimized. Examples of sub-optimization in the management of people:

> The destructive effect of grading in school, from toddlers on up through the university, gold stars and prizes in school, the destructive effect of the so-called merit system, incentive pay, M.B.O. or M.B.I.R. (management by imposition of results), M.B.R. (management by results), quotas.

Other examples of sub-optimization, causes of loss:

Competition for share of market.

Barriers to trade.

Fortunately, precise optimization is not necessary. One need only to come close to optimization. As a matter of fact, a precise optimum would be difficult to define. The Taguchi loss function will apply. The loss function at the bottom (minimum loss) will be a parabola. One may move away a short distance along the curve in either direction from the optimum, but rise in the vertical only an imperceptible distance.

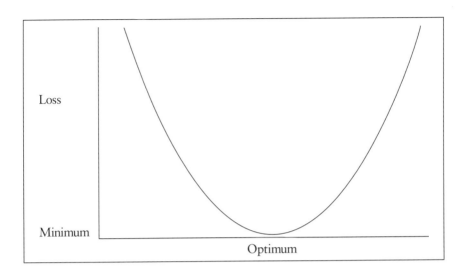

B. Some Knowledge of Statistical Theory

Some understanding of variation, including appreciation of a stable system, and some understanding of special causes and common causes of variation, is essential for management of a system, including leadership of people.

1. Variation there will always be, between people, in output, in service, in product. What is the variation trying to tell us about a process, and about the people that work in it?

2. Understanding of the capability of a process. When do data indicate that a process is stable, that the distribution of the output is predictable? Once a process has been brought into a state of statistical control, it has a definable capability.

3. Knowledge about the different sources of uncertainty in statistical data.

   How were the data obtained?

   Built-in deficiencies.

   Blemishes and blunders in interviewing, or in measurements.

   Errors in response; non-response.

   Errors of sampling.

4. There are two mistakes in attempts to improve a process, both costly:

   Mistake 1. To treat as a special cause any fault, complaint, mistake, breakdown, accident, shortage, when actually it came from common causes. (Tampering.)

   Mistake 2. To attribute to common causes any fault, complaint, mistake, breakdown, accident, shortage, when actually it came from a special cause.

5. Knowledge of procedures aimed at minimum economic loss from these two mistakes. (Shewhart control charts.)

6. Knowledge about interaction of forces. Interaction may reinforce efforts, or it may nullify efforts. Effect of the system on the performance of people. Knowledge of dependence and interdependence between people, groups, divisions, companies, countries.

7. Understanding of the distinction between enumerative studies and analytic problems. The interpretation of results of a test or experiment is an analytic problem. It is prediction that a specific change in a process or procedure will improve output in the future, or that no change at all would be a wiser choice. Either way, the choice is prediction.

8. Knowledge about loss functions in relation to optimization of performance of a system—in particular the Taguchi loss function. Which quality characteristic is causing the most loss to the whole system—has the steepest loss function—and hence is the most critical for management to work on?

9. Knowledge about the production of chaos and loss that results from successive application of random forces or random change that may individually be unimportant. Examples:

   Worker training worker in a chain.

   Executives working with best efforts on policy, but without guidance of profound knowledge.

Committees in industry, education, and government, working without guidance of profound knowledge.

10. Enlargement of a committee does not necessarily improve the results of the efforts of the committee. There is no substitute for knowledge. Enlargement of a committee may not bring in profound knowledge.

11. As a good rule, profound knowledge must come from the outside, and by invitation. Profound knowledge can not be forced on to anybody.

C. Theory of Knowledge

1. Any rational plan, however simple, requires prediction concerning conditions, behavior, comparison of performance of each of two procedures or materials.

   For example, how will I go home this evening? I predict that my automobile will start up and run satisfactorily, and I plan accordingly. Or I predict that the bus will come, or the train.

   Or, I will continue to use Method A, and not change to Method B, because evidence that Method B will be a lot better is not convincing.

2. A statement devoid of prediction and explanation of past events conveys no knowledge.

3. There is no knowledge, no theory, without prediction and explanation of past events.

4. There is no observation without theory.

5. Interpretation of data from a test or experiment is prediction—what will happen on application of the conclusions or recommendations that are drawn from the experiment? This prediction will depend on knowledge of the subject matter. It is only in the state of statistical control that statistical theory aids prediction.

6. Experience is no help in management unless studied with the aid of theory.

7. An example is of no help in management unless studied with the aid of theory. To copy an example of success, without understanding it with the aid of theory, may lead to disaster.

8. Communication (as between customer and supplier) requires operational definitions.

9. No number of examples establishes a theory, yet a single unexplained failure of a theory requires modification or even abandonment of the theory.

10. There is no true value of any characteristic, state, or condition that is defined in terms of measurement or observation. Change of procedure for measurement or observation produces a new number.

11. There is no such thing as a fact concerning an empirical observation. Any two people may have different ideas about what is important to know about any event.

D. Knowledge of Psychology

1. Psychology helps us to understand people, interactions between people and circumstances, interaction between teacher and pupil, interactions between a leader and his people and any system of management.

2. People are different from one another. A leader must be aware of these differences, and use them for optimization of everybody's abilities and inclinations. Management of industry, education, and government operate today under the supposition that all people are alike.

3. People learn in different ways, and at different speeds. Some learn best by reading, some by listening, some by watching pictures, still or moving, some by watching someone do it.

4. A leader, by virtue of his authority, has obligation to make changes in the system of management that will bring improvement.

5. There is intrinsic motivation, extrinsic motivation, over-justification.

   People are born with a need for relationships with other people, and with need to be loved and esteemed by others. There is innate need for self-esteem and respect.

   Circumstances provide some people with dignity and self-esteem. Circumstances deny other people these advantages.

   Management that denies to their employees dignity and self-esteem will smother intrinsic motivation.

   No one, child or other, can enjoy learning if he must constantly be concerned about grading and gold stars for his performance, or about rating on the job. Our educational system would be improved immeasurably by abolishment of grading.

   One is born with a natural inclination to learn and to be innovative. One inherits a right to enjoy his work. Psychology helps us to nurture and preserve these positive innate attributes of people.

   Extrinsic motivation is submission to external forces that neutralize intrinsic motivation. Pay is not a motivator. Under extrinsic motivation, learning and joy in learning in school are submerged in order to capture top grades. On the job, joy in work, and innovation, become secondary to a good rating. Under extrinsic motivation, one is ruled by external forces. He tries to protect what he has. He tries to avoid punishment. He knows not joy in learning. Extrinsic motivation is a zero-defect mentality.

   Over-justification comes from faulty systems of reward. Over-justification is resignation to outside forces. It could be monetary reward to somebody, or a prize, for an act or achievement that he did for sheer pleasure and self-satisfaction. The result of reward under these conditions is to throttle repetition: he will lose interest in such pursuits.

Monetary reward under such conditions is a way out for managers that do not understand how to manage intrinsic motivation.

Index

moving average charts, 130, 289–92
moving range charts, 130, 287–92
mR charts. *See* moving range charts
mythology, age of, 9–11
  competition in, 41
  Deming on, 9, 253–54
  emphasis on measurement, 203–4
  lack of balance in, 173
  performance appraisals, 71–72
  process model in, 71–72

National Aeronautics and Space
    Administration (NASA), 172
*National Excellence: A Case for
    Developing America's Talent,*
    64–65, 185
The New Economics (Deming), 41,
    179–80, 182, 186–87
Newman, Frank, 59, 63
Newsweek, 8
New York (state)
  school district rankings, 35
  standardized testing, 7, 92–93
New York City School Board, 209
normal curve. *See* normal
    distribution
normal distribution, 121–23
  lessons of, 125–27
  limitations of, 128
  three-sigma limit, 122–23, 124–25
normal variation, 103–4. *See also*
    common cause variation
np charts, 130, 230–31, 296–97

OBE (outcome-based education),
    12, 209
obligations, of school boards and
    administration, 171
  adopting new philosophy, 195–96
  applying, 191–92
  changes in purchasing practices,
    198–99

constancy of purpose, 192–95
  process improvement, 199–200
operational definitions, 83, 155–56,
    158
optimization, 23, 24, 311–12
Out of the Crisis (Deming), 12,
    237–38
outcome-based education (OBE),
    12, 209
Oxy Petrochemicals, 248–49

parents. *See* families
Pareto diagrams, 93–97, 260–62
Pareto principle, 94–95
Pareto, Vilfredo, 94
p charts, 130, 136–37, 296–99
performance. *See also* grades;
    incentive pay systems
  appraisals, 71–72, 212–13
  student, 213–14
  systems perspective on, 9–11
  teachers', lack of measurements,
    38
Perreault, Sr. Jeanne, 198–99
philosophy for education, 175
  adopting, 195–96
  barriers to, 175–76
Poisson distribution, 128
population, 120
preschool preparation, 56–57
problems
  of organizations, 192
  solving, 200
processes. *See also* projects, process
    improvement
  administrative, 70
  capability of, 132–33, 163–64,
    293–95
  classrooms as, 72–73
  common cause variation in,
    106–7, 132
  customers of, 25–26, 89